S0-FBO-253

"With great thoughtfulness and prudence, renowned biblical scholar Gerald L. Borchert brings his broad experience to reflect on the pregnant tensions that abound in the Christian faith and practice, calling the body of Christ to a well-reasoned, principled, often both/and approach to counteract many prevailing binary, univocal perspectives. That overarching unity is foundational to the church's mission to the world. I highly recommend this book."

—*James Hart*
President, Robert Webber Institute for Worship Studies

"If you are a thinking person who wants guidance from a biblical scholar who engages with many of the perplexing issues of life, this book is for you. Scriptural insights combined with fascinating illustrations together reflect the author's career of scholarship combined with relevance and applied wisdom to issues facing the Christian community today… Interesting, indeed! I certainly commend him for an intriguing book."

—*Harry Hiller*
Director, Cities and the Olympics Project;
Faculty Professor of Urban Sociology, University of Calgary

"In this engaging theological exploration, Gerald Borchert demonstrates that the tensions existing in our understanding of the Bible, faith, and theology are not something that should confound or confuse. Rather, tensions are opportunities to re-examine, challenge, and strengthen core beliefs. In a conversational and appealing style, Dr. Borchert explores theological topics that are often given only superficial attention. His fresh questions, insightful exegesis, and piquant observations frequently produce within the reader 'ah ha' moments. As one has come to expect, this work is grounded in a solid and thorough biblical foundation."

—*David May*
Landrenau Guiillory Chair of Biblical Studies
Central Baptist Theological Seminary

"Gerald Borchert's *Tension* is a feast for head and heart. He shares with the reader the fruit of many decades of faithful ministry, teaching, and scholarship, winsomely addressing key issues the thinking Christian faces: God's grace or human faith? Assurance or warning? Acceptance or judgment? I know of no better source for answering these vexing questions in a way that leaves the reader satisfied."

—*Eric Bolger*
Vice President for Academic Affairs, College of the Ozarks

"Gerald Borchert, a biblical scholar, who reads widely and thinks deeply, sensitizes the reader to a wide array of theological and ethical issues that defy easy answers or simplistic approaches. This highly accessible work will challenge both laity and clergy to wrestle with perennial tensions in the Scriptures and Christian tradition, and, having wrestled with them, to emerge with a much more broadly informed and finely tuned perspective on the most relevant concerns of our day."

—*Craig McMahan*

University Minister, Dean of the Chapel and
Assistant Professor of Religion, Mercer University

"Once again, Gerald Borchert gifts to the church a well-reasoned and biblically vibrant way to live faithfully amid the contentiousness so prevalent in Christianity today. Thankfully, he does not suggest a *via media* or compromise as a solution. Real tensions are not even to be overcome. Rather, Borchert brings his masterful knowledge of scripture, vast ministry experience, spiritual insight, and personal humility to enable the reader to live in the tensions that will always be our reality."

—*Constance M. Cherry*

Emeritus Professor of Worship and Pastoral Ministry
School of Theology and Pastoral Ministry, Indiana Wesleyan University

"Gerald Borchert's *Tension* addresses a crucial question for Christians: How do we think and live in a divided world? Drawing on academic research and pastoral wisdom, Dr. Borchert teaches us how to embrace personal and collective challenges. He shows us that tension is integral to God's creation. Just as muscles grow through resistance, the Spirit trains us to embrace polarities. This book provides valuable biblical insights and timely application for individuals and the church. It's an honor to support his work."

—*William D. Shiell*

President and Professor of Pastoral Theology, Northern Seminary

"We are often taught that discomfort indicates something is wrong, and tensions must be resolved either this way or that to return us to comfort. Modern teachers insist, however, that tension can lead to creative possibilities if we allow them. Borchert shows that New Testament writers knew in their day that tensions raised by discussions of good and evil, gender, sexuality, present and future, etc., push us to more creative understandings and deeper faith. "

—*Mitzi Minor*

Mary Magdalene Professor of New Testament, Memphis Theological Seminary

"As followers of Christ, we live in the tension that God's kingdom is present, yet not fully consummated. This reality has always sparked dialogue among those who call Jesus 'king.' In this book, Gerald Borchert and his fellow contributors invite readers into conversations about common tensions in contemporary Christian thought and life. If you find yourself in the midst of those tensions, read this book. It is a wonderful way to begin that process and will make you think more deeply about how your faith intersects with your way of being in the world."

—*Greg Henson*
President, Sioux Falls Seminary

"If the Bible gives you a tension headache when reading passages that rattle your sense of justice or puzzle your quizzical mind, this book is for you. Refusing to remove such tension, Borchert puts into perspective biblical and theological stress factors, and he fine-tunes the tension, so that you can continue the journey of faith humbly and clear-headed. This book is medicine for the soul plagued by perplexity."

—*Jack Van Marion*
Senior Reformed Pastor; Professor of Worship
Robert Webber Institute for Worship Studies

"A unique approach accessible for the educated lay person or minister and that shows appreciation for the many healthy tensions in biblical theology… Written in an informal, personal style, Borchert sprinkles his analysis of these theological tensions with numerous anecdotes and personal stories. It is a work of uncommon maturity and wisdom drawn from the author's many decades of teaching and deep theological reflection."

—*Garland Young*
Vice President, Dean, and Professor of the
Practice of Religion and Greek, Milligan University

Gerald Borchert's collaborative volume *Tension* calls us to attention before a host of perplexing truth issues in theology and ethics (e.g., Bible and science, sexual diversity, good and evil, Christian wholeness, security and citizenship). He invites us, as finite beings, not too quickly to choose (logical) sides, but instead to seek new syntheses that integrate paradoxes that can (un)comfortably straddle polarizing differences. I heartily encourage you to accept this invitation and join him in this engaging work of dealing creatively with these tensions."

—*Ralph Korner*
Academic Dean and Associate Professor of Biblical Studies, Taylor Seminary (Canada)

Tension: Empowering Christian Thought and Life

Gerald L. Borchert

with

Drs. Ross Brummett, James R. Hart, John Hurtgen,
David May, Craig McMahan, Mitzi Minor, R. Jackson Painter,
Jack Van Marion, and R. Garland Young

© 2021

Published in the United States by Nurturing Faith Inc., Macon GA,
www.nurturingfaith.net.

Library of Congress Cataloging-in-Publication Data is available.

ISBN: 978-1-63528-141-5

All rights reserved. Printed in the United States of America

All translations of biblical texts have been rendered from the Greek and Hebrew texts by the author unless otherwise noted, although he readily admits that his thought processes have been influenced by a combination of the King James and Revised Standard Versions of the Bible. The nuances and understandings, however, are his.

Webber Institute Books

Webber Institute Books (WIB) serves as the publishing arm of the Robert E. Webber Institute for Worship Studies (IWS). The Institute was founded by the late Robert E. Webber for the purpose of forming servant leaders in worship renewal with the perspective that "the way to the future necessarily runs through the past." IWS is the only school in North America dedicated solely to graduate education in biblical foundations, historical development, theological reflection, and cultural analysis of worship. Its vision emphasizes that its graduates will "participate intentionally in the story of the Triune God" to "bring renewal in the local and global church by shaping life and ministry according to that story." In scope it is "gospel-centered in nature and ecumenical in outlook, embracing and serving the whole church in its many expressions and variations." Those interested in obtaining further information concerning the Institute should consult www.iws.edu.

Webber Institute Books are published by agreement with Good Faith Media (www.goodfaithmedia.org) to provide a means for disseminating to the general public varying and differing views concerning the many aspects of worship and Christian life. The ideas expressed in these published materials wholly remain the views of the authors themselves and are not necessarily those of IWS or the publisher.

Such exchange of ideas hopefully will enhance worship renewal within the various segments of the Christian church. Moreover, in keeping with the hopes and dreams of Bob Webber, may all that is done through this publishing enterprise enable Christians to reject the narcissistic patterns prevalent in contemporary society and give the glory to God who sent Jesus, the Christ, to provide for human transformation and in concert provided humans with the divine triune presence through the Holy Spirit.

Robert Myers	**Gerald L. Borchert**
General Editor	Founding Editor

James Hart
President, IWS

Abbreviations

AB	Anchor Bible
BAR	*Biblical Archaeological Review*
BECNT	Baker Exegetical Commentary on the New Testament
CBQ	*Catholic Biblical Quarterly*
CorBC	Cornerstone Biblical Commentary
EvQ	*Evangelical Quarterly*
HTR	*Harvard Theological Review*
ICC	International Critical Commentary
Int	Interpretation
KJV	King James Version
LCC	Library of Christian Classics
LNTS	Library of New Testament Studies
NAC	New American Commentary
NIB	New Interpreter's Bible
NICNT	New International Commentary on the New Testament
NIGTC	New International Greek Testament Commentary
NIVAC	New International Version Application Commentary
NLT	New Living Translation
NTL	New Testament Library
OTl	Old Testament Library
PRSt	*Perspectives in Religious Studies*
RevExp	*Review and Expositor*
SBT	Studies in Biblical Theology
SP	Sacra Pagina
TDNT	*Theological Dictionary of the New Testament*
WBC	Word Biblical Commentary

Other Religious Works by Gerald L. Borchert

Today's Model Church (Roger Williams Press, 1971)
Dynamics of Evangelism (Word Books, 1976)
Paul and His Interpreters (TSF/ IBR/ InterVarsity, 1985)
Spiritual Dimensions of Pastoral Care (Westminster Press, 1985)
Discovering Thessalonians (Guideposts, 1986)
Assurance and Warning (Broadman Press, 1986; Word N Works, 2006)
The Crisis of Fear (Broadman Press, 1988)
"John" in *Mercer Commentary on the Bible* (Mercer University Press, 1995, 1996)
John 1–11 and *John 12–21*, New American Commentary (Broadman & Holman, 1996, 2002)
"Galatians" in *Romans and Galatians*, Cornerstone Biblical Commentary (Tyndale House, 2007)
Worship in the New Testament: Divine Mystery and Human Response (Chalice Press, 2008)
"Revelation" in *NLT Study Bible* (Tyndale House, 2008, 2017)
Jesus of Nazareth: Background, Witnesses and Significance (Mercer University Press, 2011)
Assaulted by Grief: Finding God in Broken Places (Mossy Creek Press/Carson-Newman University, 2011)
The Lands of the Bible: Israel, the Palestinian Territories, Sinai & Egypt, Jordan, Notes on Syria and Lebanon (Mossy Creek/Carson-Newman University, 2011)
The Lands of the Bible: In the Footsteps of Paul and John (Mossy Creek/Carson-Newman University, 2012)
Portraits of Jesus for an Age of Biblical Illiteracy (Smyth & Helwys, 2016)
Christ and Chaos: Biblical Keys to Ethical Questions (Nurturing Faith, 2020)
Translator for "Galatians," "Romans" in *New Living Translation* (Tyndale House, 1996, 2004, etc.)

Contents

NEW COVENANT PERSPECTIVES
ON LIVING INTO A TRANSFORMED LIFE

NEW COVENANT LIVING INTO THE FUTURE

Acknowledgments

I have had many superb doctoral students during my years of teaching. In designing this present work, I undertook an interesting project in which I asked nine of those now judicious representatives in the academy and in various churches and denominations if they would join me in a combination work. They have since their earlier studies become outstanding professors and academic administrators in their own right.

I asked each of them to take a number of chapters of my preliminary manuscript and add their insights, critiques, and suggestions in an effort to make our joint ideas as sustainable and as irenic as possible. I promised to integrate their ideas into my previous work. They happily and readily responded to my offer. One was unable to fulfill the assignment but gave me some crucial advice, and so is included among the others.

Their responses were beyond my expectations in terms of their forthrightness in critique, their helpful additions, and their suggested amendments. I have sought, as best as I know how, to integrate their ideas into this work. Yet it still remains open to improvement because we are merely mortal and fallible.

Naturally, since I am the writer, I take full responsibility for everything that is written here. If this work is deficient, then the result is attributable to me. If you have positive reactions to this combined work, then commendations should be directed to my colleagues. But beyond these reflections, I hasten to say that this project was a delightful learning experience not only for my associates but especially for me. Their incisive comments reminded me that we are never beyond the need for gaining new insights from those who at one time may have been part of our instruction. Indeed, in this project, several of my former students reminded me of some advice I had earlier delivered to them. So, please understand my deep indebtedness to these gracious colleagues who have assisted me in this study on tension as it relates to biblical theology and ethics or Christian thought and life. Thanks to those honored friends, Drs.:

- Ross Brummett—Professor of Religion and Vice President of Student Affairs, Carson-Newman University
- Jim Hart—President, Robert Webber Institute for Worship Studies
- John Hurtgen—Dean of the School of Theology and Professor of New Testament and Greek, Campbellsville University

- David May—Landrenau Guiillory Chair of Biblical Studies, Central Baptist Theological Seminary
- Craig McMahan—University Minister, Dean of the Chapel, and Assistant Professor of Religion, Mercer University
- Mitzi Minor—Mary Magdalene Professor of New Testament, Memphis Theological Seminary
- R. Jackson Painter—Professor of New Testament, Simpson University
- Jack Van Marion—Senior Reformed Pastor and Professor of Worship, Robert Webber Institute for Worship Studies
- Garland Young—Vice President for Academic Affairs, Dean, and Professor of the Practice of Religion and Greek, Milligan University

As always, I wish to pause and thank my beloved wife who has been a professor of Christian education and ministry supervisor to many students and who throughout our joint academic life has been an amazingly perceptive critic of my work and patient with the time demanded by the many revisions to my various writings. Thank you, dear Doris!

I am also exceedingly grateful for the unanimous endorsement of the editorial committee of Webber Institute Books for their affirmation and inclusion of this work in their worship and spirituality series.

Likewise, I express my gratitude for the gracious words of those other colleagues who have provided kind recommendations for this study.

Then, to Jackie Riley, my gracious editor at Nurturing Faith/Good Faith Media, who once again has evidenced great gifts of understanding and perception with my manuscript, and to her co-worker Vickie Frayne for her work on the footnotes, typesetting, and cover design, I express my very sincere gratitude. And last but certainly not least I want to thank Bruce Gourley, the managing editor of Good Faith Media, who negotiated the publishing of this joint analysis on "tension" in empowering the thought and life of Christians.

Thank you everyone for your assistance, and may God use this work for a blessing to others.

Engaging Tension by the Christian

Considering the Challenges of Tension

Tension—it seems to be present in almost every aspect of our cosmic reality. We wrestle with tensions and polarities in living, in making decisions, in relating to people, and in many aspects of our thinking and acting. To be a human is to face tension! Having a choice by its very nature involves some elements of tension. And God has not removed our necessity of making choices. Indeed, Christians, like all humans, are confronted daily with the requirement to make choices that can have consequences—many impact our lives and those around us. Some are very serious and may have wide human significance—even eternal implications!

The challenge for humans is to understand the significance of tension and the implications that follow from some of the choices we make and the way we relate to the options that engage us. Hopefully this study will alert us to the pervasiveness of tension and to the need for examining where we stand with respect to the choices we make and the implications of living with freedom. Welcome, friends, to this study of tension, which is a crucial aspect of human reality and of Christian thought and life—or theology and ethics.

A Personal Reflection: Science and Tension

When I was a child of eleven or twelve, our family moved about two hundred miles south from Edmonton, Alberta to Calgary. One of the parks in our new city contained a small museum of fossils and many concrete replicas of dinosaurs. My beloved younger brother (Don, who later became a philosopher) and I played with friends on those concrete replicas for several years, never doubting their former existence or the fact that they preceded us humans by millennia. Because I asked many questions about dinosaurs, my parents, who were wonderful Christians, gave me an encyclopedia about those dinosaurs. Even though I had problems at that time reading many words in that volume, that book became a treasured possession that I still have today. But during that time, we listened on the radio to some preachers, including the premier (similar to a U.S. governor) of our province of Alberta, telling us that the God who created the world did so in a very short time. I have to admit that this boy was a little confused by those different messages. I later understood there was a tension or a set of polarities engaging my early thinking.

By my first year of high school, Alberta was experiencing an oil boom. The school board, seeking to be relevant, inserted into the science program an elective course in geology. I was thrilled and literally gulped down the information about geological levels such as the pre-Cambrian and Devonian periods. Then after law school, seminary and doctoral studies at Princeton, I was called to a seminary post in South Dakota and I was asked to work a circuit speaking on the Bible and science. That opportunity led to a number of discussions and questions. My response to people with questions was always the same. "I believe firmly in God. And God does not lie in either 'the stones' or 'the Bible.'"[1] The problem is not with most of our records; it is with the people who read and interpret both the stones or stars and the Bible.

Now, as a former lawyer, I am quite aware that such a remark is a faith statement. But do you see that my answer is a response to living with a tension? Instead of accepting and dealing positively with tension, however, many people seek their solutions to tensions or polarities by lining up on one side or the other (such as "science" and "scripture") and focus, as combatants in a battle in which they seek to obliterate the arguments of the other side.

But we all make faith statements or pronouncements—whether they are positive or negative—including scientists! Charles Darwin was correct in some things, but I suggest he was not correct in everything. The same would be true of an Einstein, a Newton, or a Copernicus. These marvelous scientific adventurers stand as monumental figures in history. There is no question that they have stretched our minds into new vistas of reality. But there are other factors and realities of which they and we are not authorities.

Our task as humans is to recognize what is science and what is not. The task likewise is to recognize what the Bible claims to be hard truth or reality and what it does not. Our further task, therefore, is to recognize what is true biblical

---

[1]When I was going through graduate studies, I was fortunate to read Alan Richardson's *The Bible in the Age of Science* (Philadelphia: Westminster, 1961) that helped me develop some understandings of the real tensions that exist in the disciplines and the frequent unhealthy mindsets that result from reading only one side of the conflict. There have, of course, been a number of popular books written since that time such as Michael Gullam's *Amazing Truths: How Bible and Science Agree* (Grand Rapids: Zondervan, 2015) and the earlier work of Bernard Ramm, *The Christian View of Science and Scripture* (Grand Rapids: Eerdmans, 1954) that are quite irenic. See also the dialog in J.B. Stump, ed., *Four Views on Creation, Evolution and Intelligent Design* (Grand Rapids: Zondervan, 2017). What I trust is that Christian young people in reading scientific and religious literature on these subjects will not assume that it is always fair and unbiased. But hopefully they will weigh the materials and judge carefully how they use the information presented.

exegesis (interpretation) and what is merely an assumption concerning statements in Scripture. Our task is to work at understanding what statements are rooted in observable fact and what are theological or scientific reflections. In this pursuit of understanding, it is not a question of truth but the kind of truth that is present in an issue. Sometimes this task is difficult for people, especially in this era when the Western reader's entire social setting is very different from that of the biblical periods. William Paley and others tried desperately to bring science and the Bible together for their generations, and they should be commended for their efforts to take both God and the natural world seriously. But many have failed to remember that the Bible does not purport to be a textbook on science.

The 1925 Scopes Trial and the forceful arguments of William Jennings Bryan in Tennessee may have seemed like a victory to some, but it was only a tragic detour for the human mind. The more recent attempts to employ the Bible as the prevailing authority in such matters as creation will continue to fail, not because of good intentions but because of sad misunderstandings concerning the Bible's purpose. To bend either the truth of science into a philosophy or to bend the truth of the Bible into a book of science is a misrepresentation of God and God's world.

Therefore, it is essential to remember that the writers of the Bible serve primarily as witnesses to the reality of authentic life with God that was revealed to them in their settings. For example, when one reads the four gospels, one must understand, as I have indicated in my work on *Portraits of Jesus for an Age of Biblical Illiteracy*, that these four documents are marvelous testimonies concerning Jesus and life.[2] I repeat: they are first and foremost testimonies about Jesus, and each has a unique perspective about God's chosen liberating representative for humanity. They are far more than mere factual accounts or photographic images of Jesus, the Son of God. All of them are written with a purpose of presenting genuine portraits of Jesus that will lead the readers to comprehend and act accordingly by becoming faithful, transformed followers of Jesus as Lord.[3] We can argue about elements of truth in terms of facts all day, but until we recognize both the nature and focus of the phenomenological world that is the context of scientific analysis and the corresponding nature and focus of the biblical documents in

[2]Gerald L. Borchert, *Portraits of Jesus for an Age of Biblical Illiteracy* (Macon, GA: Smyth & Helwys, 2016). See also my earlier works, *Jesus of Nazareth: Background, Witnesses and Significance* (Macon, GA: Mercer University Press, 2011) and *Worship in the New Testament: Divine Mystery and Human Response* (St. Louis: Chalice Press, 2007), 9–57.

[3]While the text of John 20:30–31 spells out the purpose for the Fourth Gospel most clearly, each of the gospels is intended to bring about authentic faith in the reader. See Gerald L Borchert, *John 12–21*, vol. 25B, NAC (Nashville: Broadman and Holman, 2002), 317–320.

exegesis and interpretation, there will hardly be a rapprochement between the disciplines.

A Personal Reflection: Security and Tension

With these thoughts concerning faith statements in mind, I leave the subject of science and the Bible and instead turn to one specific tension in the biblical message—quite aware of various presuppositions. This subject of security has suffered greatly from the failure of Christians to take seriously the Bible's holistic picture when well-meaning Christians make statements akin to "once saved always saved."

Now I understand that the security of the believer is a very crucial concern that I will discuss at length in chapter 7, but after reading the Bible for a number of years I still recall, when I was much younger, asking my friends where that idea of "once saved always saved" appeared in the Scripture. They would often give me a number of texts that reflected assurance statements such as John 10:27–28, but I would then ask what they did with the warning texts of the Bible. Their responses usually amounted to the feelings that those warning texts such as Hebrew 6:1–6 and 1 Corinthians 10:6–11 did not apply to Christians.

As I indicated, I certainly intend to deal with that subject further, but my purpose in raising this issue here is to point to the fact that there is a significant tension in the Bible that has a great bearing on how we perceive the biblical concept of salvation or wholeness. We all seek for security, but what we are given in the Bible are both assurance and warning texts. The presence of both can create for many Christians tension, yet it can be empowering.

When I was a professor of New Testament at a seminary in Louisville and one of my colleagues was upsetting the constituency with his emphasis on apostasy (the so-called theology of "falling away"), I was approached by several of my faculty colleagues and encouraged to set down in writing my views for the denomination in hopes that it would calm troubled waters. I did so![4] But the problem is that many people refuse to accept tensions in the Bible. They will usually do all in their power to eliminate tension from their minds. Yet, reality demands that we confront honestly the existence of tensions not only in the Bible but also in life.

---

[4]Gerald L. Borchert, *Assurance and Warning* (Nashville: Broadman Press, 1987; repr. with new introduction, Singapore: Word 'n Works, 2006). In this work, I focus primarily on the dialogical letter of Paul known as 1 Corinthians, the Gospel of John, and the sermon of Hebrews.

The Intersection of Tensions and Our Mindsets

But the security issue is not the only tension/polarity in the Bible and in our theological constructs.[5] And these tensions need to be recognized because they have created and will create upheavals in the church and in society. Recognizing their presence in the Bible and in life, therefore, is crucial. Now we are people who are moving from modern mindsets with their rationalistic perspectives into this emerging era that was earlier designated by some as a postmodern period.

Our problem is that most still seek to deal with tensions by fleeing to one side of a given polarity. Such a pattern has been inherited from our Western forebearers who focused on thinking by division or differentiation. Accordingly, many stoutly resist recognizing the value of accepting the contribution of both sides of tensions. Tensions are easily viewed as alternatives that must be confronted and a selection or choice needs to be made. Instead of choosing one side, however, we need to think more about developing new syntheses that arise in the interaction of polarities, as Hegel argued many years ago in his dialectal thinking. Now, I am not a Hegelian but a further question must be raised: Do tensions always need to be resolved, or can we at times live creatively with them and recognize that there may be strength within tensions?

As one of my former students in reading this work reminded me, tension is related to ambiguity and people can have either a strong aversion to ambiguity or have a higher tolerance for it. And dealing with ambiguity points to the classic work of Eric Fromm's *Escape from Freedom* in which he detailed the reasons why people often choose totalitarianism rather than liberty—because of their lack of tolerance for ambiguity.[6] Resistance to ambiguity and search for easy answers is an ever-present danger that haunts democracies—even the American political system today.

The longing to settle tensions can create emotional and mental stress for us as humans that can engender in us confusion and block clarity in our perceptions. Education is supposed to aid us in dealing with such patterns of stress, but willingness to see alternatives can be viewed by others who resist ambiguity as a lack of decisiveness. But tension is not limited to intellectual aspects of the human persona. Tensions function in respect to moral behavior as well so that we may state our commitment to certain principles such as equality and yet act counter to our declarations. We may say we care for the poor, but the use of

---

[5]Earlier, Malcom Brown noted this phenomenon of tension in his work, *Tensions in Christian Ethics: An Introduction* (Downers Grove, IL: InterVarsity Press, 2010).

[6]Eric Fromm, *Escape from Freedom* (New York: Avon Mass Media, 1972).

our money reflects an entirely different way of life. Likewise, attitudinally we may believe we are emotionally balanced, yet may harbor attitudes of animosity, impatience, and intolerance for those who think differently than we do.

Of course, there are legitimate alternatives that demand our choice such as good and evil (which I will discuss shortly). I would hardly suggest dealing lightly with evil, sin, hate, war, drugs, or similar degrading elements in society. But I would argue that there are many aspects of reality that we will not readily resolve and so we will have to learn how to develop theologies and perspectives that can hold such tensions in a fragile, uneasy balance since we are neither omniscient nor omnipotent—which interestingly can create another tension in thinking about God.

Humans may consider themselves in our era to be almost "almighty" or "all knowing" because we can develop new machines that are able to split atomic particles or allow us to leave the gravity of the earth. Humans can manufacture tiny communication devices that would boggle the minds of our ancestors, and we have discovered new insights into quasars and black holes that would leave our forebearers gasping. But these innovations and discoveries generally only add to our Adamic temptation of thinking ourselves to be "like God" (Gen 3:5). So, the issue of supposed omniscience is one with which we must deal honestly. In this process, we dare not forget our own fallibility.

When we turn to the Bible, we recognize that it reflects our fallibility in the way that a mirror reveals our earthly warts and pimples. If we ponder its message, it becomes clear that a fundamental tension emerges from the fact that the Bible deals with people like us humans who are frail mortals and yet are in some amazing way related to and impacted by the eternal, immortal God who created and sustains us.

The God of the Bible, who became more clearly revealed in Jesus, is not like the pagan gods that are generally mere creations of the human imagination (cf. Rom 1:23) and possess frail imperfections like their mortal creators. The biblical God is quite different and has sometimes even been designated as "the wholly other one."[7] This true God, "the other one," provided an incredible act—the incarnation—in sending Jesus, the Christ, who became human in order to reconcile rebellious, error-stricken humans to God's self (2 Cor 5:19).

Not only is his incarnation virtually incomprehensible to us, but his willing death and resurrection provided a means for our forgiveness, far beyond our

---

[7]Karl Barth frequently referred to the biblical God as *der ganz Anderer*. For those who wish to familiarize themselves with his ideas in brief, the English translation of his summary work can be helpful. See Karl Barth, *Dogmatics in Outline*, trans. G.T. Thomson (London: SCM Press, 1949), especially p. 38 where he asserts that "God is not only unprovable, unsearchable, but also *inconceivable*." (Italics in the original.)

understanding. In attempting to describe this reality, the brilliant Apostle Paul was forced to employ word pictures to describe what in theology we have termed "the atonement" (the act of bringing us rebellious humans into an acceptable relationship with the immortal God). None of Paul's word pictures, nor all of them together is/are really adequate to describe what happened in the death and resurrection of Jesus. So, we struggle to comprehend this amazing mystery.

God, as the incarnate Jesus, gave himself to an actual death and resurrection in order to bring about this reconciliation of humans to God's self and to model reconciliation for us with other humans. To say that this act creates tensions in our thinking is an enormous understatement—namely, bringing together the two realms of the divine and the human in our theological reflections.

This struggle for precision, especially concerning Jesus and his work led to historic battles among the early Christians (see chapter 5) that are not absent between brothers and sisters of faith today. I simply remind you that our struggles over words in attempting adequate definitions often prevent us from reflecting the model of Jesus (cf. Phil 2 5–11), which means that our words become hollow echoes of the gospel to others. Reading and embodying the Bible's message implies entering the spirit and life pattern of God's incarnate Son. But a failure to embody the spirit of Jesus into our living will likely mean, as interpreters, that we will misrepresent the purpose of our inspired texts.

Yet, if and when we think we may have gained a correct meaning, it still behooves us to admit in all humility that we with our twenty-first-century mindsets may not have fully understood either the text or ourselves. So, we need to respect all those who differ from us in the past and present as they, like us, labored to comprehend the meaning of the biblical texts and their life applications. This task is indeed an onerous one.

But seeking to understand the biblical message is also a thrilling assignment as the Holy Spirit leads us through the maze of past, present and future tensions in order to bring us to a sense of personal and corporate purpose for living in this created universe as transforming agents for our Lord.

Reflecting on Time and Early Christian Thought

Before I move forward in our discussion, I should briefly raise the question of the ancients in their understanding of "time" and the "future" (topics to which I will return in chapter 9). I suggest that it is imperative for us to remember that the parameters of our thinking are quite different from the thought processes of the people who heard Jesus or of the early readers who received the biblical writings. And the issue of the "future" reminds me that a number of years ago, one of my seminary classmates, Tony Campolo, told me that many of the young people in the Black and Hispanic communities where he was working did not use the future tense when they were speaking about themselves or their intentions. They normally used the *present tense!* It was almost as though their minds were fixed in the present. That idea hung in the back of my mind until one of my colleagues reminded me of the important work being done by sociologists on peasant populations and the relationship of their thinking to the ancients in the Mediterranean world at the time of Jesus.

Most of us in the Western world have been socialized into a future orientation where we have been forced by our culture to focus our lives on distant goals not immediately attainable. But that orientation does not fit the stories of the New Testament. So, as Bruce Malina asks, "What happens when a future-oriented American reads [about]. . . the coming of the Son of Man?" And we can continue to ask: How do we respond when we read something such as this scripture: "Truly, I say to you, this generation will not pass away before all these things take place" (Mark 13:30, Matt 24:34, Luke 21:32)?[8] Would the early Christians not read this message a little differently than we do? Malina would respond: Very differently! The reason is that, like peasant communities of today, they would be present-oriented. And that distinction makes a great difference in the way many Westerners read their New Testaments.

Indeed, the sociologists would remind us that even the elite Romans were not future-oriented, but their primary preference was a past orientation. They and their ancestors were not concerned about "long-range planning in any field."[9] Thus, as Carroll Quigley has argued, the Roman rulers "never found logical obstacles to action, because they cared nothing for logic" and they "had no plans for world conquest [but they] ... became rulers of the world in fits of absent-mindedness."[10] So, the early Christians would hear "Let the day's own troubles be sufficient for the day" (Matt 6:34) and "Give us this day our daily bread" (6:11) a little differently than we might. And when we read "Jesus Christ is the same yesterday and today and forever," Malina asks, does that text from Hebrews 13:8 not simply mean "an endless day, hence an endless present?" And he asks:

---

[8]Bruce J. Malina, *The Social World of Jesus and the Gospels* (London: Routledge, 1996), 181.

[9]Ibid., 182–83.

[10]Carroll Quigley, *Weapons Systems and Political Stability* (Washington, DC: University Press of America, 1983), 374.

"Did anyone [then] experience the alleged tension between the 'already and the not yet' that some scholars argue they were supposed to have experienced?"[11]

As you read your Bible and engage in this study on "tension" in theology and ethics, please bear in mind that the first century Christians may have received the messages of Jesus and the New Testament a little differently than we in the twenty-first century receive them. Try to remember that when Mark quoted Jesus as saying "the kingdom of God is near (*engiken*)," Mark was likely not thinking of some distant future. He was oriented to the present, while we are much more future-oriented. Accordingly, let us understand that while there are many inherent tensions in theology and ethics, some of our tensions may be the result of our reading ancient works that are oriented differently than we think.

Pursuing the Tensions That Impact Our Lives

With these introductory remarks in mind, let me mention a few of the tensions that are present and should be considered further as we proceed.

There is the age-old disturbing problem that if God is good, why do humans suffer? When something tragic happens, is it a result of our sin? Or, is it because of someone else's sin? This concern, of course, also raises the issue of why good people suffer. And those questions of course lead to the subject of theodicy that raises the concern of how we as humans face the reality of issues such as climate change. These subjects point to the more personal questions of integrity and why do we, as humans, have tensions within ourselves. Why do we act like we do when our better selves tell us that we should or should not do what we are doing?

And in this era when matters of discrimination have frequently been on the front pages of newspapers and made lead statements on television, what should we do with the fact that there continues to be discrimination not only in society but also in the church? We proclaim that Jesus came to remove the barriers between Jew and Gentile, slave and free, rich and poor, and male and female (cf. Gal 3:28) and yet, why does the church seem so unable to live with the reality that in Jesus Christ such differences have been eliminated?

Then what about divorce and remarriage, when in some places up to fifty percent of marriages are failing? Some of our recent ancestors thought that divorce was virtually an unpardonable sin. And, I should not forget the question of how homosexuals fit into this issue of no distinctions.

---

[11]Malina, *The Social World*, 185. This tension, he would argue, is a creation of nineteenth-century northern European biblical interpreters and their heirs.

Naturally we must ask: How do God and Jesus figure into the bringing about of a change in humanity? What shall we say about the nature of Jesus and what theologians call the incarnation? And what does it mean to be saved or find wholeness in this life? Then I suppose we might ask: Can we actually find wholeness in this life? What is the role of grace and faith in our understanding of salvation? Do we ever act as if faith is more significant than grace, or the reverse? And what does Paul mean by walking in newness of life? How does such walking relate to obeying God's precepts?

Of course, there is the matter of dealing with the tension over security and the seemingly contradictory statements of the biblical texts on assurance and warning. Indeed, is it possible to be secure?

And what does it mean to live like a Christian? What characteristic is most Christlike? And how do we relate to the Spirit? Indeed, how does the Spirit of God fit into the pattern of Christlikeness? Is prayer important in this pattern? What about forgiveness? Is it really necessary for me to forgive? Why? What if I do not forgive? What about my personal life and time? How do I conceive of my time and its relationship to God? Then what about the church as a new covenant community? And how do we treat the sacraments or ordinances of the church?

There is also the question of Christian citizenship. What happens when obedience to Jesus and our national interests collide? Which standard or flag is ours?

And finally, what should be the hope of those who belong to Christ or the church? Is such a hope realistic in this "me-centered," "immanent-oriented" society? How can humans be sure about such a hope?

Approaching Our Study of Tension

I trust these and other preliminary reflections will set your thoughts into high gear. Hopefully they will stir your mind and challenge you to reflect more on the tensions and polarities that may be present in your theologies and the way you approach life. Some of these tensions may be easily discernible, while others may not be so evident in your thinking. Wherever you are on the spectrum, I suggest that there is a need to reconsider the issues concerning tension as we look to the challenges of the future.

A hard look at how we tend to deal with tensions today can be very instructive because it can force us to look at both sides of issues in new ways. I believe that such a reflection on tension can provide a stimulus to engage complex issues of dissonance and assist us in realizing that some of our old, simplistic answers may not bring satisfaction today as they once may have offered. My sense is that many of our simplistic answers are often in fact not really answers to our complex lives. Further reflection may force us to realize the need to abandon a few of our most cherished and/or embedded theological views and adopt newly chosen deliberative perspectives—which can affect the way we will live into the future and relate to both God and others differently.

It is already obvious that the world that is emerging is challenging Christians and churches to demonstrate the validity of their proclamations. Can this challenge awaken us into seeing new vistas of engagement? It is not that Jesus changes, but perhaps we may need some rebooting of our views. Hopefully glimpsing anew our current situation will stir up a reconsideration of many questions such as the way we use our resources, the way we relate to time, the way we care for the poor among us, the way we deal with our earth and its fragility, the way we approach health issues and toxic patterns of living, the way we deal with disagreements among us, the way we perceive truth, the way we sense Jesus touches our lives, our society and even how we with God's leading can be involved beyond our current circle of engagement. Perhaps we can gain some further insights that will help us engage in concerns that we will face with a more holistic perspective than we have had in the past.

I think we need repeatedly to ask: Is our theology ready to deal better with old tensions and accept the fact that new tensions loom in the future? Perhaps, seeing the incredible power that is present in dealing more effectively with both sides of tensions may be more productive. Dynamic power may be present if we are a people who are willing to accept and creatively integrate such tensions into new combinations. Will we be among the new explorers of Christianity?

Welcome then to this study of tension! Hopefully, you will be challenged to reflect on some new aspects of living with God and respond more perceptively to tension. Prayerfully, you will be directed to new dimensions of accepting the legitimacy of these tensions in your life. Confidently, may you reject easy answers to complex questions and recognize that God will be with you in your struggle for clarity. And may we all be open to discovering that God can lead us into the emerging concerns that are not yet fully on the radar screens of our lives.

… So, let us begin with one of the most fundamental tensions: the issue of good and evil.

Chapter 1

The Problem of Good and Evil

Tensions in Understanding Good and Evil, Climate Change, Suffering, Theodicy, and Violence and Forgiveness

The Reality of Evil and Its Consequences for Humans

The problem with humanity is that we readily recognize evil in the world when it pertains to others or in its corporate and national or international aspects, but it becomes much more difficult to accept its presence in our own lives and in matters pertaining to our personal commitments. As a result, we tend to minimize the nature of personal evil and focus our discussions on the errors, rebellions, and evils of others. We also use surrogate expressions in referring to this reality such as the dark side (which I will do). We likewise usually overlook our engagement in personal evil and often refuse to call sin "sin."

Instead, we generally refer to sin by conjoining it to our concepts of "mistakes" or "errors" or even our personal "foibles." Moreover, we readily portray the Devil as a comic medieval figure dressed in red or black tights and carrying a pitchfork, and thus redefine who Satan is. Yet we still know that evil is not something with which we should toy. Dealing with evil is not a game. And evil is not merely the absence of good. Evil is a powerful reality that impacts all of us as humans.

Now I will briefly review the difficult issue of theodicy below, but at this point let me simply remind you: According to the opening chapters of Genesis, only God was at the beginning and beyond that mystery we are instructed that God "created" or "formed" (*bara*; Gen 1:1) all other realities. These "formed" realities were declared "good" (*tob*) by God, which implies that evil must be the distortion or opposite of "good." Among the concepts connected with evil is the reality of temptation. The biblical understanding of temptation is not the same as sin or disobedience: the latter is a willful act that opposes the good purposes of God.

One of my former colleagues, when he was teaching Old Testament, made the point that the Bible portrays this reality of the distortion of good through a clever Hebrew wordplay. The human creatures were "image bearers" of God, and were "naked and unashamed" (*arum*; 2:25), but their problem occurred when they encountered in the Garden of Eden the most deceptive of God's creatures (*arom*; 3:1)—the serpent! And they succumbed to the temptation of this sly, figurative snake (who in Rev. 12:9 is also identified as the destructive, evil dragon called the devil or Satan[1]).

The defense offered to God by the man and the woman in blaming someone else (the serpent and the spouse) for succumbing to temptation (Gen 3:1–13) has been repeated myriads of times. But shifting blame is no defense, as is evident from the subsequent divine judgment rendered on all the participants in that early Genesis story, including the punishment on the tempting agent (3:14–24). Playing the blame game, however, is merely an indication of the human propensity to rationalize or excuse disobedience and involvement in evil activity.

Excusing the actions of others is also another way humans attempt to rationalize their own disobedience and involvement in the patterns of evil (cf. Rom 1:32).[2] Thus, one finds an intriguing archetype of an excuse in the musical *Jesus Christ Superstar* wherein Judas is represented as the tragic figure who was simply trying to force Jesus into assuming his intended destiny of being a messianic figure. But the biblical message is that humanity has repeatedly followed the same patterns of dealing with the ways of evil or the so-called dark and foreboding side of human activity. Accordingly, the God of the Bible has sought in various ways to counteract the destructive nature of submitting to what the Jewish rabbis defined as the powerful inclination to evil (*yetzer harah*). Ultimately the sending of Jesus became the divine answer to this common human problem (cf. Rom 3:21–26, 5:6–11; 1 Cor 10:13), but the more complete answer must also wait for our further discussion later in this chapter and elsewhere.

Yet not all bad events or so-called "evil happenings" can be directly connected to yielding to temptation or the sins of humanity. These other phenomena are often labeled as "natural disasters" or what in the practice of law we frequently define as "acts of God." Some would define these phenomena as natural evil as over against moral evil.[3] It is interesting to note, however, that the Apostle Paul viewed the condition of the natural world as a reflection of the fallen state of humanity when he said, "the creation was subjected to futility" ("meaninglessness," *mataiotēti*)" but that the day would come when even the creation would be "liberated" along with "the children of God" (Rom 8:20–21).

---

[1] For an excellent discussion of the story in the Garden of Eden, see Walter Brueggemann, *Genesis*, Int (Atlanta: John Knox, 1982), 40–54. For a helpful discussion of the figures related to the devil throughout the Bible, see Stanley H.T. Page, *Powers of Evil: A Biblical Study of Satan and Demons* (Grand Rapids: Baker, 1995).

[2] See also the comments of Joseph A. Fitzmyer, *Roman,* vol. 33 in AB (New York: Doubleday, 1993), 289–290 and James D.G. Dunn, *Romans 1–8*, vol. 38A, WBC (Dallas: Word Books, 1988), 76.

[3] I am here purposely avoiding the use of evil in reference to natural disasters although I am fully aware that moral action can create natural disaster, as in the case of climate change that I discuss later in this chapter.

Humans and Their Relationship to Creation

Perhaps one contemporary indication of the significant interconnection between the sad state of humanity and the current state of the world is what we today refer to as the "greenhouse effect," involving the significant melting of the ice cap and its attendant results. Of course, there are many people who refuse even to acknowledge this interconnection and seek for other explanations that will excuse humanity's corporate involvement in climate change.

But the current reality of our world reminds me of an interesting set of observations made by Walter Brueggemann in discussing the story of the garden of Eden in Genesis 2. Clearly in creating Eden, God's intention was good: humanity would find this garden to be a "pleasant" paradise setting for both life and service (Gen 2:9). But in this setting of serenity, there was a clear choice for humans to make that involved a prohibition. That prohibition concerned the tree of the knowledge of good and evil (Gen 2:19). In this analysis of the creation story, Brueggemann notes, humans were given three distinct but interrelated messages: (1) a *permission* to live in a wonderful setting supplied by God; (2) a *vocation* or task to be performed by humans; and a *prohibition* to avoid.[4] These three messages, I believe, are in fact a crucial window into the way humanity relates to God and to the created order.

In seeking to understand the way humans act toward the creation, I cannot help but vividly recall the number of teaching experiences I had in both Singapore and Malaysia when the sky was filled with a dense gray haze that sometimes made it difficult to breathe. The reason for that haze is the burning of huge tracts of forested land in Indonesia so as to turn the jungles into plantations so that wealthy property owners can turn their forests into moneymaking enterprises.

Even though burning of forests is illegal, clearing the land takes a great deal of time and money. As a result, the forests somehow become torched when authorities are not watching. For some Indonesians, the jungles are a stumbling block to progress. So, why not burn and transform the areas as quickly as possible, even if the pollution is a major problem for those in nearby countries? The winds generally blow away from Indonesia, so why not get the job done?

This last comment reminds us that distant nations are not necessarily concerned about the well-being of nearby nations. Concern for others is not usually in the national interest, especially if it does not involve matters of money and wealth for them. Moreover, if a nation is more populous or more powerful than the nation complaining, the likelihood of a correction being made is slim

---

[4]Brueggemann, *Genesis*, 46.

at best—and the United Nations is not generally ready to step into the situation unless it is supported by a powerful coalition that supports the complaint. But even in interpersonal relationships, I suppose that it will continue to be a pattern with humans because they have strayed from the way of God.

Humans and the Climate Change Problem

Perhaps there is a lesson to be learned from the previous illustration as we turn to the concern over climate change.[5] In many parts of the world, the increase in the use of fossil fuels is having a major impact on weather patterns as temperature indices are rising throughout the world and the ice in the polar regions of the earth is melting at an unprecedented rate. Even small increases in ocean levels can have major effects on the fierceness of ocean surges and on the increasing threats of rising water levels in densely populated oceanfront communities throughout the world. With heat indices rising throughout the globe, the amount of arid land is also growing. The impact of this change could easily become catastrophic in the western coastal states of the United States as fires are now common. It could also lead in the future to further wars as nations throughout the world seek to grab lands from others and the poor become expendable.

With the growing population trends and the shriveling of inhabitable land, the possibility of further conflict is obviously on the horizon. But nations will likely turn to blaming their plight on more immediate, short-range problems and will not likely be prepared to admit the legitimacy of the early warnings until the deserts grow and major cities are inundated with unwelcomed water or related problems. The issue will not go away until humans admit that they are contributing to the change and are willing to admit they have not heeded the warning signs. Only such admissions will lead to costly changes in behavior. For the present there may still be the possibility of a reversal, but the time may soon come when correction is of little avail. Will humans wake up? The question is still open. But disconcerting is the large number of evangelical Christians who refuse to accept the warnings.[6]

---

[5]For a review of the climate-change debate, see Michael S. Northcott, *A Political Theology of Climate Change* (Grand Rapids: Eerdmans, 2013); Kristen Poole, *Christianity in a Time of Climate Change: To Give a Future with Hope* (Eugene, OR: Wipf and Stock, 2020); and the encyclopedic work Ernst M. Conradie and Hilda P. Koster, eds., *T&T Clark Handbook of Christian Theology and Climate Change* (London: Bloomsbury T&T Clark, 2020) that reflect a wide range of denominational perspectives concerning the issues involved. See also Bill Gates, *How to Avoid a Climate Disaster: The Solutions We Have and the Breakthroughs We Need* (New York: Knopf Doubleday, expected 2021). For various threats to humanity see, Toby Ord, *The Precipice: Existential Risk and the Future of Humanity* (New York: Hachette Books, 2020).

[6]Robin Globus Veldman, *The Climate Change Skepticism: Why Evangelical Christians Oppose Action on*

As I introduced this segment by reflecting on the global situation of Paul's day, I remind you again that the apostle sums up the situation quite clearly for his Romans readers that the whole creation reflects the sad state of humanity as it cries out in the hope of being set free from its decaying bondage. Indeed, Paul pictures creation as "groaning" like Christians groan for the future day when all will change to reflect the way of God (Rom 8:21–23),[7] Will we heed the warning signs?

Evil, Suffering, and Dealing with the Dark Side

The problem of evil provides for the Christian one of its most insoluble tensions. We understand the existence of evil, but we are at a loss to explain how it came to be—because God is good (Ps 25:8, Mark 10:18). So, here is the tension. We can see the results of evil and can fathom certain aspects of its presence, but some parts of the equation do not compute for us concerning the reality of God and the presence of evil. In attempting to explain the problem, some religious think-ers—for example, the Gnostics—reduced the issue to an innate problem in their godhead.[8] Christians, however, generally refuse to accept that twisted solution. The best minds have wrestled with this problem and have not been able to provide acceptable solutions. Creative possibilities have certainly been tried, but all have generally been rejected because certainty is lacking. It is for this reason that I have begun this work with this most vexing of our human tensions—namely, the problem of evil. And I will expand on this issue for humans in chapter 2. But without further introduction, I turn now to one of the derivative tensions.

The Problem of Suffering and Dealing with the Dark Side

The issue of suffering raises for all humans an exceedingly complex tension. Rabbi Harold Kushner discussed part of this important tension in his best-sell-ing book *When Bad Things Happen to Good People.*[9] The issue cuts to the very heart of our concepts of fairness and justice. And we ask how can a good God allow such patterns of reality to exist? Dealing with this issue of suffering is not something new. The existence of evil raises for all of us questions of "Why?" Such

---

Climate Change (Oakland: University of California Press, 2019).

[7]For further comments on these verses, see Dunn, *Romans 1–8*, 470–479. See also Fitzmyer, *Romans*, 504–511.

[8]See my further discussion on this issue later in this chapter.

[9]Harold S. Kushner, *When Bad Things Happen to Good People* (New York: Random House/Anchor, 2004; originally published New York: Shocken, 1981). See also the earlier work of Leslie D. Weatherhead, *Why Do Men Suffer?* (New York: Abingdon, 1936).

questions do not go away. We can explain some forms of pain and suffering, but some aspects of the negative factor in our creation leave us begging for answers.

The Killing of the Canaanites vs the Book of Jonah

Readers of the Old Testament have frequently asked Christian ministers and teachers: Why did God allow the people of Israel to slaughter the Canaanites and others but particularly the children (cf. Num 21:3; Deut 9:3, 20:16–18)? Does the Bible not tell us that God did the same to Sodom (Gen 19:24–25), and did not the Israelite warriors do so to Jericho (Josh 6:21)? Answers have frequently been given to the effect that when the cities were "devoted" to God (utterly destroyed), it was because God was concerned about the contamination of the Israelites by an "unholy" people—namely, those who engaged in detestable practices. Certainly the early Israelites seemed to have yielded easily to the ways of their neighbors as is evidenced by the fact that the "high places" of fertility worship were seldom removed except by a few kings, primarily by the most resolute Josiah (2 Kgs 20:4–14). But that answer probably does not satisfy all the queries.

Yet, as one scans the Book of Jonah, a very different picture of God seems to emerge. The prophet Jonah was commanded by God to go and warn the people of Nineveh that because of their sins God was going to destroy that city. Of course, that city symbolized for Israelites both the enemy and the epitome of evil and barbaric ways. When Jonah refused to obey God and rushed away on a ship headed in the opposite direction, God used a great storm and a monstrous fish to redirect his disobedient prophet to Nineveh. When the prophet finally did his preaching and the people repented in sackcloth and ashes (note also that the animals were so clothed! Jon 3:6–9), Jonah became disgusted and sat down in the hot sun outside the city waiting for its destruction. And when it did not come, God's servant became even more angry! Then, to protect the unruly prophet from the scorching heat, God in a single day provided a plant to offer shade and thereafter promptly dispatched the plant via a worm—a process that only increased Jonah's anger toward God.

The point of the story comes in God's response to Jonah's disgust when the Lord says: "You pitied the plant." But then God asks the searing question, "Should I not pity Nineveh?" Also, God reminds Jonah of a crucial fact that the city contained 120,000 "who were unable to distinguish their right hand from the left, besides the cattle" (Jon 4:10–11).

Naturally, a number of questions arise as a result of the Book of Jonah, the first being its presence in the Old Testament canon. Does this message seem to be the same one that is repeatedly given through the time of the conquest when the people of Israel were told to destroy the people in the land where they were going? That question is especially pertinent since the Assyrian conquerors were particularly ruthless in dealing with captured enemies. Do you sense the difference? Why was God graciously concerned about these enemies of Israel in Jonah and not earlier? Indeed, is it not amazing that the Book of Jonah actually made it into the Jewish canon when the Gentiles, the *goyim*, were despised even in the time of Ezra? Was a new picture of God emerging in this book?

Illustrations Related to Suffering

Perhaps every family may have a story that could touch in some way on the uneasy and messy questions that pertain to this discussion. Here are a couple of illustrations:

A Child and a Minister. My grandfather died soon after my mother was born, and my grandmother later married a man who was a self-proclaimed preacher. Soon thereafter my grandmother contracted cancer. Her new husband called on his church to pray earnestly for her. When she died, he considered that his prayers went unanswered. From that point forward, he wanted nothing more to do with God and indeed nothing more to do with my mother. So, she was shipped off to relatives and was shunted from one relative to another for years. But my grandmother had instilled into her, even as a young girl, a genuine trust of God through Jesus that sustained my mother through her very difficult years of childhood and into her teenage life. Yet her stepfather could never recover from his feeling that if there was a God, that God was unjust to him and uncaring. In turn, he abandoned a mere child. The question, then, is: What kind of a God did her stepfather honor, and what kind of a God did my mother honor? Do you see how our experiences in life impinge upon our tensions in understanding who God is and about suffering that is in the world?

The Philosopher's Twisted "Club-foot" Theory. The wife of well-known philosopher, Edgar Brightman,[10] died of cancer. The pain of witnessing his wife dying left this searching philosopher with numerous questions, particularly the question: What is God really like? In his struggle the philosopher thought he

---

[10]See the theory of the finite God advanced by Edgar Brightman, *A Philosophy of Religion* (Englewood Cliffs, NJ: Prentice-Hall, 1940), 240–242, 305–307. For a brief reflection on Brightman's thinking, see the work of his student Peter Bertocci, *Introduction to the Philosophy of Religion* Englewood Cliffs, NJ: Prentice-Hall, 1951), 415–418 and 430–432.

found an answer in his theory of the "club foot" of God. He posited that God, the creator, was good but that God was also deformed and that every time God took a positive step in creation the club foot would come along and mar the creative work. This club-foot theory of God was thus the way this philosopher solved the great problem of theodicy and the reality of evil, illness, suffering, and bad things happening to good people. The answer to the problem of theodicy was for him one that in God there are both positive and negative, or good and evil, attributes coexisting together.

The Twisted Gnostic Solution

Such a solution that attempts to combine good and evil in the divine is in fact a modern modification of an ancient attempt to confront the same problem. The early Gnostics developed elaborate schemes in their search for an answer.[11] Some clearly posited the existence of an eternal horizontal dualism akin to ancient theories of two sets of gods such as were familiar in Mesopotamia—namely, two gods: one of light and one of darkness who struggled incessantly. Since the area was close to the equator where day and night seemed to be almost equal and constant, a proposed resolution would come through the final defeat of darkness. For the Iranian Gnostics the ancient good god (*Ahura Mazda*) would ultimately triumph over the dark god (*Ahriman*) through the efforts of those who had been enlightened from above. But this system was hardly as captivating as the other views that were developed by the proponents of a vertical dualism.

In one example of this vertical view the good god and his godhead (called the *pleroma* or "fullness") was composed of a number of *syzygies* or couples of gods. One of the least of these gods (a female who was called *sophia* or "wisdom") was viewed as straying from her partner in an effort to reach the ultimate depth (a male). As one might guess, she was unable to attain her goal and nearly died in trying. But her unworthy desire was thereafter unwelcomed in the *pleroma* and therefore excluded from that realm. That excluded desire (the little wisdom) became the demiurgical sub-god and the source of a subordinate godhead known as the realm of the planets or fates. It possessed some incomplete light particles that became the object of the struggle between the two super realms. This demiurgical god then, through the secretive efforts of the upper realm,

---

[11]For a survey of the various views of Gnosticism, see the work of my former teacher, Hans Jonas, *The Gnostic Religion* (Beacon Hill, MA: Beacon, 1958). For a brief summary, see Gerald L. Borchert, "Insights into the Gnostic Threat to Christianity as Gained through the Gospel of Philip" in Richard N. Longenecker and Merrill C. Tenney, eds., *New Dimensions in New Testament Study* (Grand Rapids: Zondervan, 1974), 79–93.

was encouraged to create the world with its humanity. It was a clever ploy of the upper godhead to recover the lost particles of light that were thus passed on to some humans. This demiurgical god did not understand that there was a so-called good godhead above and considered her(him)self as the ultimate god. This demiurge was indeed regarded as a jealous god similar to a concept that they identified with the deity in the Old Testament. The message of the New Testament was also then twisted appropriately to differentiate between the two gods, as Marcion did in his restructuring of Christianity.[12]

The separation of one original realm into two realms provided these Gnostics with the philosophical basis for a solution to the problem of evil, illness, and pain. The original god works for good and the latter for evil. While this solution may look very different from that of the modern philosopher in the illustration above, the philosophical difference is actually quite minimal.

The Remarkable Book Called Job

Job in the Old Testament also attempted to tackle the problem of suffering.[13] It is virtually impossible to date this biblical wisdom work, and one can only assume that Job represents a righteous Jew, although such is not absolutely clear. After a brief introduction of the rich, righteous man named Job, the scene shifts from earth to the heavenly court.

In this segment, the focus of the book turns to a rather strange conversation between God and God's adversary (the Satan). This Satan doubts that God's perspectives on righteousness are correct. So, the Adversary challenges God to a kind of wager that God's ideal man, Job, is only faithful because of the blessings he has received—a not unknown theory even among some Christians, Jews, and indeed many others! The Satan argues that if Job loses everything, he will surely curse God (Job 1:6–12). God takes the challenge and gives the Satan a free hand at stripping Job of his riches and family that have provided him with status in the community. In addition, Job is struck with various maladies. Yet, the Satan cannot kill him. Ultimately Job's wife also deserts him and tells him to curse God and die. This text, however, indicates that Job does not yield to such a sinful and wicked suggestion (1:13–2:10).

With these momentous changes in Job's life and fortunes, his three "friends" (Eliphaz, Bildad, and Zophar)—who act as representatives of the traditional

---

[12]For a quick summary of Marcion's views see Wayne E. Meeks, ed., *The Writings of St. Paul* (New York: W.W. Norton, 1972), 184–93.

[13]For a helpful commentary on the book of Job, see J. Gerald Janzen, *Job*, Int (Atlanta: John Knox, 1985).

understandings of suffering and wisdom—are then introduced. The Adversary, the Satan, who is a type of necessary stage figure, is then removed from the scene and does not reappear in the book (2:11–13). At this point, the Hebrew also moves from prose to poetry that is indicated in many modern translations. These three friends then challenge Job with various bits of advice so that he will confess the errors of his ways and humble himself in order to receive a reprieve from his sufferings. Job's problem, however, is that he cannot perceive where he has gone wrong with God or others, so he remains unmoved by his friends' simplistic analyses of his plight.

In the midst of these interchanges between Job and his friends, Job clearly asserts his trust in his Redeemer (*goel*) and that in spite of anything that may happen to him, he will be justified and see God (19:25–27). But his advisers do not seem to hear Job's struggle. Eliphaz voices a pious refrain that Job should submit himself to God and then everything will turn out well. But if Job fails to do so, God will humble him still further (22:21–29). In desperation, Job responds that if he can only discover where God is, he will willingly set his case before God (23:3–4) because he cannot understand why things do not seem to balance out. Why are the unjust not punished by God (24:1–25)? After a brief reminder from Bildad that humans are hardly righteous in God's presence and are merely maggots or worms (25:4–6), Job sums up his defense in a long discourse by arguing that even though he cannot explain the reason for his horrible situation, he is confident that he has lived his best in the sight of God (chs. 27–31).

With the conclusion of his three counselors' advice and Job's defense, another figure, Elihu (a younger, self-righteous spokesman) appears on the scene and angrily attacks Job for justifying himself with God and refusing to heed his advisers (32:1–5). Elihu seems to represent the self-confident, religious types who are bent on defending God by insisting (a) that God uses suffering to discipline humans (33:8–30), (b) that God is never wrong or unjust (34:10–20), (c) that Job cannot claim he is righteous before God (35:1–8), and (d) that God is really unknowable unless humans are responsive in the midst of suffering (chs. 36–37).

Finally, the Lord appears and asks Job where he was when the world was formed and whether he was able to hold the stars together or fully comprehend and control all the animals on earth (chs. 38–39). If Job cannot respond positively to such questions, then how can he expect to argue with the almighty God (40:1–2)? After many more questions the biblical writer does not ease the tension but concludes his description of God by reminding the reader that there is no human on earth to be compared to God, who is even the ruler over human pride (41:33–34).

The answer of Job is exceedingly brief. Job's response is that the Lord can certainly do whatever God wants and that he did not previously understand the wonder of God. He had heard about God previously, but now that he has recognized the true reality of God, he hates himself and repents in "dust and ashes" (42:5–6).

The Book of Job ends by returning to prose with the Lord's condemnation of Job's three friends and the requirement of their repentance for condemning Job with pious platitudes and with the need of Job's prayer for them. It also ends with a restoration of Job's prosperity. Whether the book originally concluded with the "happily ever after" ending typical of fairy tales is questioned by some scholars. What is absolutely clear, however, is the classic importance of this book in its wrestling with the great question of suffering and that easy answers are no answer at all!

The Perspective of Jesus on Suffering

We turn now to the New Testament and the story of the blind man in John 9.[14] The disciples in this account see a man who has been blind from birth, and in the typical pattern of Jewish thinking of the time they ask Jesus the reason for his sad condition. In their view, someone is to blame and Jesus, the sage, will probably know whether it was the man himself in the womb or his parents (9:2). What other alternative is there for his condition? But to their surprise, Jesus does not blame anyone. Instead of looking to the past and blaming someone, Jesus simply indicates that God will work in Jesus to provide the man with sight—for Jesus is the "light of the world" (9:3–5). Then Jesus spits in the dirt and puts mud on the man's eyes, in the way that God breathed into the dirt to make the man/Adam (9:6; cf. Gen 2:7). After the blind man washes in the pool of Siloam, he is able to see.

But the religious critics among the Jews are more concerned about the fact that this healing takes place on *Shabbat* (Sabbath) than that the man can now see (9:7–14). So, they are determined to condemn the healer who has broken the Sabbath law. Accordingly, they seek an explanation from the healed man and his parents concerning his original state. When he does not cooperate with their plan to condemn the healer, the religious leaders excommunicate the man from the synagogue as a sinner even from the womb (9:15–34).

---

[14]For a fuller discussion of this text, see Gerald L. Borchert, *John 1–11*, NAC (Nashville: Broadman & Holman, 1996), 320–326.

This story is a superb illustration of how difficult it is for humans to deal with the inherent tension that exists in suffering. We all want an explanation of "why." Moreover, we typically bring our preconceptions to the question. When we have difficulty solving the inherent tension in the issue, we manufacture a rationale for the situation. Blaming someone or something is our easy way of responding. But such a pattern does not usually solve the problem. It may positively spur us on to find ways of avoiding the condition in the future, but there are many situations with which we, as people of faith, will of necessity continue to struggle.

The story of the blind man reminds me of several examples of children who were born with birth defects into the families of some of my former colleagues, one of whom shared his experiences in a book he and I wrote, *Assaulted by Grief: Finding God in Broken Places*.[15]Now it may help us to justify our thinking and answer the question of "why" for such tragedies, as in the case of the thalidomide babies. We can blame those deformities on poorly vetted medications. But most of our experiences with birthing problems do not leave us with such an option, as was attempted by the disciples in the earlier story. Yet using the blame game does not remove the pain we experience. Grief is not answered by logic. It remains etched in our minds and lives, but healing can begin in the context of a caring community. And this is one reason, I firmly believe, that God gave us families and a community we call church. God knew we needed caring human faces in which we can see smiles through tears, hear voices that comfort us, and a visible presence that will kindly listen to our repeated refrains of trying to resolve our losses and hurts.

As we look to the future, we may be able to alleviate some aspects of pain and suffering. We will not eliminate all the negative elements in life, however, and we will not in this world live forever. Eternal life belongs to another realm. In the present context, we will still have to deal with such unresolved questions. But perhaps God may enable us to recognize the legitimacy of tension in our struggles with pain, suffering, and the problem of both evil and nonmoral tragedy. Yet when we understand Job and when we understand Jesus, we begin to fathom the reality that God does not wish evil upon us and that God is actually with us in our suffering. You may argue about Jesus being abandoned on the cross, but I trust you will sense that God never actually abandoned Jesus when he was on the cross—even though it genuinely felt like it in his painful death (John 16:32)! So, let us remember that easy answers are usually no answer at all.

---

[15]For our work, see David E Crutchley and Gerald L. Borchert, eds. *Assaulted by Grief: Finding God in Broken Places* (Cleveland, TN: Carson Newman University/Mossy Creek Press, 2011).

Confronting Tension in the Issue of Theodicy

In the previous paragraphs I have attempted to illustrate for you a few of the crucial concerns that have vexed countless writers and thinkers who have dealt with the tension in good and evil that assails Christians and others in our world. But now it is time to deal forthrightly with the age-old issue of theodicy that has perplexed philosophers and ethicists for centuries. In this discussion I am indebted to my brother, Donald Borchert, the editor-in-chief of the *Encyclopedia of Philosophy* (2nd ed., 2006), who has summarized the issues related to theodicy in chapter 5 of his very helpful work on *Embracing Epistemic Humility*.[16]

The ancients wrestled with the reality of both good and evil, as I illustrated in my references to early Gnosticism (which includes Manichaeism). The Stoic philosophers earlier had thought that they could resolve the tension, but Epicurus (341–271 BC/BCE) posed a dilemma that involves the general assumptions that God is good, God is omnipotent, and evil exits. "This dilemma," D. Borchert argues, "inflicts a fatal blow on any theodicy that, like Manichaeism, is based on a dualism of an eternal omnipotent force of good vying with an eternal force of evil."[17]

And so we turn to the options. The first type of thinking D. Borchert identifies is "Augustinian Theodicy." Augustine had early in his life been enamored with the views of Manichaeism but after he abandoned that perspective, he sought to redefine evil as "non-being." He also sought by using "aesthetic motifs" to explain away evil on a "sub-rational level of creation" and limit evil to the "rational level of creation" so that "sin and its penalty are only evils in God's world." But attempts "to define evil out of existence are defeated" by our experiences.[18]

The second approach D. Borchert defines as "Heilsgeshichte Theodicy," which adds another dimension to the earlier triad—namely, that God has a purpose and uses evil as a means of instruction. The German term "*Heilsgeshichte*," which roughly means "salvation history," implies that in the end the saving purposes of God will be obvious. Such a view, therefore, implies an eschatological or "post-death" dimension. But such a view requires a great trust that learning in the face of traumas actually takes place and will be evident in the *eschaton*. But, as D. Borchert suggests, a visit to a place such as the Holocaust museum Yad Vashem in Jerusalem might be "the 'knock- out' blow" to this view![19]

---

[16] Donald Marvin Borchert, *Embracing Epistemic Humility: Confronting Triumphalism in Three Abrahamic Religions* (New York: Lexington Books, 2013), 141–185.

[17] D. Borchert, *Embracing*, 151.

[18] Ibid., 148–152, 173.

[19] Ibid., 158–159, 173.

The third option is what he entitles the "Divine Retribution Theodicy." This view can be linked to the ancient *Upanishads* and the *Law of Karma* and is also related in Indian literature to the reincarnation (*samsara*) cycle. But he reminds us that *Karma* and *samsara* can equally be disassociated from a divine being. One can also see this option entrenched in Israel's post-Sinai cycle in relation to the period of the Judges and beyond in which obedience and faithfulness to the covenant lead to prosperity, whereas disobedience and unfaithfulness result in retribution. We can also see such a view expressed in the speeches by the "friends" of Job that I have treated earlier. Such views have even been associated with some contemporary Christian preachers. But D. Borchert then suggests that this view may "sacrifice God's goodness" to divine wrath.[20]

And that perspective leads to the fourth view that D. Borchert terms "The Best of All Possible Worlds," which has been associated with the work of Gottfried Leibniz, "who coined the word 'theodicy.'" But this view is also foundational to the thinking of Islamic theologian and mystic Muhammad al-Ghazālī" (b. about 1058) who combined the views of two earlier Islamic theodicies. The Mu'tazalites argued for a strong view of free will and that humans—not God— were the authors of good and evil, whereas God is just, does no wrong, and does everything for a purpose. The goal of theodicy here is to discover the "good purpose behind every event." The other source for al-Ghazālī was the challenge from the Ash'arite school that focused on the infinite power of God so that all events both good and evil are the result of God's will. But D. Borchert asks, "How can a morally sensitive human consider worshipping and adoring a God whose wrath trumps [God's} goodness?"[21]

The fifth and final view is the "Limited God Theodicy" that D. Borchert suggests goes back to Plato and later was carefully reasoned by John Stuart Mill (1806–1873), who was impressed by arguments that focused on the divine designer. Accordingly, Mill concluded that such an "intelligent will is not omnipotent," which removes the Stoic dilemma by denying the second assumption of God's omnipotence. But for God to accomplish the divine purposes, the assistance of humans is needed, and D. Borchert argues that such a "trade-off" was seemingly acceptable to philosopher and psychologist William James (1842– 1910) and more recently to Rabbi Harold Kushner. Yet the distinguished British Idealist, F.H. Bradley (1846–1924), recognized that the cost of such a view was human assurance of good will, joy, and peace. And D. Borchert adds that while

---

[20]Ibid., 160–165, 174.
[21]Ibid., 185–170, 174.

such a view enhances the worth of humans, it "seriously compromises the hope, trust, and assurance that God's purposes for humankind will be realized."[22]

What then is the answer to theodicy? D. Borchert turned in his work to the Book of Job, as I have done above, and advised a sense of "epistemic humility" before the divine mystery of God.[23]Humility before "mystery," however, does not mean that we are left in limbo. Instead, I believe that we Christians have been given some important guidelines to deal with the great tensions of life and to those tensions this book is directed. Before moving forward, however, I would remind you that this discussion about evil is not merely an academic exercise. Evil is real, and it can be both devastating and very painful.

Spiritual Evil and Violence vs. the Way of Forgiveness

Stories of violence are constantly confronting us as we seek to live with integrity. We long to conduct our lives in a secure society where protection and safety are not a question. But the reality is that violence is all around us. The television monitor repeatedly blares out reports of violence, and our lives are forcefully impacted by those who have been tragically devastated by the violent actions of others.

Two of my colleagues at different times have found their daughters murdered. One in fact lost his daughter while I was writing an early version of this chapter and was editing the book I mentioned above.[24] Our minds are filled with questions about why such things happen. Our immediate reactions become not only the big question of "why," but also "How could I have protected her better?" "What else could I have done?" "Why does society not wake up?" And the questions continue to multiply.

Here again we are faced with another evidence of the problem of evil in our midst. Here again we are confronted with the dark reality of sin and rebellion against the ways of God. The obvious answer, of course, is for all of us to repent and change our ways, but we know such a solution is rather "a pie in the sky," unrealistic hope in this world. Even we as Christians do not cease sinning and we need to repent and change our ways. Some "pious prigs" may twist reality and claim that they have ceased sinning, but the Johannine writer knew differently. He knew that all those who said they had ceased from sin were liars and truth did not reside in them (1 John 1:8–10). The Petrine writer, however, tells us exactly

---

[22]Ibid., 170–172, 174.
[23]Ibid., 172–173.
[24]Crutchley and Borchert, eds., *Assaulted by Grief.*

when our sinning stops. It terminates with our death (1 Pet 4:1)! I should, of course, add that sin, evil, and violence will actually only conclude with the *parousia* of Jesus and the inauguration of the new heaven and earth (cf. Rev 21:5–8). Until then, we can only approximate safety in this life.

The Defeat of Evil and the Declaration of Forgiveness by Jesus

Jesus took very seriously the power of evil in the world. He recognized the work of Satan present even in the well-meaning words of Peter when the apostle told Jesus that it was not necessary to suffer. Moreover, according to Matthew, this exchange amazingly took place at a high point in Jesus' ministry, after Peter's inspired confession (Matt 16:23; cf. also the temptations of the devil at 4:1–11, especially 4:8–9).

And as the hour of Jesus' crucifixion approached, Jesus knew the hour "had arrived" "for the Prince of the world" [God's enemy] "to be defeated (*ekblethese-tai*—'thrown out'" [John 12:31]).[25] Yet in this proleptic defeat of evil at the cross, Luke tells us, a completely unanticipated event occurred that powerfully epitomized the reality of Jesus who, as he was dying, cried out: "Father, forgive them (*aphes autois*) for they do not have a clue what they are doing" (Luke 23:34). It has since come to be understood as the great "declaration of forgiveness"— the theme of new life in Christ. And not long thereafter that model declaration of Jesus became a pattern that was repeated in the death of Stephen, the first Christian martyr (Acts 7:60). And I have a suspicion that Stephen's reenactment of that forgiveness model must have had a powerful impact upon the firebrand Saul/Paul, the Sanhedrin's official inquisitor and executing attorney (Acts 8:1; cf. Paul's self-evaluation in 1 Cor 15:9) and who later was to accept a similar pattern to that of his earlier victim.

This model of freely given forgiveness without any strings attached will not go unnoticed in the world because it challenges the very foundation of the human desire for reparation and/or revenge. But the model was pressed further by Jesus. When Peter asked Jesus how many times he should forgive his brother, Peter thought he had become truly generous when he suggested "seven times." After all, it went beyond the customary "three times" in Jewish tradition! The answer of Jesus was completely overwhelming: "seventy times seven" (Matt 18:21–22; some mss. read seventy-seven times). It meant that human followers of Jesus were supposed to meet the limitless standard of God in their relationships with others.

---

[25]See my comments and Excurses 12 and 13 on John 12:30–33 in Gerald L. Borchert, *John 12–21*, vol. 25 B, NAC (Nashville: Broadman and Holman, 2002), 55–60.

Do you and I really want to adopt such a standard with others who mistreat us? The answer probably is: "Not really!"

There is, however, a slight problem with our typical responses. We should not forget the prayer that Jesus taught his disciples. In that prayer one of the petitions is: "Forgive us ... as we also have forgiven...." (Matt 6:12). In other words, Jesus sets the standard so high that when we pray, if we do not forgive, we may in fact be bringing a curse upon ourselves or at the very minimum we may be excluding God's forgiveness to us. Now, I am not sure I like that kind of alternative. Do you? It creates another tension for us. Yet that perspective is in fact the Christian one![26]

When I was still in seminary and serving my first church, I asked the people in my Sunday school class to tell me about their Christian standards. Most of the people told me: "Our standards are the Ten Commandments and the Sermon on the Mount." As a response, I then asked them if they "had actually studied the Sermon on the Mount, because it seemed very difficult for me—to say nothing of the fact that this petition was in the Lord's Prayer."[27] You see, Jesus did not offer his followers an easy way in life. That fact is precisely why I find the tensions in my Christian life to be quite taxing.

The Power of Forgiveness: Challenging Illustrations

In concluding this chapter, I turn now to some examples of forgiveness and inquire as to how you would have acted in similar circumstances.

First, do you remember the Amish story in Nickel Mines, Pennsylvania, where a man shot ten little children before he shot himself? Do you remember that some of the Amish parents actually went to the funeral of the killer to support his widow and children? And do you recall that the Amish also gave money to support the murderer's family? Were these actions merely kind gestures, or do they say something about the way Christians are called to act? How would you and I fit into such a pattern?

Second, do you remember that Elizabeth Elliot returned to Ecuador to continue the work that a group of missionaries had begun among the tribe of Auca Indians after her husband Jim and four other missionaries had been killed

---

[26]See also Jesus' parable of the unforgiving servant in Matthew 18:23–35, as well as my further explication of the Lord's Prayer in chapter 9.

[27]For comment on Matthew 6:14–15, see Robert A. Guelich, *The Sermon on the Mount: A Foundation for Understanding* (Waco TX: Word Books, 1982), 297–298. See also my comments on the Lord's Prayer in chapter 9, as well as the work of Charles H. Talbert, *Reading the Sermon on the Mount: Character Formation and Decision Making in Matthew 5–7* (Grand Rapids: Baker Academic, 2006).

by those primitive people?[28] The men had rejected the gift of Auca women as a peace treaty. No doubt, the missionaries were probably a little naive and did not understand the sociological implications of such a rejection; they needed more education related to the culture. But what do you think about Elizabeth's willingness to return? Would we be willing to do so? Her action was a living demonstration of forgiveness in response to violence.

Third, I turn to a personal experience I had with Corrie Ten Boom when as a young professor, I was asked by a college to be one of two guest speakers in the opening convocation. During the evening activities prior to that event, I remember vividly the meaningful fellowship of about thirty people in the small dining room of the college. As we concluded the meal holding hands, we sang together, "There's a Sweet, Sweet Spirit in this Place" and I felt something like an electric pulse while holding that dear little woman's hand. Later, Corrie told me some stories concerning her life in the Ravensbruck concentration camp and how that after the war, in a Munich church she met one of the most ruthless camp guards.[29] She said she had a great struggle within herself not to publicly castigate that guard for his previous activity. But when he came up to meet her, she prayed earnestly that Jesus would help her forgive him. Her attitude seemed to change, and a peace came over her. At that point she was honestly able to tell him she forgave him. "That song we just sang," she said, "expressed my feeling in those moments of forgiving that German guard." I shall never forget that encounter with the blessed Christian woman who modeled the caring love of Jesus. She and her family were stalwart Dutch resisters who sought to rescue Jews who were trying to escape the extermination camps, and most of her family succumbed to Nazi brutality as a result.

So, the question continues with me: Could I do likewise for those who were fleeing death and then forgive my captors who wiped out my family like that Dutch woman? What about you? Is such not the pattern of the Lord Jesus and his follower Stephen? And was it not also the pattern of Joseph who earlier was sold into slavery by his brothers (Gen 50:15–21)? Who will be the next witness to respond to violence by the God-given gift of forgiveness?

And what about African-American leaders such as Martin Luther King Jr., John Lewis, and others who sought equality and who forgave those who brutal-

---

[28]See the touching testimony of Elisabeth Elliot in *Through Gates of Splendor* (New York: Harper, 1957).

[29]For the moving perspectives of Corrie Ten Boom, see *The Hiding Place* (Washington Depot, CT: Chosen Books, 1971); *Prison Letters* (Old Tappan, NJ: Revell, 1975); and *Tramp for the Lord* with Jamie Buckingham (Fort Washington, PA: Christian Literature Crusade, 1974).

ized them in their nonviolent marches that were turned into chaotic repressive actions by proponents of white racism? That problem has still not been eliminated today! So, what will you and I do?

The world may be following the ways of evil, but the servants of Christ Jesus are called to a very different pattern of response than is usually expected of humans. If the church of the future is to make a lasting impact in the world, the followers of Jesus will have to adopt the model of their Lord and will have to demonstrate that they can return blessing, goodness, and forgiveness for evil.

… And this discussion leads me to some thoughts on human nature.

Chapter 2

Problems with Human Nature

*Tensions in the Integrity of the Self: Living with Two Inclinations
and the Weakness of Analogies*

Paul's Understanding of Humanity: A Critical Argument

I turn now to the issues of tension involved in the human self or the human persona. As I discuss this matter, I think you will sense that there are important insights to be gained from the Apostle Paul, especially in Romans, which can help us understand why we experience tension as we negotiate living authentically in this world. I must first acknowledge my sincere gratitude for the doctoral seminars that focused my thinking on this subject by my former graduate professors Wayne Oates and Seward Hiltner, under whom I was privileged to study at Princeton. They, of course, are not responsible for the ideas I discuss in this chapter, but they challenged me to reflect on this subject seriously. I have detailed some thoughts earlier and am here expanding on those ideas considerably.[1]

In my earlier writing I argued that Krister Stendahl, the former dean of Harvard Divinity School, was undoubtedly correct in his criticism that much of Pauline interpretation since Martin Luther was driven by an underlying presupposition that when Christianity moved from the Jewish Semitic world to the Hellenistic European world, the understanding of Paul's view of the law—especially in Romans—was not fully comprehended.[2] I certainly agree here, but as Stendahl continued, he focused on the fact that Paul had a robust conscience and hardly had a typically split human psyche. At the point of a Pauline robust conscience, I sincerely took issue with Stendahl and I still do today. That view from my perspective has led to unfortunate interpretations of Paul and sin, especially in reference to Romans chapter 7, which I will discuss later. First, however, I must outline some basic considerations of Paul's arguments with both Hellenistic and Jewish views concerning humanity and sin.

---

[1]Gerald L. Borchert, "Romans, Pastoral Counseling and the Introspective Conscience of the West," *RevExp* 83 (1986): 81–92.

[2]Krister Stendahl, "The Apostle Paul and the Introspective Conscience of the West," *HTR* 56 (1963): 199–215. Reprinted in *Paul Among the Jews and Gentiles* (Philadelphia: Fortress, 1976), 78–96.

As most readers of Romans recognize, Paul reached a strategic summary of the first section of Romans at 3:23 when he unapologetically stated that "all have sinned and fall short of the glory of God." The way he arrived at that conclusion was to analyze both the Hellenistic and Jewish concepts of humans and their disobedient relationship with God, subjects to which I now turn.

I do so with the clear understanding that Paul was in a dialogue with his imagined opponents here. In other words, Paul was debating the issue of human authenticity in what Rudolph Bultmann many years ago termed a Diatribe (as in the Diatribes of the ancient Cynics and Stoics). Paul's goal was to make clear that no one can stand before God as righteous. The point was that everyone needed the divine help from God's unique agent, Jesus, to gain divine acceptance. So, to that debate I now turn.

A Hellenistic View of the Person: Paul's Critique

The Greco-Roman view was that the human self could be divided into two parts. In this bipartite view the person could be regarded as body and soul. The body could be pictured as a container or even a tomb that at death could be sloughed off and the eternal soul would be freed and seek wings, as Plato indicated, so that it could then attempt to join or be absorbed into the eternal soul.[3]

But Paul argued for a tripartite view that is more complex in his analysis of Romans 1:18–32. In this view the "mind" (*nous*) that was seated in the head, the top part of the human, closest to the eternal realm, would have been considered the most important aspect of the self and very much akin to the divine. The second part that Paul identified as the "heart" (*kardia*) could be regarded as the seat of the "will" (*thelēma*) and was obviously located in the central part of the human. The third and lowest part of the person, Paul identified as the "passions" or "desires" (*pathē*), which involved the stomach and particularly the sexual organs. They would be regarded like the body in the bipartite view as completely foreign to the eternal realm and would accordingly need to be discarded at death.[4]

How then did Paul handle the Hellenistic view? He first made it clear that humans should be able to understand the existence of God because of what could be seen and known in nature (now designated in theology as general revelation). Humans, however, tend to suppress this true knowledge of God and choose instead

---

[3]Plato, Phaedrus, 245–255.

[4]Bruce Malina, *The New Testament World: Insights from Cultural Anthropology* (Louisville: Westminster, 2001), 69. From his sociological perspective, Malina suggested that humans had three zones: (1) the zone of emotion-fused thought, (2) of self-expressive speech, and (3) of purposeful action, but I not able to coordinate these three with Paul's thinking here.

to manufacture their own representations of god (idols and the gods of the imagination or the pantheon who were basically super humans but who were laced with frailties like all humans). So, instead of humans achieving the Greek goal of being "wise" (*sophoi*), they actually became stupid (*emoranthēsan*) or spiritual morons by replacing the glorious God with created substitute gods (1:18–23).

Accordingly, Paul announced three unambiguous judgment refrains that "God delivered (*paredōken*) them to their desires."[5] Humans have thus degenerated through three disintegrating stages of their selfhood (1:24, 26, 28).

To summarize, Paul wisely did not begin with the mind (*nous*) but indicated that because humans had not acknowledged God appropriately, God first allowed their *hearts* or wills (*kardia*) to become distorted and thus their lives and practices became inauthentic (1:24–25). Then, in turn, their *passions* (*pathē*) became twisted so that they misused their bodies—undoubtedly eating and drinking too much, but more specifically by engaging in inappropriate sexual activity. Thus, Paul concluded that they warped their natural desires into unnatural ones, including homosexual patterns (1:26–27).[6] These unnatural practices then led them into the contorting of their *mind* (*nous*) so that they could no longer think or reason clearly concerning their deformed actions. As a consequence, they engaged in a host of evil practices from greediness, gossiping to quarreling and even to murder. But, in addition, they "conspired" to entice others to evil practices—as a justification for their own perverted actions (1:28–32). The picture that Paul painted of a twisted humanity was clearly pathetic. Yet Paul did not regard the situation to be hopeless.

As a brief digression, I should add here a brief comment on Romans 12. After discussing the transformation through Jesus in subsequent chapters of Romans, Paul reached what for the Greeks would have been a very strange and perhaps incredible statement concerning humans, namely that the transformation process should also reach to the mind (*nous*), that part of the human most like the divine (12:2). Because Paul knew that every part of the human needs to be touched by God's renewing power, he called the believers in Rome to give every aspect of the self in commitment to God's sanctifying process—including the mind!

---

[5]See also the analysis of Romans 1:24, 26–28 by Joseph A. Fitzmyer in *Romans*, vol. 33, AB (New York: Doubleday, 1993), 272–273. He views Paul as speaking protologically, by which he means "seeking to give a logical explanation of the dire condition of pagan[s]." He takes issue with those such as Käsemann, Reicke, and Nygren who argue that Paul asserts a natural theology here. While Paul argues for such a perspective in 1:19–20, his logic here relates to God's judgment on the sinful activity of humanity.

[6]For my extended discussion on how we as Christians should relate to those with homosexual preferences, please see chapter 11 in Gerald L. Borchert, *Christ and Chaos: Biblical Key to Ethical Questions* (Macon, GA: Nurturing Faith, 2020), 103–114. Also, see p. 64ff.

A Jewish Perspective of the Person: Paul's Critique

Then Paul turned to the basic Jewish view of the self, which was quite different from the Hellenistic perspectives discussed above. The Jew understood the person to have two fundamental inclinations known as the *yetzer hatov* (the inclination to good) and the *yetzer hara* (the inclination to evil)[7]. These two inclinations were present and challenged humans throughout life. Accordingly, people were responsible to make the correct decisions. Judgment or blessing naturally was supposed to follow, depending upon the people's responses. The Jews believed that they could make the correct decisions but also understood that they had not always been faithful to God.

The history of the people of Israel was a sufficient testimony for his argument to confirm their previous failures. Thus, after the exile the Jewish rabbinic leadership proclaimed the absolute necessity of a full commitment to the law. Such a perspective, they believed, was absolutely essential to avoid another exilic experience. This view of the law, accordingly, led them into legalism (which I shall discuss elsewhere) and a full confrontation with Jesus who announced that he was "Lord over the Sabbath"—one of the most significant aspects of the Jewish law (Mark 2:28).

In dealing with this Jewish view of the self, Paul addressed the well-known fact that the Jews thought they were better than the Gentiles (*goyim*).[8] In contrast to this perception, however, Paul forcefully condemned the Jews for their pride or superior attitude.[9] And he reminded them that it was not their self-oriented proclamations of heritage concerning the law or their earlier blessings that counted with God, but rather their actual responsive lives and actions that were evaluated by God.

God was impartial in the divine analysis of human activity and did not make superficial judgments about human commitments. Acceptance of Jesus' sacrifice and responsive obedience was what counted with the Lord because God in Christ fully understood the secret lives of humans (Rom 2:1–16). Outward show meant nothing. Inward attachments of the heart to God were crucial. Thus, like the Gentiles, they stood under condemnation.

---

[7]For a contemporary interpretation of these early Jewish inclinations, see Rebbezim Tziporah Heller and Sara Yoheved Rigor, *Battle Plans: How to defeat the Yetzer Hara* (Brooklyn, NY: Masorah Publications, 2009).

[8]See the old Jewish prayer discussed in chapter 3 concerning the Gentiles and Paul's response in Galatians 3:28. See also my commentary on "Galatians" in Roger Mohrlang and Gerald L. Borchert, *Romans and Galatians*, vol.14, CorBC (Carol Stream, IL: Tyndale House, 2007), 247–248, 299–300.

[9]For a helpful discussion of Jewish religious pride in Romans 2, see James D.G. Dunn, *Romans1–8*, 78–84 and 90–92. See also Joseph A Fiztmyer, *Romans*, 298–303.

With these preliminary matters out of the way, Paul confronted the obvious inconsistencies that he witnessed between the Jewish boasting about their relationship with God and their actual practices. The Jews, Paul argued, were more like twisted blind guides, inauthentic teachers, law breakers, worship thieves, and hypocritical "Jews" whose circumcision was merely external show and God was concerned with actual Jewish integrity (2:17–29). Paul understood clearly the difference between the true nature and the name of being a Jew (2:28), and that is why he distinguished between children of the flesh and children of the promise (9:8) and why he asserted so strongly that there is in reality no distinction between Jew and Greek when it comes to God's promise of salvation (10:12).

So, in case they misunderstood him, Paul as a Stoic rhetorician launched into a series of diatribe-type questions and asked whether the Jew had any advantage or circumcision had any significance. His answer may surprise us, but it was "Much!" The problem was not with their heritage; it was their lack of integrity. They would get what they deserved (3:1–8)!

Consider here the old Jewish prayer in which they thanked God that they were not made Gentiles (*goyim*; see chapter 3). Then note Paul's pertinent question: Were the Jews any better off than the Gentiles? Paul's answer now was an astounding "Absolutely No!" (*ou panatos*). Judgment is fairly distributed by a just God (3:9). The problem was not God's faithfulness to the covenant but with Jewish credibility. Paul's harsh judgment was that they actually had no actual "fear of God" (3:18; cf. Ps 36:1).[10]

The result should be clear. Paul's evaluation was the same for both Gentiles and Jews. Everyone has sinned (3:23), so therefore everyone needs to be transformed by God through Jesus Christ (3:27–31; 5:8, 18–21). But that evaluation raises the knotty question of the nature and extent of the transformation needed When you have thus reflected on the universality of sin with Paul and the need for transformation, a fundamental question probably arises in your mind concerning the nature and extent of the change within humans necessitated as a result of justification, or being declared righteous before God.

---

[10]For the view of Mark D. Nanos on the law, see *The Mystery of Romans: The Jewish Context of Paul's Letters* (Minneapolis: Fortress, 1996), 37 and *Reading Paul Within Judaism: Collected Essays* (Eugene, OR: Cascade Books, 2017), 63–106. I would remind us that since the Second World War and the annihilation of many Jews in subsequent nuanced works such as W.D. Davies, *Paul and Rabbinic Judaism* (London: SPCK, 1958) and E.P. Sanders, *Paul and Palestinian Judaism* (Philadelphia: Fortress, 1977) that there has been an effort to protect Jewish thought patterns and diminish the conflict statements concerning the Jews in the New Testament. While Paul would never say that the law was negative, the face-off with the Jews over the interpretation of the law was intense in the first century. Such antagonism should not, however, mark continued scholarship.

Romans 7– 8 and Our Misguided Perception of Human Psychology

This critical question concerning the human self was then forthrightly addressed by Paul in Romans chapter 7, which is frequently misinterpreted by Christians. And that brings me back to Krister Stendahl's important paper presented to the American Psychological Association in 1961[11]

In that work, Stendahl argued that when Christianity moved from its matrix in Judaism to Europe, Paul's concept of law in Romans was not fully understood in the West and received little comment until Augustine became the first major exponent of the introspective Western conscience. It was then adopted by Luther in his struggle with guilt that he designated as the second use of the law—namely, that it functions as a schoolmaster to crush one's self-righteousness.

In his analysis Stendahl opposed the tendency to modernize Paul and he saw little warrant for viewing Paul as having a troubled conscience. This essay brought a screeching halt to mystical and existential interpretations of Paul and a needed corrective to the anthropological interpretations of Paul advocated by theologians such as Bultmann and the guilt-ridden views of Soren Kirkegaard. They of course, were a needed corrective to the parched years of scholastic debates over sin and salvation. But Stendahl's corrective did not mean that insights gained from psychology and sociology were inappropriate, especially in the light of his own over emphasis on Paul's robust conscience. This is the point at which I have taken issue with Stendahl and those who have followed him.[12]

With these comments, I turn now to Romans 7 and 8. Interpreters, in an effort to protect skewed views of salvation, frequently argue that Romans 7 merely concerns Paul's perspectives as a non-Christian, prior to justification. But I contend that such a view is totally wrong and does not begin to grasp the depth of Paul's perception concerning the self!

From my point of view, Paul was not only a bright rabbi and a superb theologian but also a brilliant psychologist. His analysis of humanity's selfhood and the striking tension he articulated in Romans 7 preceded and may be more helpful than some of the significant views of Jung, Freud, and their successors that I studied at Princeton with Seward Hiltner and that I will attempt to use as an analogy and then also attempt to indicate its weakness.

---

[11]See Stendahl, "Paul and the Introspective Conscience," 199–215 or *Paul among the Jews and Gentiles,* 78–96.

[12]See my further study in Borchert, "Romans, Pastoral Counseling and the Introspective Conscience," 85–88. Gerd Theissen wrestled with similar issues of the human persona in chapter 11 of his work, *Psychological Aspects of Pauline Theology* (Minneapolis: Fortress, 1987), but my sense is that the "robust conscience" of Krister Stendahl has haunted most New Testament analyses and studies on this subject.

So, let me attempt to summarize what I think Paul was saying in Romans 7 and 8. For purposes of trying to help readers understand my analysis, let me make some tentative comparisons with designations used by some popular psychologists. But I wish to make clear that in this exercise I am not suggesting that these comparisons are factual, nor would I even begin to suggest that Paul was thinking like Freud. The comparisons are merely employed to assist in our understanding of the text since many readers are familiar with psychological terminology.

Thus, when you read the word "I" in your English versions of Romans 7, think of the Greek word "ego"that is also used by psychologists in discussing the self. And when you see the words "law" (*nomos*) and "commandment" (*entolē*), think of the psychological idea of the "super-ego." Then, when you see the word "sin" (*hamartia*) in the text, think of the psychological concept of the "id."With these preliminary identifications in mind, I will add some additional factors so that we should be ready to consider the rich insights of Pauline psychology. Again I say: Do not identify Paul with Freud!

The human self (the ego) is faced with the incredible problem or tension of attempting to stand between the poles of God's standard (the super-ego) that is good—clearly *not bad* (7:7)—and the temptations of sin (the id) that for humans can be designated as not good but bad. These bad tempting influences normally seek to manipulate God's standards and raise questions concerning the legitimacy of them (7:7–8). Such was the pattern of the sly serpent in the Garden when it subtly asked the woman if God had given any rules about the fruit on the trees that was forbidden. Then following the question, the serpent slyly challenged the command of God (Gen 3:1–5). Now the self or ego does not merely have inclinations to good and evil, as the Jewish psychological perspective above might have argued. The situation is much more complex and serious than the human ability or capacity to decide between good and evil. The reason for the problem, as Paul makes clear, is that sin or the id in fact has captured the will of the ego or the self. Accordingly, Paul explained, humans are sold to sin (Rom 7:14).

As a result, the human self ("ego") is tremendously confused. The ego knows God's standards ("super-ego") and wants to obey them, but it cannot do so because of its bondage to sin (or the "id," cf. 7:15–20). In total distress, the self or ego cries out for help: "I am distressed (or I am a failure)!" "Who can release me from this bondage?" (7:24). If you have dealt with any potentially suicidal persons, you will easily recognize such an agonizing call. But what we need to understand is that this call is a universal cry of humanity. We say things such as "I hate myself." But notice what we have actually done in such a statement. We have been able to separate the "I" or the ego from the "self" and in so doing, the "I" can actually judge the "self," just as God does!

In other words, the weakness of the analogy is that Paul indicates there are *two egos* that are conversing—the "I" that is acting as the self and the "I" that is judging like God! Here then is the brilliance of the Apostle Paul. Naturally, he turned to Jesus Christ as the one who would rescue him, but there is more. Paul not only thanked God for the rescue, but he also admitted that even in the rescuing process he was still a split person (7:25). He was a person *living in tension!* Yes, we are as James clearly recognizes "double-minded" (*dipsuchos*—1:8; 4:8)!

At this point, you might be tempted not to agree with my evaluation of Paul and in opposition you might ask: "Have we not become entirely new, transformed creations in Jesus (2 Cor 5:17)?" Or, to follow Stendahl, you may ask: "Do we not have a strong sense of self-affirmation and a robust conscience?"

Rather than retreating into theological platitudes for the answer, I suggest that you ask yourself another question in response: Do you still continue to sin once you become a Christian? Of course, you do (see 1 John 1:8–10). Remember that 1 John warns against those who say they do not sin. That text was purposely written to Christians who might have thought they had advanced as humans to a superior stage of sinlessness or perfection.

So, the answer to the earlier question of becoming a totally new creation should be obvious. As Christians, even though many of us have experienced what Paul calls being justified, we hardly attain sanctification in this life. Being sanctified is a process in this life. Like Paul, when we have been justified—having been declared righteous—we begin to walk in a new way of life with God in Christ Jesus. That means, once we have been justified, we are in the process of becoming transformed—becoming sanctified (Rom 6:19). We have not yet been perfected; we have not yet died and been glorified.[13] How then do we cope with the fact that we are split or double-minded people?

Paul also had the answer but unfortunately, in the development and transmission of the New Testament, the scribes decided to place a chapter number at this strategic point in the discussion. The answer actually comes in Romans 8.

The answer is that we are not condemned for being split persons (8:1). Nevertheless, we have been given a resource for dealing with our split natures. That resource is the Holy Spirit. Our task then is to use that resource (or to be used by that resource) to cope with our bifurcated natures. We are to walk with/

---

[13]For a further discussion of the stages of salvation see chapter 6 on "New Covenant Wholeness."

in the Spirit and walk neither under the domination of sin (the so-called "id") nor according to mere rules and commandments (the so-called "super-ego"). The way of rules can easily be manipulated by sin and the pressures of the flesh (8:2–11). But the Holy Spirit helps us to live with our tension-filled selves and teaches us how to "walk" with God (see chapter 6) in this new way of life (Rom 6:4)![14] Paul genuinely understood the nature of the Christian life and did not make unfounded claims of easy living as a follower of Jesus.

Conclusion

In this era when writers are debating issues concerning the nature of the church that is on the horizon, it is absolutely essential for us as Christians to admit that we are still weak and that we sin. But even though we are faced with great inner tensions and are not yet perfect, we are now pilgrims on a journey with our Lord Jesus, the one who is perfect and who died to bring us ultimately into perfection, salvation, and wholeness. Accordingly, even though we are not perfect humans, we do have an incredible message for the world. God loves humans and wants them to experience the journey to wholeness not only personally but also in communities and in creation. Moreover, our communities and our creation can be transformed and sustained if we pay attention to the patterns of God in the world. Hopefully we and our communities can discover the power that comes from God in Christ as we seek to live the new life through the presence of the Holy Spirit.

… And this statement concerning new life leads me to the troubling nature of our making distinctions among humans.

---

[14]For further discussions about "walking" with God and conducting one's life, see my chapters 6 and 9 on "New Covenant Wholeness" and "New Covenant Living." See also my further comments on "walking" in "Galatians" in Mohrlang and Borchert, *Romans and Galatians*, 253.

Chapter 3

Problems with Making
Racial and Economic Distinctions

Tensions Created by Differences in Race and Economics

Paul's Summons to Freedom and Human Response

Galatians is one of my favorite books in the Bible. I was part of the team that translated that epistle for the *New Living Translation* of the Bible (NLT), and I subsequently wrote the commentary for the publisher on this early epistle of Paul.[1] Galatians maps out an important set of perspectives for Christian living and relating to people who we may think are a little different than we are. Because it was Luther's favorite book of the Bible, he lovingly called Galatians his "Katerina" after the name of his wife. Galatians provides a key to what I have to say in this discussion on tensions related to making distinctions concerning other people.

The apostle Paul thundered, "For freedom Christ has set you free," and later added "only do not use your freedom as an opportunity for worldly patterns (Gal 5:1, 13). These words are strategic for understanding how we should be related to a world seething in various forms of cultural captivity. They are also crucial for Christians who proclaim a commitment to the Bible. The sending of Jesus into the world was God's most significant act in history. Therefore, this act of God must form the basis for our lives as Christians.

Yet, how do people generally react to this message of "freedom" in Jesus? The answer is that they usually dwell in the swamp of making distinctions and building walls of privilege both in their communities and with God. The Galatian Gentiles adopted a one-upmanship perspective and readily accepted the perverted idea of their pseudo-teachers that they could gain a higher status with God than others through circumcision. But Paul, who grew up espousing such a concept of privilege, later found it to be an unholy bondage. Therefore, he forcefully condemned the Galatians for their "Jesus plus" views and their superiority ideas as absolutely stupid (3:1), a new slavery (5:1), and worthy of God's eternal curse (1:8–9). Indeed, Paul concluded that teachers who proclaimed such false ideas of gaining superior points with God should not merely be circumcised

---

[1] Gerald L. Borchert, "Galatians," vol. 14 CorBC (Carol Stream, IL: Tyndale House, 2007), 245–342.

but be castrated (5:12).[2] Those are among the most caustic remarks in all the Pauline letters! And by the way, circumcision is not really the issue. Paul knew that circumcision was intended as a mark of commitment to God, but it became for Jewish men a sign of privilege.

Let us, therefore, examine this idea of privilege beyond mere circumcision and focus on relationships between people. In doing so I am reminded of a Jewish prayer book I found in a bookstore in Jerusalem. In it was the old three-fold Jewish prayer: "Blessed be God, I thank thee God that Thou hast not made me a Gentile." Next, "Thou hast not made me a slave." And finally, "Thou hast not made me a woman." A footnote states: The women will pray: "Blessed be God, I thank thee God that Thou hast made me what I am."[3] (Women, how do you react to that prayer? We will address that issue in the next chapter.)

After I found that prayer book, I walked over to the Western Wall where I often prayed and where the women are still separated from the men, as they are in Orthodox synagogues. And there was flashing in my mind the remarkable words of Paul in Galatians: "There is neither Jew nor Greek, bond nor free, male and female because you are all one in Christ Jesus." (3:28). That statement by Paul follows the same order as found in the old Jewish prayer! Do you think the order is a mere coincidence? Or do you think that Paul may have actually prayed words such as those before he became a Christian? Does that idea not send shivers down your spine when you think about how we Christians treat others?

So, we should be asking: What about Christians making distinctions of privilege in the church today? The proud Pharisees loved titles, long robes, and other evidences of prestige (Matt 23:1–11; Mark 12:38; Luke 11:43; 20:46). Jesus, however, condemned such people as being nothing but whitewashed tombs (Luke 11:44, Matt 23:27). Moreover, James identified such distinctions as inherently unchristian and evil (Jas 2:4). Yet such patterns of elitism continue today in churches, to say nothing concerning society.

Accordingly, I turn now briefly to the issues of race and economics before I tackle the knotty questions of sexuality in the next chapter.

---

[2]Borchert, "Galatians," 313–18.

[3]P. Birnbaum, ed. and trans., *Daily Prayer Book, Ha-Siddur Ha-Shalem* (Jerusalem/New York: Hebrew Publishing, n.d.), 15–18.

Language and Racial Tensions[4]

Racial and color distinctions scarcely trouble little children. As the song in the musical *South Pacific* puts it, "You have to be taught!" Differentiating other people from ourselves is one way of establishing our perceived superiority. The task is made much easier if their faces and bodies are a little different than ours and particularly if their skin color is different. If their language is different, then we can easily reason that their language is less adequate than ours, especially if our language is the one used by the majority in our context. Of course, even if we are not in the majority, we can easily counter such a view by claiming that our language is the language of heaven!

The Significance of Different Languages

But when you travel around the world and if you have taught in many places as I have done, you soon wish that you could speak many languages. While I have struggled with eight languages throughout my years in the academy, I just wish I could communicate fluently in many of the world's tongues because, unless you can speak to others in their native/cultural language, you really do not understand how others think. It is in other countries that I have come to realize the significance of what the Bible was trying to communicate in both the tower of Babel story (Gen 11:1–9) and in the account of the miracle of hearing at Pentecost (Acts 2:1–12).

But language differences, as color disimilarities, can also be the means or cultural tools for making distinctions. Both can serve as convenient bases for isolating other people and treating those others as stereotypically inferior. It is then a minor task to wall them off from social advantages. To assume then that those of the subgroup are satisfied with their station in life generally tends to relieve those with privilege from any sense of responsibility for the welfare of the underprivileged. But Jesus knew that the mind can be very deceitful and excuse the abuses by the privileged.

---

[4]For some reflections on the issues of race, see Jim Wallis, *America's Original Sin: Racism, White Privilege, and the Bridge to a New America* (Grand Rapids: Baker, 2017); William James Jennings, *The Imagination: Theology and the Origins of Race* (New Haven: Yale University Press, 2010); David Maxwell, *Race in Post-Obama America: The Church Responds* (Louisville: Westminster/John Knox, 2016); and Jennifer Harvey, *Dear White Christians: For Those Still Longing for Racial Reconciliation* (Grand Rapids: Eerdmans, 2014). See also Samuel K. Roberts, *African American Ethics* (Eugene, OR: Wipf and Stock, 2008; Cleveland, OH: Pilgrim Press, 2001).

An Illustration Reflecting Racial Differences

Concerning people of another color, I remember very vividly traveling from western Canada to the southern United States with my parents when I was a young boy and entering a store where I saw two sets of bathrooms and two sets of water fountains with one set marked "Colored." I asked my parents what that was all about. My wise dad took me aside and explained that "the folks down here make distinctions among people. They think that somehow black people are a little less human than whites and if they drink from the same fountain, they will catch something that will contaminate them, or hurt them." I thought for a few minutes, then looked at my father in sheer astonishment and asked if they had ever sung in church, "Red and yellow, black and white, they are precious in his sight." My dad responded, "Someday they will understand!"

My dad was undoubtedly correct, and some things have indeed changed since I first came to the South. But the hearts of many people still make such outward distinctions and the words of Paul still have not been realized. Clearly it is difficult for us to resist the temptation of making distinctions because we love to identify with people who are just like or almost like us and have similar perspectives to those we esteem.

Evangelism and the Tension of Crossing Bridges

At this point a tension in evangelism confronts us. We have been called to share the gospel with all the people in the world (cf. Matt 28:19), but we would just as soon evangelize those who are somewhat like us or whom we can make more like us. We like to deal with people of "our" kind. We may say we love others, even though they are different from us, but because our love patterns are superficial, it is hard for us to adopt the same strategy as Jesus in the incarnation. You see, Jesus became like us in order that he could help us to become like him!

Some early church growth strategies tended to emphasize the difficulties in crossing too many bridges in evangelism and focused not on an incarnation model, but on a strategy for success in gaining converts. Yet it pointed to a genuine problem among humans because it seems difficult for a church to cross more than one or at the most two bridges in its task of evangelism. I recognize that we are not Jesus who was able to cross multiple bridges in order to come to earth as a human, and I hardly wish to denounce genuine efforts in reaching people for Christ. But having taught a number of Ph. D. students in evangelism and related fields, sometimes I wondered with them whether some of our strategies were not really self-protective—basically because we may fear people who are different than we are. Therefore, I must ask myself continually the question: Do I actually want people who are different from me to be in the same church or faith community with me? That question has haunted me in teaching young ministers.

I thank God for the great strategies that mission boards have been developing concerning reaching the unreached people in other lands, but our Western democracies are gaining many immigrants of those unreached people in our own communities. Reaching them is a major task, and it takes a fundamental change in perspective to reach them.

While some people in the world and in the church are ready to welcome into their communities those who are ethnically and racially different than they are, many even in the church still resist such mixtures because they fear cultural assimilation. Sometimes it is easier to support missionaries who do their work in another country far away than it is to support evangelism that brings different kinds of people into our local churches where the universality of the gospel may be realized. And this problem does not simply apply to churches in North America. In my travels around the world, I have seen a similar resistance. But I always give thanks to God for those Christians who are learning that people of other colors, races, and economic status who are a little different do not infect them negatively by their presence.

Indeed, rather than assuming that the trajectory may be negative for races and colors working and worshiping together, I have found that it can be exceedingly beneficial, empowering, and enlivening. Jesus was a master at building bridges, and we need to take seriously this tension-challenge of our differences and embody the incarnation model of Jesus who became like us so that we could become like him!

Economic Tensions

Closely associated with racial tensions are the tensions related to economics in society and the church. Riches and wealth determine the status a person has in society and the privileges that accrue to that person as the result of money. Money can open people's mouths or close them in deceit, just as Matthew informs us that, after the resurrection of Jesus, the Jewish authorities bribed the guards at the tomb to assert the foolish claim that the terrified disciples had the courage to steal the body of Jesus (cf. 28:11–15).

In the perspective of Jesus, money and wealth can present a dangerous detour to following the way of God not only because riches can provide humans with a false sense of earthly independence but also because they mask our poverty in the realm of the spirit. Such indeed was the case in the illustration of the rich fool who tore down his barns and built bigger ones so he could retire and his "soul" or self could take it easy. But God required his life that night (Luke 12:13-21).

Similarly, when the rich man inquired what he still lacked in order to be acceptable to God, Jesus informed him that he should sell what he had and give his wealth to the poor. Then he would have the eternal treasure he was seeking. But I am sure that man did not quite anticipate such an option (Mark 10:17–22, Matt 19:16–2, Luke 18:18–25). Indeed, the response of the disciples—like the response of most people in the West today—was one of shock. Jesus even elevated the shock to the point of making it almost impossible for a wealthy person to enter the kingdom of God by using the maxim-like statement about the camel and the eye of a needle (Mark 10:24–26, etc.). While interpreters may wrestle with the tension of what seems here to be impossible, the correct interpretation is that salvation or wholeness is impossible for humans to achieve. But God actually did in the incarnation of Jesus what for humans was impossible!

Yet the tension remains, even for Christians, because you cannot buy your way into heaven. Therefore, even Christians must take seriously the scathing words in Luke's beatitudes when Jesus says "Woe to you who are rich," because of what is coming to you (Luke 6:24)! That, of course, is the point in the story of the rich fool (above; 12:13–21). He was badly out of touch with his destiny! But when you think about our reality, there are not many humans who do not desire more money or wealth. It is undoubtedly the reason that the Wisdom writer of Ecclesiastes warns that it is pointless ("vanity") to love wealth or money, since such a person is never satisfied (Ecc 5:10) and why the Pauline writer concludes that the love of money is the root of all evil and it leads people to wander from the path of faith (1 Tim 6:10).

But the love of money and wealth that is the current mindset of most people, especially in our narcissistic West—where the theme of "me first" is dominant and leaves the poor very vulnerable. Moreover, the distinctions in wealth or the lack thereof are growing at an exponential rate. The question that confronts the church today as always is: Where does its mission fit into helping lift the plight of the poor (the *anawim* of the first century) rise from the swamp of degradation? Do not forget that Jesus designated them as the blessed and promised them the kingdom of God/heaven (Luke 6:20, Matt 5:3). For Christians and the church to take a blind eye to the poverty around us is theologically inconceivable, and yet we often suffer from a paralysis of spirit. There are, of course, modern prophets who remind us of our blindness, but many times we really are unwilling or incapable of listening to their pleas and criticisms.[5]

Slavery and Economic Tensions

The next tension Paul addressed involved the distinction that the old Jewish prayer made between the free Jew and the slave.[6] In this respect, it is interesting to recall that, in their argument with Jesus, the hostile Jews claimed a theological thesis that as descendants of Abraham they had never been in slavery (John 8:33). Of course, that statement was a theological myth created to affirm their so-called innate relationship with God. In discussing the situation, Paul was much more down to earth and addressed the new Christians who were slaves (cf. 1 Cor 7:17–24). He used the circumcision issue to assure them that they were acceptable to Christ, making the incredible statement for a Jew that "neither circumcision nor uncircumcision counts for much." What counts, Paul asserted, is one's new relationship to God (7:19).

Did he wish for slavery to continue? Obviously, no! Instead, Paul told them that if they could gain their freedom, they should surely do so and not become a slave to any person (7:21, 23). Yet if they were slaves, they should not be troubled because Christ still accepted them. Their slavery did not minimize their Christian standing with God. But Paul would have acknowledged one acceptable type of slavery: being a slave to Jesus, as he called himself (Rom 1:1). Then what about slavery between Christians? When discussing Philemon's relationship to Onesimus, Paul told the slaveholder to treat the slave as a brother (Phlm 16).[7] Now,

---

[5]See for example Ron J. Sider, *Rich Christians in an Age of Hunger: Moving from Affluence to Generosity*, 6th ed. (Grand Rapids: Thomas Nelson/Harper-Collins, 2015; revision of 1977) and his *The Scandal of the Evangelical Conscience: Why are Christians Living Just Like the Rest of the World?* (Grand Rapids: Baker, 2005). See also Craig Blomberg, *Christians in an Age of Wealth* (Grand Rapids: Zondervan, 2013); and Jeremy K. Everett, *I Was Hungry: Cultivating Common Ground to End an American Crisis* (Grand Rapids: Baker, 2019).

[6]During New Testament times, Rome and other major cities were filled with captured persons who served their masters as slaves, frequently as household servants. Some were well educated and even functioned in various trades, business positions, and as teachers for the household. Some, of course, were menial workers, and some like those Jews who were captured and forced to build the ramp on Masada were more like the slaves who served the plantations primarily in the Americas during the seventeenth, eighteenth, and nineteenth centuries. For a helpful perspective on slavery, see Willard M. Swartley, *Slavery, Sabbath, War and Women: Case Issues in Biblical Interpretation* (Scottdale, PA: Herald Press, 1983), 31–64 and 192–228.

[7]For a further interpretation of this brief personal letter of Paul to Philemon, see Scot McKnight, *The Letter to Philemon*, NICNT (Grand Rapids: Eerdmans 2017), especially 95–108; Murray J. Harris, *Colossians and Philemon* (Grand Rapids: Eerdmans, 1991), 265–276. See also the helpful introductory summary of slavery in the Hellenistic world in W. Hulitt Gloer and Perry L. Stepp, *Reading Paul's Letter to Individuals: A Literary and Theological Commentary on Paul's Letters to Philemon, Titus and Timothy* (Macon, GA: Smyth and Helwys, 2015).

Paul would hardly have marched in some parade to end slavery. In his setting such an act would not only have been ineffective, but the Roman authorities would also have regarded him as guilty of *maiestas* (treachery or treason). But to treat a slave as a brother was logically the beginning of the end to slavery.

Yet not long ago many Christians refused to acknowledge their errors both in Europe and in the Americas because of the economic benefits of slaveholding. And they argued from their interpretations of the Bible that since slavery was not forbidden but was actually practiced in biblical times, then it should be permitted. Indeed, it was frequently argued as a permissible idea because of the curse of Ham's son Canaan. For these folks, Ham's indiscretion virtually legitimized enslaving blacks (Gen 9:25).

But the tide of time began to change in England because of stalwart figures such as William Wilberforce and the radically transformed slave trader John Newton who in 1779 penned the hymn that stole the hearts of many Christians—"Amazing Grace." Yet it took a war (usually designated as the Civil War in the North and the War Between the States in the South) and an economic shift and mechanization of the cotton industry to bring a termination to slavery in the United States. Yet it continues elsewhere in the Americas.[8]

Unfortunately, the end of slavery in the United States did not bring an end to discrimination among people. There are still other ways for people to benefit from the repression or subjection of others, especially if the others are a minority. Economics and power are always strong motivations for benefitting some at the expense of others.[9] The tension that arises from the desire for personal and corporate benefit can easily expand into international-wide systemic problems. Attempting to be authentically Christian in such a context can almost be overwhelming, but Jesus did not say that our mission would be easy. Indeed, it is countercultural; change will be difficult and unpopular, and the challenge can be dangerous. The tension between personal benefit and the authentic Christian treatment of others remains for us a constant struggle in living for Christ with integrity.

---

[8]For a disturbing account of the church's involvements and the collusion and dark relationships and practices with the power brokers of Latin American, see Eduardo Galeano, *Open Veins of Latin America: Five Centuries of the Pillage of a Continent*, trans. Cedric Belfrage (New York: Monthly Review Press, 1971, 1973).

[9]For some additional thoughts on the subject of ethical tensions and dilemmas as we face the future, see Brent Waters, *Just Capitalism* (Louisville: Westminster/John Knox, 2016); David M. Bell, Jr. *The Economy of Desire: Christianity and Capitalism in a Postmodern World* (Grand Rapids: Baker Academic, 2012).

Contemporary Slavery and Christian Responsibility

While we can rejoice that in most of the world slavery has been terminated, yet there are still evidences that it has not been eradicated, even in America! Children are still captured and carried off to places other than in democratic countries where they are used for various purposes including war and sexual pleasure. [10] We also periodically discover examples of such slavery even in the Western world. Women are still enticed into marriage or fake unions and used for the satisfaction of men. Some are subjected to the horrible process of so-called "female circumcision" to protect their owners/masters. People are given jobs for long hours and at such pitiful wages so that improvement in their condition is virtually impossible.

And the stories continue to confront us with the presence of human greed and inhumanity. Truly Jesus Christ came to set people free from all such bondage and enslavement. But freedom is a fragile quality that must be carefully sought, maintained, monitored, and preserved lest it vanishes like smoke because of the insatiable human desire for power, prestige, possessions, and personal satisfaction!

In this era when people are struggling for acceptance, recognition, and freedom, Christians are duly summoned to represent the liberating Christ and envision the possibility of a God-inspired church that prophetically stands against systems of power and abuse that still enslave and impoverish countless people.

… Our calling, therefore, is to a church that embodies the reality that we are all one in Christ Jesus.

---

[10] See for example the important works of Wendy Stickle, Shelby Hickman, et al. *Human Trafficking: A Comprehensive Exploration of Modern Day Slavery* in Global Issues in Crime and Justice (Thousand Oaks, CA: Sage, 2019); Molly Dragiewicz, *Global Human Trafficking* (New York: Routledge, 2015); Nita Belles, *In Our Backyard: Human Trafficking in America and What We Can Do to Stop It* (Grand Rapids: Baker, 2015); and Rachel Lloyd, *Girls Like Us: Fighting for a World Where Girls Are Not For Sale: A Memoir* (New York: Perennial, 2012).

Chapter 4

Problems with Making Sexual Distinctions

*Tensions Related to Sexuality and the Acceptance of Women,
Divorcees, and Homosexuals*

The Status of Women and Patterns of Repression[1]

Perhaps some of the foremost concerns that raise tensions among Christians currently are issues related to sexuality.[2] For ease of dealing with this subject of sexuality, I have divided this chapter into three major segments, but all three of these sections continue the subject of making distinctions and the difficulties humans have with the full acceptance of other humans. The first two sections are focused primarily on the treatment of women, although divorce today clearly involves both partners and indeed others—primarily the children of divorced couples. The third section deals with the varied group frequently designated as homosexuals, although there are many distinctions among them.

These issues have their roots in the historical repression of women and are reflected in the third segment of the old Jewish prayer concerning women and the Pauline alternative (Gal 3:28) that I introduced in the previous chapter. While some Christians may argue that the perspectives in the Bible are consistent and scarcely change from Genesis to Jesus, that view is patently false. The perspective on women in most of Genesis is that women were regarded as little more than possessions to be enjoyed and used by men somewhat akin to a chattel or thing.

The Status of Women and the Tension in Genesis

Genesis 1:26–31 indicates that God made humanity both male and female in the divine image as the height or pinnacle of the created order on the sixth day before God rested and established the seventh day and made it holy (2:3).

---

[1] For a helpful discussion on this issue, see William Loader, *The New Testament on Sexuality* (Grand Rapids: Eerdmans, 2012) and his subsequent work, *Making Sense of Sex: Attitudes Towards Sex in Early Jewish and Christian Literature* (Grand Rapids: Eerdmans, 2013). See also the earlier important work of Louis William Countryman, *Dirt, Greed and Sex: Sexual Ethics in the New Testament and Their Implications for Today* (Minneapolis: Fortress, 1988).

[2] For the feminist perspective, see Rachel Sophia Baard, *Sexism and Sin Talk: Feminist Conversations on the Human Condition* (Louisville: Westminster/John Knox, 2019).

Interpreters have then often highlighted the fact that the remainder of Genesis 2 separates the forming of man and woman. It is often stated that God formed man first and made a special effort to breath into this dusty created thing the divine breath of life (Gen 2:7). But since the man was lonely, God built woman out of one of man's ribs (Gen 2:21–22). Accordingly, some argue that in this biblical text women are said to be subordinate to men and are merely meant to be "supporters" of men (2:18). This line of thinking then suggests that Genesis 3 indicates the woman was the first to sin by taking the fruit from the forbidden tree and then tempting her husband (the man) to sin. Phyllis Trible, however, in her defense of women argued that woman is the height of the created order—since she is made last.[3] So the arguments go.

But Walter Brueggemann correctly asked if such arguments were the actual purpose of Genesis 2 and 3. Was not the purpose of this second story to reflect on the nature of relationships within the creation for man and woman, as well as suitability or fitness (2:18) between the two? Was not God's goal to emphasize harmony in the story? And was it not confirmed by the note concerning their unashamed nakedness before each other (2:25)? Also, did not the story of their joint disobedience bring a severing of true fitness and openness between the two humans? In addition to the breaking of harmony between the humans and the created order, was there not a shattering of open communication between them and God (3:1–19)? Yet that was not the end of the story. God still cared for them![4]

Clearly this canonical story in Genesis contends that sin and disobedience are to be viewed as having changed the equation of relationships. Man was no longer able to enjoy the creation without sweaty work (3:17–19), and woman was made to suffer pain in childbirth and became obligated to serving man (3:16). From that point it became worse, as murder (4:8–12) and all sorts of corruption and violence followed (6:11). Even the judgment stories in the form of a flood that eliminated most of humanity (6:9–8:19) and the dividing of people through the short-circuiting of communication patterns at Babel (11:1–9) could not restore the broken relationships with God or with other humans.

So, God selected a man named Abram/Abraham and tried to set humans on the correct path. Yet for all of Abram's faithfulness, the reality of broken relationships between man and woman was evident. He sought to follow God but when he went to Egypt, he manifested his fear and in self-defense used his wife as a bargaining chip with the pharaoh (12:10–20). In a society where large harems

---

[3]See Phyllis Trible, *God and the Rhetoric of Sexuality* (Philadelphia: Fortress, 1978).
[4]See Walter Brueggemann, *Genesis* in Int (Atlanta: John Knox, 1982), 50–52.

were the pattern of powerful rulers, we might ask: Can anyone blame this man (Abram) for seeking to protect his skin—even though he could be called the father of the faithful? But did he learn from his early experience? No! Even as the new Abraham, he still repeated his defensive mode concerning his wife with Abimelech (20:1–7).

And what about Lot offering his daughters to be raped in order to protect his male guests (Gen 19:5–8)? Or consider Laban toying with Jacob for Rachel and replacing her with Leah (29:15–30). Of course, such were the customs in antiquity. Even women had come to view their roles primarily as son-bearers and as obedient to the master/husband of the house. When wealthy women were married their female slaves could also serve as "son-producers" for their mistresses according to Eastern custom (e.g., Hagar with Abraham and Zilpah and Bilhah with Jacob).

Since women were not much more than chattels[5] and were expected to be obedient to their husbands, there developed an implied understanding among men that wives had to be absolutely faithful to their husbands—even after death they were to raise up a son for their dead spouse. Witness the state of affairs in the story when Judah was ready to have his daughter-in-law stoned for her apparent unfaithfulness until it was revealed that Judah himself was the man who got her pregnant (Gen 38;12–30)! Men did not regard themselves under the same restrictions of faithfulness, even though the laws of adultery were intended to apply to both males and females.

Women in the Hellenistic World

To summarize the many and various Hellenistic views of women would be impossible in this brief context, but the work of Mary Lefkowitz and Maureen Fant is a superb resource for a study on this important subject.[6] An inscription concerning a deceased woman named Amymone, the wife of Marcus, from the first century BC/BCE in Rome reads: "best and most beautiful, worker in

---

[5]Notice that the tenth commandment includes a neighbor's wife among the neighbor's property that was not to be coveted (Exod 20:17). Young females who had not had relations with men were considered by Israel's soldiers to be legitimate spoils of war. But women who had relations with men were viewed as contaminated and were expected to be destroyed (Num 31:17). Bonnie Thurston in her detailed study of *Women in the New Testament* (New York: Crossroad, 1998), 14–15, has argued that women under the eligible age (12) had virtually no rights and could be sold into slavery or contracted for marriage. Money or property of a married woman generally belonged to her husband, and he was generally the only partner who could seek a divorce. A woman's testimony in court was regarded as defective. See also Willard M. Swartley, *Slavery, Sabbath, War and Women: Case Issues in Biblical Interpretation* (Scottdale, PA: Herald Press, 1983), 152–228.

[6]Mary R. Lefkowitz and Maureen B. Fant, *Women's Life in Greece and Rome*, 3rd ed. (Baltimore: John Hopkins University Press, 2005).

wool, pious, chaste, faithful, a stayer at home." These words summarize a general description of a good woman in that era.[7] It reminds one of Proverbs 31 where a woman's value or virtue is reckoned in her faithfulness and service. A starker Hellenistic view can be cited from the poet Hipponax in the sixth century who reflected that "The two best days in a woman's life are when someone marries her and when he carries her dead body to the grave."[8]

Yet the Hellenistic world was in a period of great transition from the concept where women were regarded merely as chattels to their assuming rights of ownership and of gaining positions of importance in employment and public life, even in roles as varied as gladiators and health care professionals.[9] In that sense it was similar to emerging patterns of women during the twentieth century in the democratic world. The dark ages after the fall of Rome and the collapse of learning, however, witnessed a clear decline in the freedom of women. In that context the church became a repressive force against women's equal rights and freedom.

The question before us then is this: What will the future bring in the way of women's roles and rights? Can the Western world sustain its twentieth century progress into the twenty-first century? Or, will the growing role of women in society again collapse? Women have not yet fully emerged as the powerful force they could be, but that possibility is unfolding in our contemporary world. Will Christians be in the vanguard of such an emergence and therefore support the genuine liberation of women, or will the church demonize such efforts? These are unanswered questions, but they are indeed worthy of pondering.

The Woman Caught in Adultery and the Samaritan Woman[10]

At this point it is appropriate to introduce the pericope of the woman caught in adultery that appears in most of our Bibles in the Gospel of John after 7:52, but in some ancient manuscripts after Luke 21:25. It is, as I have noted more at length in my commentary on John, a legitimate canonical story concerning Jesus that I believe is looking for a home.[11] One may ask: Where was the man in the charge of adultery?

---

[7]Ibid., 17.

[8]Ibid., 27.

[9]Ibid., 129–69 and Wayne E. Meeks, *The First Urban Christians: The Social World of the Apostle Paul* (New Haven: Yale University Press, 1983), 23–25, 70–72.

[10]For an analysis of each of these texts in John 4 and John 7:53–8:11, see my extended discussions in G. Borchert, *John 1–11*, 369–76 and 195–216.

[11]See my comment on this issue in G. Borchert, *John, 1–11*, 369–70.

But I contend that the response of Jesus to the men who were ready to stone the woman is far more telling: "The one of you that is above sin, let him throw the first stone!" When Jesus made that statement and started to write in the dust, these self-righteous men left the scene, beginning with the older ones first (John 8:3–9). Think about this situation of adultery for a moment and then ask yourself: Why did all the men leave? Was this a set-up for entrapment that failed? The evangelist does not answer our question. But Jesus caught the men in their self-righteousness. Do you think this pericope reveals to us something about the views of men in that early Jewish community?

I would also have you reflect for a moment on the story of the Samaritan woman who met Jesus at the well in John 4:7–42. This woman obviously had become rather loose. Not only had she gone through five husbands, but she no longer needed a marital arrangement (4:16–18). After she was confronted by the searing words of Jesus, she forgot her reason for coming to the well and rushed off to tell the men (*anthrōpois*) to "Come, see a man who told me everything that I have done!" (4:28–29). Now while the Greek word for men is generic, if you were among those men, what do you think you would have done if a woman of bad reputation had made such a statement about her life? Do you not wonder why the folks of the village were anxious to meet Jesus?

Paul's Rabbinic Argument about Women

Let me here reflect on the issue of Paul and women very briefly. While Paul does not deny the role of women in publicly praying and prophesying, he does enjoin them to wear veils—"because of the angels" (1 Cor 11:10). Most people today either read over that text and promptly forget it or conclude that Paul must have been a bit twisted in his mind. Yet I caution you to remember that Paul had also been a prominent Jewish rabbi who undoubtedly tried to make sense out of Old Testament texts. The rabbis at that time had developed many strange arguments in trying to interpret difficult texts. One of the most difficult passages was Genesis 6:1–4 concerning the sons of God viewing the daughters of humans and lusting after them. The text for Paul probably involved a rabbinic explanation for the presence of strange people in our world who were called the *nephilim*, which is usually translated as "giants." In this mythical scenario, however, the full veil worn by women became viewed by the Jewish rabbis as a man's means of protecting his women from the lusting eyes of others—obviously even angels!

Today we hardly worry about the lusts of non-earthly beings such as disobedient angels or the sons of God who fathered the *nephilim*. Yet their current perceived absence does not mean that earthly predators do not stalk and attack women. Nor does it mean that we would necessarily blame the evil spirits directly for violence. But our lighthearted statements such as "the devil made me do it" could well be more serious than we sometimes suppose.

Now as a former attorney, I would hardly attempt to sue the devil or put such a spiritual, demonic scoundrel in jail for someone's crime. We frankly do not usually regard the evil spirit world as proximately or immediately responsible for such violence. But evil is evil. What is important here, however, is that Paul's view of women was clearly part of his first-century rabbinic context.

We know that women such as Phoebe, Priscilla, and Junia(s),[12] had important roles (Rom 16:1–7) in the early church. Yet when Paul came to establishing order in the churches and focused the role of women in 1 Timothy 3:8–15, in dealing with the independent-minded churches of Ephesus and Asia he would again turn to his rabbinic support. The texts of 1 Timothy and Titus particularly remind us of some of the Corinthian problems, but to pursue this matter further would lead me to a long digression such as was undertaken by William Mounce in his extended discussion of the above 1 Timothy text, yet that discussion could have focused more on rabbinic thinking in order to clarify the issue.[13]

Tensions in Divorce and Remarriage

With the above thoughts in mind, I turn now to the issue of divorce and remarriage, a subject that has kindled fiery arguments and splits in churches—including the well-known incidents surrounding the multiple marriages of King Henry VIII and the split establishing the Church of England.

A Personal Reflection on Divorce

I was blessed with having had a wise father who was the leading layman in our large church in Calgary, Alberta, Canada. He allowed me to raise all kinds of questions and challenged me to ponder difficult issues without giving me simplistic answers. During my teenage years I had a friend whose dad was also a fine Christian man but who had never held a leadership position in our church. So, I asked my father about him. Without answering my query, he told me that he had been divorced and Mr. X did not think that the Bible allowed him to hold a leadership position. I read and reread the texts from the Pastoral Epistles and compared them with

---

[12]See James D.G. Dunn, *Romans 9–16*, vol. 38B, WBC (Dallas: Word Books,1988), 886–890.

[13]See William D. Mounce, *Pastoral Epistles*, vol. 46, WBC (Nashville: Thomas Nelson, 2000), especially 120–149.

the forgiving texts elsewhere. Those verses remained in my mind for many years as I asked myself repeatedly if Jesus was a stern legislative ruler who would hold a grudge for a past mistake. That question troubled me for years.

Divorce and Hope

In responding to the issue of divorce, I turn first to the third great antithesis (Matt 5:31–32) in what is generally called the Sermon on the Mount. To understand the six antitheses in this section of Matthew (5:17–48),[14] remember that they involve Jesus' confrontation with the patterns that the Jewish legal experts developed for interpreting the various aspects of the Torah Codes. In this third antithesis Jesus waded into the swamp of the Deuteronomic Code pertaining to husband-and-wife relationships, particularly their interpretations of Deuteronomy 24:1–4. Typical of Jesus, he affirmed the biblical text and emphasized the fact that both men and women were subject to such a law, not just the women. But I believe there are three different issues involved here: the divorce document, the indecency associated with divorce, and the concept of divorce itself.

A divorce document was given to women because men tended put women out of the house without any rights and left to fend for themselves. Many would then be forced to turn to prostitution and any man could pick them up as Judah did with Tamar (Genesis 38). The divorce document provided women with the right to begin their lives again without interference from their former husbands, and actually granted grace to a woman in the context of pain and abandonment. I think that sometimes we read these stories and do not fully understand the horrible nature of women being abandoned that should impact our understanding concerning the gracious nature of the freedom to start life over again with the divorce document.

By the time of Jesus, men tended to interpret the issue of indecency very loosely, as the privilege to escape from their marriage commitments—especially by the followers of Hillel. Failure to bear a son or disliking the looks of a woman when she became older would qualify. Even such matters as poor cooking became legitimate grounds for setting aside a wife. In the apocryphal book called Sirach or Ecclesiasticus, the writer advises his readers concerning inadequacies in a wife. He speaks of an unworthy (indecent) woman as being both a dragon and a lion (25:16) and likens her speech to the venom of a poisonous snake (25:15).

---

[14]For an excellent discussion on these antitheses, please see Robert Guelich, *The Sermon on the Mount: A Foundation for Understanding* (Waco, TX: Word Books, 1982), 134–271. See also Donald A. Hagner, *Matthew 1–13*, vol. 33A, WBC (Dallas: Word Books, 1993), 102–136.

She is one who inconsiderately gives her husband's dinner to the neighbors (25:18), and causes her husband grief because of her impudence (25:22–23). She is like sandpaper with her constant chattering (25:20), and her beauty is merely used to capture him (25:21). Since she does not obey her husband, Sirach advises his readers that she should be dismissed (perhaps here a divorce is meant, but it is not clear [25:26]). Compare these words with the well-known text in Proverbs 31:10–31 concerning the woman who is a dutiful servant.

Many Christians misunderstand the biblical perspectives on divorce and remarriage.[15] We in the church frequently view the Mosaic concept of the divorce procedure to be a negative action, whereas it was in fact a means for rescuing abandoned women. For example, with the document in hand a woman could remarry and if she prospered and her husband died, the former husband was prevented from claiming any right to her newly acquired property. Remember that the general understanding of the Torah text at Deuteronomy 24:1–4 assumes the right for a man to dismiss his wife, but in doing so he had to supply her with a document guaranteeing her freedom. The former husband was forbidden from forcing her to marry him again. It was the Mosaic means of protecting a woman.

Part of our misunderstanding related to divorce grows out of two Hebrew words: *Shalach* means "abandoning" or "putting away" one's wife, such as was the tragic pattern practiced when men dismissed the wives of their youth (Mal 2:14–16). *Keriythuwth* means the severing of the marriage bond and supplying the wife with a writ of divorce. The woman with such a divorce document in hand had the right to be married again without the consent of the former husband. The latter word is used in Jeremiah 3:8 when God finally has had enough of the people of Israel playing the harlot with foreign gods and as a result sends them into exile with a writ of divorce. The separated ones are therefore pictured as a divorced woman, and God (representing the husband) legally would be denied the right to take her back (Jer 3:1–5). Naturally the knotty question for Jeremiah (God's spokesman) was: Could God retake or remarry the divorced Israel as his wife (3:6–10)? It's a fascinating question. Even God is here set into a tension context.

---

[15]Please see my discussion in Gerald L. Borchert, "1 Corinthians 7:15 and the Church's Historic Misunderstanding of Divorce and Remarriage" in *RevExp*, 96 (1999): 125–129 as well as my discussion on "Divorce and Remarriage" in *Christ and Chaos: Biblical Keys to Ethical Questions* (Macon, GA: Nurturing Faith, 2020), 95–101.

The Perspectives of Jesus and Paul

When Jesus came on the scene, the Jewish leaders, in an effort to trap him or at least to "pigeonhole" him, posed all sorts of questions to him about the legitimate rules for divorce. Would he follow the strict interpretations of indecency argued by Rabbi Shammai or the more lenient interpretations of Rabbi Hillel? Perhaps you can recognize that the rabbi's questions were not very different from those Christians who want to assign guilt for the failure of a marriage. Today, would he prefer to allow divorce based on the common consent of the parties?

Jesus knew all the arguments and when his disciples asked him to define the legitimate grounds for divorce, his brief response in Mark 10:10–12 may have seemed like a dismissal to the disciples. Would Jesus follow the strict view of Shammai who argued that divorce was only for adultery (cf. Matt 5:31–32)? Yet Luke 16:18 even omits the exception clause. My view is that the disciples totally misunderstood Jesus. For him both separation and divorce were tragedies. Neither was God's original intention in creating man and woman. God's desire was for them to become one, and that unity is the reason a man leaves his parents and is joined to his wife (Mark 10:6–8). (Note that it is the man who leaves his parents and is joined to the wife, not the reverse [Gen 2:24]).[16] Then Jesus added the crucial warning against anyone breaking that marriage bond (Mark 10:9).

Did the disciples really want to accept the views of Jesus or of God's original intention in marriage? I think the answer must be a clear No! Matthew provides the clue to this answer. Remember that women had very few rights in the minds of Jewish men. So, Jesus responded to the arguments of these legal casuists because he added that the Mosaic provision for the divorce decree was given because of the "hardness of their hearts" in seeking to get rid of their wives (Matt 19:8).

Then having listened to Jesus' disputation with the Pharisees, the disciples in a pathetic response must have thrown up their hands in exasperation and said to Jesus that if they could not do with their wives as they wished, then "it is preferable not to marry" (Matt 19:10). You can almost hear Jesus thinking: "Too bad,

---

[16]This summarizing statement concerning the marriage relationship between a man and woman almost takes the reader by surprise, and most commentators who reflect on this verse normally acknowledge that the general Semitic pattern is for the wife to be joined to the husband's family rather than the reverse. Even John Skinner in writing *Genesis* for the ICC during the period when the History of Religions School was in vogue (Edinburgh: T&T Clark, 1930), 69–70, hardly argued that the text pointed back to a earlier matriarchal period. Moreover, there is little support for the idea that it represented a theological "pre-Fall" relationship—as suggested by Kenneth A. Matthews, *Genesis 1–11:26*, NAC (Nashville, Broadman & Holman, 1996), 222–25. I have generally said that it is an intriguing statement, just like the conversation of Jesus with the disciples concerning marriage (Matt 19:10–12).

boys!" But is not his response virtually the same: "Not everyone can adopt this perspective, but only those to whom it is given!" (19:11).

Clearly divorce is to be viewed as a tragedy because what at one point was expected and promised by the couple to be a wonderful union ended in pain, and a fractured relationship. So, is it then an unpardonable sin as some Christians have thought in the past? No! Even the Apostle Paul recognized that some marriages do not work out, particularly between Christians and non-Christians. Therefore, he advised that if the unbelieving spouse could not live with the Christian, then the Christian was "not bound" (1 Cor 7:15). Paul meant that a peaceful termination of the marriage should be allowed, leaving the Christian person free to get on with the rest of life. If such a life involved remarriage for a Christian, then like every marriage, it should not to be entered lightly. Every Christian marriage should be undertaken as a serious covenant not only between the parties but also with the one who created them (Gen 2:24–25).

The New Testament also briefly addresses the issue of church leaders being "the husband of one wife" (1 Tim 3:2, 12; Titus 1:6). Please remember not to read twenty-first-century cultural patterns of the West into the first-century Mediterranean culture. For example, in the Africa bush country and elsewhere, important men frequently have more than one wife. Christian missionaries then have often insisted that monogamy is the absolute standard for church membership. While most Christians would affirm that standard, tension questions arise such as should a new Christian husband put away all but one wife, the other wives would face a situation similar to patterns of the dismissed wives in the Old Testament who had little basis for livelihood. Who would care for those wives? The missionaries? And when these new Christians read that Abraham and Jacob had more than one wife, they may wonder why it is necessary to "be the husband of one wife." Then some rural leaders (men) purposely postpone becoming Christians until they have married the needed complement of wives for their leadership status. You see, humans are not above manipulation.

While I could have chosen to mention some Western patterns of manipulation, I chose the above example to stretch your thinking since they do not apply directly to you. But for many of us, rules usually apply to others and not to us—or, do they? Remember that Jesus understands our common patterns of manipulation.

I should add at this point that patterns are changing in Africa, especially in urban areas, so that advertisements for positions in local papers will often read something of this nature: "This job implies that the employer will cover the expenses of only one wife." Do you understand the interconnection between economics and marital patterns? Sometimes I have to ask, Which is the most powerful: Christian ethics or economics?

A Personal Postscript: A Letter

Before I close this brief discussion on divorce and remarriage, I wish to share with you an unprompted letter that I received from a woman who had traveled with me on one of my Holy Land seminars:

> Dear Dr. Borchert:
> I am sure you won't remember me, but you lectured on our bus in the Holy Land.... I had almost made up my mind to skip the evening lecture but you helped me in what you said. I want to say thank you. Why? Because you made me feel like a human being after all!
> I grew up in an orphanage, married my high school sweetheart and I thought it was for life.... It was a nightmare but I gave him chance after chance and after 3 children and 5 and 1/2 years, I was only a mere 82 pounds. I got a divorce.... there was such a stigma to it and most people thought I was a failure. I wasn't a Christian.... I started going to church.... I met [his name] .... I said I would join the [name] Church. I was baptized at 29, and it truly was a life-changing experience....
> Whenever the topic of divorce came up, it was very difficult and so judgmental. I attended a life and work conference and the minister there asked if anyone was divorced. I hesitated and then I admitted I was. He said, "Well I would never have married [performed the wedding ceremony for] you!" ....
> Because of my divorce, people always looked down ... and think they really didn't try to make it work.... Then you came along and gave me a new perspective. You said that divorced people can still be useful in the church.... I could finally let those unkind thoughts of other people float away....
> [Signed]

This letter states the situation better than I can. You never know when you can be an instrument in God's hand to bring healing to people who are experiencing rejection and hurt.

In closing this section, I would again add that divorce is a tragedy, but it is not unpardonable or the end of Christian life and service. For all Christians, however, the meshing of two persons creates tensions. Learning how to deal with the varying ideas, perspectives, desires, needs, and actions of each other is both the God-given responsibility and the joy of marriage. Living in that tension is the role of a Christian spouse and parent.

The Painful Tension of Homosexuality in the Church

I turn now as a professor, former dean, ordained minister, and biblical scholar to an issue that I would rather not address because—whatever I have to say—someone is bound to condemn me and perhaps to do so with great feeling. Yet, as Christians we must face the difficult issues that require nuanced answers and our best Christ-like perspectives. We need to join those who in the heat of tension seek to follow the example of our Lord. We cannot avoid offering our best opinions, somewhat in the spirit of Mark Yarhouse who has tried graciously to deal gently with clients and the church.[17] Accordingly, I am proceeding, knowing that this concern has split denominations, fractured relationships of well-meaning Christians, and left some congregations in shambles. It is as though the devil has determined that this issue today will provide a needed foothold to undo some redemptive work of Jesus in our world. So, I tread into the issue of homosexuality lightly.

Medical authorities have disagreements concerning the genetic construct or ladder of humans. Nevertheless, they generally recognize that people are born with considerable variations in their genetic codes and that absolute clarity concerning those codes is hardly yet achievable. I also wish it understood that I do not intend to bend the biblical statements, and I disagree with those who say that Paul did not understand what homosexuality was. Yet I recognize that

---

[17]See the helpful work of Mark A. Yarhouse and Julia Sandusky, *Emerging Gender Identities: Understanding the Diverse Experiences of Today's Youth* (Grand Rapids: Brazos, 2020) and his earlier works *Sexual Identity and Faith: Helping Clients Find Congruence* (West Conshohocken, PA: Templeton Press, 2019) and *Understanding Gender Dysphoria: Navigating Transgender Issues in a Changing Culture* (Downers Grove, IL: InterVarsity, 2015). Please also see my extended discussion on this divisive issue in G. Borchert "Homosexuality" in *Christ and Chaos*, 103–113. Cf. also the work of my seminary classmate, Tony Campolo, in confronting this issue in his *Speaking My Mind, The Radical Evangelical Prophet Tackles the Tough issues Christians are Afraid to Face* (Nashville: Word/Thomas Nelson, 2004), 55–76. For a further analysis of this subject, see Robert A.J. Ganon, *The Bible and Homosexual Practice: Texts and Hermeneutics* (Nashville: Abingdon, 2001). See also the subsequent exchange on the subject in Robert A.J. Ganon and Dan Via, *Homosexuality and the Bible: Two Views* (Minneapolis: Fortress Press, 2003), as well as the interesting thoughts of Megan K. DeFranza, *Sex Difference in Christian Theology: Male, Female and Intersex in the Image of God* (Grand Rapids: Eerdman's, 2015) and the interchange of views in Preston Sprinkle, ed., *Two Views on Homosexuality, the Bible and the Church* (Grand Rapids: Zondervan, 2016).

there is tension over homosexuality in the church, and that I am not writing this section of the book to stand in judgment over people on either side of this issue. I also wish to be clear that having taught in many schools and visited many others where ministers are being trained—no matter what designation the school leadership might call themselves—I have encountered those who claim, secretly at least, to be homosexual. I have also made it clear to those who have shared their feelings with me in private that I am not a homosexual and that I am happily married to a wonderful Christian woman. So, with these preliminary matters before you, I turn to this issue that has raised tension in humanity and in the church.

Suggested Perspectives on Homosexuality

While the reasons for homosexuality have not at this point been fully determined, it appears that viable theories leading to homosexuality can be rooted in genetics and/or in family systems. Although I have read a good deal of medical research that strongly suggests the genetic patterns of some persons can be mixed or what I have sometimes termed as cross-wired, I have here sought to be careful in reaching conclusions simply on the basis of theological perspectives.

Accounts such as the Bruce Jenner story should give everyone pause before assuming they have the final answers. Perhaps we should ask: "Why would a robust, medal-winning, male athlete want to have surgery to clarify his/her gender and become a woman?" In response to the shock of those who would pose this question, I would ask: "Are we still in the era where the male is regarded as superior in the subconscious minds of most people?"[18] We must be careful not to blame people, because we probably have not walked in their shoes.

Having taught in departments of counseling and sociology in several schools, I would advise caution concerning family systems in playing the blame game. It may appear from research in these fields that boys who have mothers who tend to be somewhat frigid toward their husbands and overly possessive and intimate with a son can spark an inordinate submissiveness on the part of the son, especially if the father engenders in the son a feeling of fear. A consequent failure to respect the father that is supported by the mother's excessive guardianship of the son can also be an important factor. The result may be that the son could develop a mixed influential identification (compared to the more typical relational pattern) with the mother rather than identifying with the father.

---

[18]See my further comments in G. Borchert, "Homosexuality," 108–109.

Now the concern with any analysis is that our goal is not the blame game but searching for understanding. So, for example, I have discussed the matter with some concerned mothers and fathers where from my perception the family system analysis would not seem to fit that situation. Accordingly, I would assert again that great care must be exercised in reaching conclusions concerning parents who have tried earnestly to cope with children whom they do not understand but have regarded as a little different—perhaps even from a very early age!

In like manner, research may suggest that lesbian girls may develop competitive feelings toward their mothers but—in contrast to boys—research does not confirm that girls develop an influential identification with their fathers. Rather, fathers of lesbians do not appear to have lacked ease in being affectionate toward their daughters. But generalizing is dangerous.

Yet one tendency seems to be apparent with both boys and girls in this category: the sense of loneliness or worthlessness that leads to a need for affirmation or acceptance. It is precisely at this point that the church and Christians could have an impact. But what is often experienced by persons is rejection and judgment. As a result, they are sometimes isolated from the very community that ought to be assisting them in finding meaning and purpose in living. When they find accepting communities, their self-worth is often greatly enhanced. So, they will search for groups who will accept them.

If they only find repeated rejection, they will probably react with patterns of acute self-affirmation—which only brings further condemnation upon them. Even the term "gay" is a reaction to its original meaning. Witness, for example, the display of the Gay Pride Parade that my wife and I attended while teaching in San Francisco. While I hesitate to categorize the parade, it included those who flaunted an immature sexual openness. Such behavior was an attempt at self-affirmation and could remind one of the Pauline condemnation of such action in Romans 1:26–27 and even more in the concluding quest for co-approval at 1:32. But my point here is to leave condemnation and to emphasize the fact that rejection can easily lead to a defensive reaction in the search for self-affirmation. Frequently humans, including church people, attempt angrily to address those actions without probing the reasons for them and for their own fears behind their reactions. Condemnation was not the way of Jesus. Care and concern for the hurting was the Jesus pattern. Christians are called to bring healing. Blaming is not the way.

The Problem with Polarization.[19] The above statement brings me to the situation in churches and denominations today. It is exceedingly difficult to exhibit the "mind of Christ" (Phil 2:5) when people have become polarized and bat around slogans for identification such as "welcoming and affirming" or either one. If we refuse to recognize either statement, we are probably regarded as witless "boors" by some people. If we separate the two statements and seek to adopt a posture of "welcoming" without "affirming," we are often regarded by both opposing sides as "fence straddlers." If we adopt both statements, we are probably regarded by others as somewhat devilish or in denial of Scripture. But people are not slogans. They are humans who have been created by God, and as humans they seem to have things out of joint with others and with God (Rom 3:23) and need the healing touch of Jesus.

The Issues of Isolation and Acceptance. If we as redeemed people isolate others from the community of faith and merely condemn them, then how will they find the needed healing in Jesus? When Paul addressed his Corinthian misfits, he reminded them of their former ways that included: immorality, idolatry, adultery, homosexuality (of both types[20]), robbery, greediness, drunkenness, cursing, rowdiness, and so on. But then he blessed them because they had found the acceptance of Jesus and had been transformed as any other Christian (1 Cor 6:9–11). But I greatly fear that many Christians who read Paul's list do not concentrate on the process of transformation and renewal but on the identification and condemnation of "those people" whom they have decided will not "inherit the kingdom of God." Yet they may not have realized that self-righteousness is the ever-lurking sin of the people of God. Homosexuals, like all of us, experience loneliness, but they may feel even more lonely and isolated than heterosexuals. Can we understand that flaunting one's sexuality may be a defensive posture that seeks acceptance?

---

[19]For interesting perspectives on this subject, see Karen Keen, *Scripture, Ethics and the Possibility of Same Sex Relations* (Grand Rapids: Eerdmans, 2018) and James Brownson, *Bible, Gender, Sexuality* (Grand Rapids, Eerdmans, 2013).

[20]The two Greek terms *malakoi* and *arsenokoitai* are used very infrequently in Greek literature, and some scholars have speculated that Paul may have developed the latter term for use in 1 Cor 6:10 and 1 Tim 1:10. Some scholars have argued that this term is inherently evil, while others have argued with D.S. Bailey that it merely refers to the sex act with one of the same sex. (see William D. Mounce, *Pastoral Epistles* in WBC [Nashville: Nelson, 2000], 38–39). The problem with such arguments, as my former professor James Barr (*The Semantics of Biblical Language*) who critiqued the major work of Kittle in *TDNT*, is that word studies of themselves are often deceptive unless they are used in a defining context. What is clear in these Pauline references is that these words are used in lists of actions that are rejected by Paul.

But the next question concerns the acceptance of the continued homosexual lifestyle in the church. Perhaps the best way to approach this tension is to ask ourselves: Does the church regard homosexuality per se to be on the same plane as immorality, idolatry, adultery, robbery, greediness, drunkenness, cursing, and rowdiness? And how would we relate "greediness" to the other terms in that list? On the other hand, is there a point at which homosexual behavior can become destructive? If we ask these questions, should we not also ask if there is a point at which opposition to homosexual behavior can also become destructive of community well-being? Having the mind of Christ also means analyzing our own motives in the light of Jesus.

So, do we really understand why some people become homosexually oriented, and are we interested in comprehending both sides of this tension? Medical information may provide new insights. Are we prepared to accept new insights? And how do we treat such people? Do we regard them as truly made in the image of God, even though—like with us—that image may be distorted? Moreover, what is our attitude toward church action/discipline? Is it redemptive, or is it condemnatory? These questions are very important in dealing with this painful tension in the church that not only involves the laity but also the clergy.

I honestly believe that God intended the normative pattern of relationship as being a monogamous one between a man and a woman. But all humans are broken people, and as humans we are not made from a cookie cutter. We desperately seek to be accepted by God and by others—even those who claim to be self-sufficient. Claiming otherwise is just another version of self-righteousness, and it needs the healing touch of God. The question is: Are we prepared to help God in that transforming process by being the conduits for assisting in healing?

The church of the future will have its plate full of frustration and tension concerning these issues as it seeks to be Christ's body. The challenge of course is to be like Jesus, the one who did not reject the Samaritan woman (John 4) but called her to a transformed pattern of life. As we face the future, can we as Christians accept that model?

A Postscript on AIDS and Pandemics[21]

Since AIDS has frequently been linked to homosexuality, it is necessary to pause briefly and reflect on it and the safety-fear tension that this and other pandemics create. While the Acquired Immunodeficiency Syndrome has sometimes been proclaimed by a few vocal North American preachers and Christians as a judgment of God upon homosexuals, it should be regarded as a worldwide tragedy that has affected many innocent people and it is not likely to cease quickly in its devastating pandemic effects.

Anyone who has been in Africa and witnessed how the disease has wiped out entire communities and left thousands of children orphaned can hardly be too quick to fall into a simplistic judgmental posture. I am quite aware that one of the major ways that this disease is transmitted is via unsafe sex, and having talked with nurses and doctors in Africa and elsewhere I know that many people pursue such activities without regard for its dangers. Indeed, I remember vividly one African young woman's remark when she said boastfully to her nurse that she was not worried. But the HIV virus is exceedingly virulent and has even killed health care professionals, not merely those engaged in sexual activity. As with all pandemics (including Covid-19), it is a horrendous danger to the world—particularly to people in the developing nations.

But having stated the problem in such dark terms, I do not mean that Christians should run from the situation or adopt the traditional ostrich tactic of sticking one's head in the sand concerning the problem. Some of my most self-giving former students are working with people in the hardest hit areas, seeking not only to assist in supplying the medical needs of those infected but also attempting to develop care programs for the multitudes of orphaned children. Christians need to regard the challenging tension of a pandemic not merely as a tragic unsettling situation but also as a God-given opportunity for service to both our Lord and to humanity.

The task of sharing God's love in service is of course not without the risk of contracting the disease, and it requires healthy vigilance and dependence on any knowledge and resources that are available for prevention if one takes on such a caring task. But now that the patterns of contracting the virus are better under-

---

[21]For a more intense discussion on the problem of AIDS and the ethical and medical implications involved in this and other subjects, see the important section in Arthur Zucker, Donald Borchert, and David Stewart, eds., *Medical Ethics: A Reader* (Englewood Cliffs, NJ: Prentice Hall, 1992), 334–93. See also Clifford G. Christians, Mark Flacker, et al., *Medical Ethics: Cases and Moral Reasoning* (New York Rutledge, 2017) and Kevin P. O'Rourke, OP, and Philip J. Boyle, eds. *Medical Ethics: Sources of Catholic Teachings* (Washington: Georgetown University Press, 1999).

stood, Christians are called to confront this problem as they did in serving those who were struck with plagues such leprosy not too long ago.

We can treat HIV or a Covid-19 virus as though it is nothing, and assume we are immune to its effects. But fear can also grip people with such a debilitating grasp that Christians cease to exhibit the qualities of Christlikeness. For example, when a faithful Christian contracted the HIV virus a few years ago from a then inadequately monitored blood transfusion, Christians in that community of faith shunned the entire family—including the young children who had difficulty understanding their tragic circumstance. Today we may shake our heads at this reaction on the part of those Christians, but we must remember that we are all frail, deviant humans. It is much easier to condemn others than to place our own miscues before the gracious throne of God and seek forgiveness.

Conclusion

With this brief review of issues flowing from the basic problem of good and evil in our world, the attendant tensions that have resulted from our genuine split nature as humans and our insatiable desire to make distinctions in order to assert our selfhood, I turn next to the work of God in sending Jesus, the incarnation of God's selfhood, to deal with our lack of integrity by providing healing and wholeness to us humans in this phenomenal world.

… And that transforming reality is repeatedly being accomplished today through the historic mystery of Jesus, the subject to which we now turn.

Chapter 5

The Coming of the Transforming Jesus

Tensions in Understanding the Incarnation and the Two Natures of Jesus

Approaching the Subject of Jesus

I have purposely delayed the discussion of the divine answer in order to set the stage for the divine solution by first treating the problems with humanity. Having done so, it is now appropriate to approach the central tension we face concerning our understanding of Jesus. In this approach, we must of necessity confront the strategic task of dealing with the important issue of mystery.

Now some scholars in a former school of theologians might have begun our study of Christian thought and life or theology and ethics by turning first to the subject of revelation and the understanding of God. In such a study we might seek to deduce the divine reality in terms of concepts such as "omnipotence," "omniscience," and "omnipresence" in addition to "immortality" and "invisibility." But I have purposely avoided dealing with such ideas, as least until the next chapter. The reason, as you will see, is because such terms communicate mixed and confusing messages to us in this phenomenal world. Yes I am also quite aware that the term "incarnation" is also a word that is shrouded in mystery. But I start here because it reminds me that Jesus, the Son of God, is clearly a "mystery in flesh!"

Although some attributes of God may perhaps be deduced from general revelation (e.g., the creator's sovereignty over against creation's "law of the claw" and what in the legal profession we call "acts of God" in nature), such reflections do not lead us very far in our understanding of God. We can, of course, turn to the Old Testament and gain some crucial insights into the divine reality and the way God acted with Israel. These insights, which Christians usually refer to as the theology of the Old Testament,[1] are foundational for our understanding of

---

[1] For some helpful theologies of the Old Testament, see Walter Brueggemann, *Theology of the Old Testament: Testimony, Dispute, Advocacy* (Minneapolis: Augsburg/Fortress, 1997); Bruce Waltke, *An Old Testament Theology: An Exegetical, Canonical Approach* (Grand Rapids: Zondervan, 2007); Christopher J.H. Wright, *Knowing God Through the Old Testament: Three Volumes in One*, 2nd ed. (Downers Grove, IL: InterVarsity, 2014); Robin Routledge, *Old Testament Theology: A Thematic Approach* (Downers Grove, IL: InterVarsity, 2012); and John Goldingay, *Old Testament Theology: Israel's Faith* (Downers Grove, IL: InterVarsity, 2016). Also see some important older works such as: John Bright, *The Kingdom of God* (New York:

the coming of Jesus, our interpretation of the New Testament, and the meaning of Christian theology and ethics.[2] Therefore, I frequently refer to the Old Testament in this work. Like all good Christian thinkers, I would not diminish the Old Testament as a crucial basis or foundation for understanding the message of the New Testament.[3] But, as Paul earlier argued, the Law is the basis, guardian, or "tutor" (*paidagōgos*) that directs us to understand Jesus Christ and the New Testament (Gal 3:24).[4]

Interpreting the nature and work of Jesus is not an easy task. I have spent many hours pondering and writing about the person and significance of Jesus.[5] But I inevitably come away from my efforts with the sense that I have only begun to scratch the surface of the person and work of this incredible, mysterious Jesus. In summing up his gospel, the Johannine evangelist indicated that he supposed "the whole world could not contain the books that would be written" concerning Jesus and his works (John 21:25). So, please understand that in this chapter I am trying to write about someone who, like God, is shrouded in mystery.

Abingdon, 1953); H.H. Rowley, *The Faith of Israel: Aspects of Old Testament Faith* (Philadelphia: Westminster Press, 1956); and Gerhard von Rad, *Old Testament Theology*, particularly vol. 1, *The Theology of Israel's Historical Traditions*, trans. D.M.G. Stalker (New York: Harper & Brothers,1962).

[2]Reading the Old and New Testaments together as Christian scripture is commonly understood today as a canonical approach following the lead of Brevard Childs of Yale. The following works purport to argue for a specific Christian interpretation of the Old Testament: G.K. Beale, *A New Testament Biblical Theology: The Unfolding of the Old Testament in the New* (Grand Rapids: Baker Academic, 2011); R.W.L. Moberly, *Old Testament Theology: Reading the Hebrew Bible as Christian Scripture* (Grand Rapids: Baker Academic,2015); John Walton, *Old Testament Theology for Christians: From Ancient Context to Enduring Belief* (Downers Grove, IL: InterVarsity, 2017); and Frank Thielman, *Theology of the New Testament: A Canonical Approach* (Grand Rapids: Zondervan, 2005).

[3]See, however, Rudolph Bultmann, particularly his essay on "Prophecy and Fulfillment" in *Essays on Old Testament Hermeneutics*, ed. Claus Westermann, trans. James Luther Mays (Atlanta: John Knox, 1960), 50–75, who has a negative view of the Old Testament, perhaps in part influenced by his context in Nazi Germany. See my comments in Gerald L. Borchert, "Is Bultmann's Theology a New Gnosticism?" *EvQ*, 36.4 (1964): 222–223.

[4]For my further comments on Paul's concern in this passage see "Galatians" in Roger Mohrlang and Gerald L. Borchert, *Romans and Galatians*, vol. 14, CorBC (Carol Stream, IL: Tyndale House, 2007), 297–300.

[5]See for example Gerald L. Borchert, *Jesus of Nazareth: Background, Witnesses, and Significance* (Macon, GA: Mercer University Press, 2011) and *Portraits of Jesus* (Macon, GA: Smyth and Helwys, 2016). Of the many interesting studies, see Mitzi Minor, *The Power of Mark's Story* (St. Louis: Chalice Press, 2002); Edward Schillebeeckx, *Jesus: An Experiment in Christology* (New York: Crossroad, 1986). For a fascinating dialog, see N.T. Wright, *Jesus and the Victory of God* (Minneapolis, Fortress, 1996) and Carey Newman, ed., *Jesus and the Restoration of Israel: A Critical Assessment of N.T. Wright's Jesus and the Victory of God* (Downers Grove, IL: InterVarsity, 1999).

Jesus, the Human-Divine Reality

The question of the way to human wholeness, salvation, and security is rooted for all believers in the issues surrounding the coming of Jesus. It was so for the early church, and it continues to be so for us. Jesus was born a human, a Jew in the first century of this new era that some now refer to as AD (Anno Domini) but that others out of deference to general humanity use CE (the Common Era). The New Testament writers refer to Jesus as "the Son of God" (e.g., Mark 15:39; Matt 14:23, 16:16; John 9:35; Rom 1:4; 2 Cor 1:19; Eph 4:13; 1 John 4:15) and the Gospel writers also indicate that he frequently called himself "the Son of Man" (e.g., Mark 8:31, Matt 12:8, Luke 12:40, John 5:27, Rev 14:14).[6] In these two designations resides the coming of the new covenant and the mystery of the incarnation—perhaps our most incomprehensible tension.

Confronting Two Perceptions of Jesus Christ

It is important for contemporary Christians to recognize the difference between the perspective of the first-century followers of Jesus and the way most of us think about the Incarnation. The disciples walked and talked with a man called Jesus. They watched him eat and drink of earthly substances. They knew he became tired and needed to sleep, even in a small boat on the choppy Sea of Galilee. This God-man even needed to go to the bathroom. The disciples testified that he called himself the Son of Man, yet they heard others charge him with claiming to be equal to God (e.g., John 5:18)—a charge he did not deny (10:30, 33). They knew that he was betrayed and realized he died on the cross. They were quite aware that he was buried in a stone tomb and were sure that his tragic death was the end of a strange, happy-sad story in which they were participants.

But this death was not the end! Jesus was actually raised from the dead and even displayed his former wounds to the disciples (Luke 24:39–40; John 20:25, 27). Then he commissioned them to announce that a new era had dawned, and then their sadness and fear were transformed into joy and boldness. Moreover, skeptics such as Thomas and opponents like Paul astonishingly thereafter proclaimed him to be not only the Son of God but actually God (John 20:28; Rom 1:4, 10:13; Phil 2:9–11). No one could stop the disciples from proclaiming him as the risen Lord Jesus Christ!

---

[6]There are of course many word picture and symbolic names or designations for Jesus such as suggested by Adella Collins in her work *King and Messiah as Son of God: Divine, Human, and Angelic Figures in Biblical and Related Literature* (Grand Rapids: Eerdmans, 2008).

Now those who came after that incredible experience of witnessing the risen Jesus (and we in the twenty-first century) have never seen this Jesus. We have never walked with him or talked with him. Many of us have read stories about him in the Gospels and may even have visited the land where he once walked (often designated as the Holy Land). But the way we, his later followers, have come "to know him personally" is through the presence of the Holy Spirit in our lives. So, our perceptions of this Jesus we confess as the Christ are very different from those first followers. They saw a man and confessed him to be the true incarnation of God. We have an experience of God in Christ that coordinates through the Holy Spirit with the gospel proclamations concerning this man, Jesus. Accordingly, we confess him to have been the true incarnation of God in a human. But both they and we are faced with an incomprehensible tension in our thinking. We confess what we do not fully understand!

Preliminary Ideas about Jesus: From the Jews and the Disciples

In the time of Jesus there were many theories about the coming of messianic figures, speculations that raised hope among the Jewish people. But because there were pretenders who appeared and claimed to be directly sent from God, the Jewish authorities developed patterns for investigating these figures as a means to know the possibilities concerning their authenticity and to try to determine how they could control them both for their own purposes and as a basis for denouncing fake figures and protecting themselves from punishment by their Roman conquerors.

Such an investigating committee was sent to John the Baptizer and to inquire of him whether he fit any of their packaged understandings of the coming one(s). He denied forthrightly (John 1:19–21) that he was the Messiah, Elijah (cf. Mal 3:1, 4:5–6), or the promised coming of a prophet such as Moses (cf. Deut 18:15). When they pressed John further why he was calling the people to repent and to be ready, he simply responded that he was a "voice" proclaiming the coming of the expected one and that he was completely unworthy even to be a slave of him (John 1:22–27). Such an answer no doubt must have greatly frustrated his investigators.[7]

But let me pause briefly to remind you that the Jews were very vague in their speculations. The Prophet could have been thought to be someone like Ezra

---

[7]For a further discussion of the Jewish expectations and John the Baptist, see Gerald L. Borchert, *John 1–11*, vol. 25A, NAC (Nashville: Broadman and Holman, 1996), 125–134. For an excellent discussion on the messianic figures in Qumran, see Raymond E. Brown, "The Qumran Scrolls and the Johannine Gospel and Epistles," *CBQ* 17 (1957): 403–19 and 559–74 and the follow-up work of Marc de Jonge in *Jesus: Stranger from Heaven and Son of God* (Missoula, MT: Scholars Press, 1977), especially 77–116.

who called the people back to obey the Law. The entire concept of obedience in that time had radically changed from focusing on the verb *Halak* ("walking" with God) to the noun *Halakah* (obedience to "legislated rules") and there were incessant debates concerning these rules among the rabbis.

Moreover, when it came to the expectation of Elijah, Jewish families at Passover longed for the coming of this special one from God (and still do today). Their Seder meals still anticipate his coming with an empty chair at their celebrations. It is, therefore, no wonder that at the event we call the Transfiguration (probably on Mount Hermon) Peter became ecstatic with the visionary experience of beholding Jesus talking with those two "mountain men"—Moses and Elijah (cf. Mark 9:2–8).

The third figure, the Messiah, was also shrouded in speculation. Indeed, the Manual of Discipline (1QS 9)—from the Covenanters of the Dead Sea Scrolls—indicates that they expected two messiahs: the messiah of Israel (a messianic king) and the messiah of Aaron (a great priestly messiah). Interestingly, we find both of these messianic concepts in the New Testament. For example, Paul argued that Jesus was of the seed of King David (Rom 1:3) and the Preacher of Hebrews likened Jesus to a great high priest after the order of Melchizedek (Heb 5:1–10, 7:1–17).

But even after he had performed many miracles, did the disciples understand the messianic nature of Jesus?[8] Hardly! At Caesarea Philippi when Jesus asked them who people thought he was, the answer was varied until Peter, the spokesperson for the disciples, announced that Jesus must be "Christ, the Son of the Living God" (Matt 16:16). Jesus probably responded something like "Right on, Peter!" or more traditionally, "You are blessed!" But when Jesus tried to tell them that he was ready to die, Peter responded: "No way!" At that point Jesus had to condemn his well-meaning follower as an instrument of the devil (Matt 16:23).[9]

Later, when they were gathered in the upper room Jesus poured out water and began washing the feet of the disciples. He was making good progress until he came to Peter, who protested and again said "No way!" He thought that such menial activity belonged to a slave—certainly not to a messiah. Jesus must have shaken his head and responded something akin to: "OK, but then you will have no part in my community." At which point Peter undoubtedly cried: "Well, if that is the case, then wash not only my feet, but also give me a shower!"

---

[8]For a examination of miracles, see Graham H. Tweftree, *Jesus the Miracle Worker* (Downers Grove, IL: InterVarsity, 1999).

[9]For a fuller treatment of this important text, see Donald A. Hagner, *Matthew 14–28*, vol. 33B, WBC (Dallas: Word Books,1995), 461–475.

Jesus probably smiled and said: "Feet are enough, Peter!" (cf. John 13:3–9).[10]
Did the disciples, even at this late point in the life of Jesus, really understand the
nature and purpose for the coming of the Messiah? Hardly! It took the death and
resurrection of Jesus to make clear even to the disciples what God's purposes were
in sending this human-divine agent to earth.

The Difficult Task of Defining Perceptions

But how can the divine and the human exist together in one person? That
question troubled the early thinkers, and it continues to vex theologians today
because on that assertion hang most of our Christian affirmations. As the Apostle
Paul clearly stated his conviction in 2 Corinthians 5:19, "God was in Christ
reconciling the world to the self-hood of God." But what did it mean for the
human and the divine to be joined in Jesus? Such an assertion does not compute
in our human minds.

We know that we are not gods, even though John cited Jesus in a confrontation with the Jews concerning their understanding of the Scripture by reminding
them of the earlier Old Testament text that reads: "You are gods" (John 10:34–
35; cf. Ps 82:6)[11]And, Luke cited Paul as quoting from the Greek philosophers
on the Areopagus (Mars Hill) that humans are God's "offspring" (*genos*) when
he was attempting to help the Athenian judges/debaters understand how mortals
could be brought into a new relationship with God through the death and
resurrection of Jesus (Acts 17:28). But with their mindsets of many gods, these
Greeks began to think of "death" and "resurrection" as just two more gods in
their pantheon. And while one of the council members, Dionysius, and a Greek
matron, Damaris, apparently understood Paul's thinking, most of the council-
ors were hardly prepared to accept this talk of resurrection and to give up their
views of the immortality of the soul and their concepts of the body as a tomb
(17:22–32).[12]

Moreover, we know what the Jews thought when in John they believed that
Jesus considered himself to be equal with God. They were ready to kill him, and
not merely because he broke their revered Sabbath rules (John 5:17–18). Perhaps

---

[10]For an extended discussion of this foot-washing text, see Borchert, *John 12–21*, 76–84.

[11]For some interpretations on this intriguing statement, see Borchert, *John1–11*, 343–44.

[12]Understanding the Greek view of the body is imperative to sensing Paul's argument in this text.
(See my further discussion on resurrection and immortality in chapter 13.) It is important to remember
that Socrates was condemned to death by this council and drank the hemlock because of a guilty verdict
on the charge of atheism—namely, denying the existence of their pantheon. Paul did not fall into that trap
but instead proclaimed an unknown God to them and thereby sought to alter their foundational way of
thinking. See also my further discussion on Hellenistic thinking in chapter 2.

the most astounding confession among the early disciples was the one made by the so-called doubter (I prefer realist), Thomas, when after the resurrection he is reported to have called Jesus: "My Lord and my God!" (John 20:28). For a Jew to make Jesus equal to the Lord God (*YHWH*) was almost inconceivable. Yet that was the confession of Thomas, and it has become the hallmark of Christianity.[13]

Other New Testament writers expanded our understanding with additional confessions. For example, the Preacher of Hebrews asserted that Jesus occupied the throne with God (1:3, 8) and is the "great high priest" who has gone through (*dieléluthota*) the heavens" like a victorious conqueror (4:14). Moreover, since "he has been tempted/tested (*pepeirasmenon*)" in every conceivable manner that we could be "without sin (*chōris hamartias*)," he is able to understand and sympathize with our frailties (4:14–15). Or, think of Luke who indicated that Peter proclaimed to Cornelius that Jesus would be the one who would "judge the living and the dead" and that everyone who "believes in him receives the forgiveness of sins" (Acts 10:42–43). In addition, James reminded his readers that they believed in "the glorious Lord Jesus Christ" (Jas 2:1).

The New Testament Writers and Early Faith Statements about Jesus

These perceptions were only part of a developing process that led the New Testament writers to begin formulating a more complete understanding of Jesus. Paul was instrumental in this process of defining who Jesus is with his rebellious Galatian children when he pointedly indicated that the Law (Torah) was not an end in itself.[14] The rabbis had elevated the Law virtually to the equivalent of God so that absolute obedience was demanded in their interpretations of the 613 rules that they had isolated from the Torah as *halakah*. But Paul countered that the Law was merely an instrument, a tutor (*paidagōgos*), to lead people to Christ (Gal 3:24). He also argued that as far as the timing for the coming of Jesus was concerned, the world was as fully ready as it could ever have been for the arrival of God's special emissary (4:4).

Then in Philippians—a letter that was similar to a last will and testament—Paul reminded Christians that we are called to be "minded" (*phoneite*, 2:5) like Christ of Jesus. And he detailed what he meant by that statement in the familiar hymn of the second chapter[15] when he reminded his beloved Macedonian

---

[13]For my fuller discussion on John 20:28 and the important purpose statement that follows in the Gospel of John, see Borchert, *John 12–21*, 314–320.

[14]For my analysis of the early dating of Galatians, see Borchert, "Galatians," 248–51.

[15]For an expanded interpretation and discussion of this hymn in Colossians, see Ralph P. Martin, *A Hymn of Christ: Philippians in Recent Interpretation in the Setting of Early Christian Worship* (Downers Grove,

children that Jesus emptied himself of many of his divine attributes in order to humble himself and become a human. Indeed, he died the humiliating death on the cross for humanity. God, however, has highly exalted Jesus and has given him the highest name in all creation so that humanity will ultimately bow before him and acclaim him "Lord" (2:5–11).

Finally, in the letter to a place that he had never visited (Colossae), Paul enunciated what I call the pinnacle of Paul's thinking concerning Jesus.[16] In this hymn in Colossians, Jesus is confessed as being nothing less than the image (*eikōn*; 1:15) of God and not merely someone or something created like an idol. This Jesus was the firstborn of God before all creation and actually has been active in the creation of everything. Moreover, the reason he is worshiped by Christians is that he embodied in himself the reality of God and provided for Christians the crucial example of the promised resurrection from the dead along with the model for living as the new people of God (1:11–23, 2:6–12).[17]

Among the other New Testament writers who sought to formulate a clear and lofty perception of Jesus was the Preacher of Hebrews who pictured Jesus as a messianic high priest. He also wanted his readers to understand that Jesus was far superior to any angelic visitor to earth. God of course had communicated with people, and especially with Israel, in various ways before the coming of Jesus. But when God's Son came, it was a totally different type of visitation because this Jesus had been involved in the actual creating and sustaining of this phenomenal world. In fact, Jesus mirrors the glory of God and bears the very "character" (*charaktēr*; 1:3) or "exact representation" of God's self. This Greek term *charakēr* is used only once in the entire New Testament, indicating that the Preacher had searched for a specific term that could summarize his understanding of the uniqueness of Jesus And now that he has completed his initial work of salvation, he is enthroned with God in majesty (1:1–4).[18]

IL: InterVarsity, 1997). See also Peter T. O'Brien, *Commentary on Philippians*, NIGTC (Grand Rapids: Eerdmans, 1991) and Gerald Hawthorne and Ralph P. Martin, *Philippians*, vol. 43, rev., WBC (Grand Rapids: Zondervan, 2004).

[16]See Borchert, *Portraits of Jesus*, 95–102. I recognize that there are some interpreters who consider that this letter was written by someone other than Paul, but I remain unconvinced.

[17]For an expanded interpretation and discussion of this hymn in Colossians, see Peter T. O'Brien, *Colossians, Philemon*, vol. 44, WBC (Waco, TX: Word Books, 1982), 31–63 and Murray J. Harris, *Colossians and Philemon* (Grand Rapids: Eerdmans, 1991), 41–53, as well as the earlier work of Ralph P. Martin in "An Early Christian Hymn (Col. 1:15–20)" *EvQ* 36 (1964): 195–205.

[18]For helpful works on Hebrews, see also: Luke Timothy Johnson, *Hebrews*, NTL (Louisville: Westminster/John Knox, 1980); Craig Koester, *Hebrew*, AB (Garden City, NY: Doubleday, 2001), and the brief but important work by William Johnsson, *Hebrews*, Knox Preaching Guides (Atlanta: John Knox, 1980).

It is pointless, therefore, the Preacher argued even to consider comparing the Son to angels. At this point his readers should recall that in the intertestament period angels and archangels had been viewed by the people of Israel as intermediaries between God and humans because the Jews had regarded God as so lofty and unreachable that they believed they needed some other form of communication with God (Heb 1:5–13). But the Preacher asserted that angels are nothing but mere "servants" and are hardly the true mediators between God and humans (1:14).

The high point of reflective thinking about Jesus among the early Christians probably comes in the Gospel of John that was written sometime during the reign of the ruthless Domitian in the 90s. Here Jesus is proclaimed as the very "word" of God (*logos*) who had been around from the very beginning, even before time existed. He was instrumental in creation and is "the life" and "the light" that precedes all other life. Moreover, he can never be eliminated or overcome (1:1–5). In an era of persecution, this message must have engendered confidence and support among the early Christians. This divine word had actually become flesh (*sarx*) or human—the amazing act of God—which in theology we call the Incarnation. Even though he became a human and was called Jesus, John asserted, he embodied the very nature of God's presence on earth. So, John likened Jesus to the *shekinah*, which was God's presence in the Tabernacle of Israel (1:14).[19]

But perhaps equally significant to recognize is that these texts point to an additional reality that Jesus was not only confessed but was also worshiped by the early Christians as the embodiment of God on earth—which is really what the confession of Thomas means when he addressed Jesus as "My Lord and my God" (John 20:28). The Pauline sense of assurance is also reflected in "If we have died with him, we shall also live with him; if we endure, we shall also reign with him" (2 Tim 2:11) and that nothing "in all creation will be able to separate us from the love of God in Christ Jesus our Lord" (Rom 8:39). Worship and devotion, as Larry Hurtado argued, is a powerful indicator of how the early Christians understood who this Jesus was for them.[20]

---

[19] For a further exposition of the Johannine Prologue, see Borchert, *John 1–11*, 99–125.

[20] Larry Hurtado, *At the Origins of Christian Worship: The Context and Character of Earliest Christian Devotion* (Grand Rapids, Eerdmans, 1999). For the early Gentile Christians, commitment to Jesus meant a "replacement cultus"—a new religious commitment and a renunciation of a former way of life. See also Hurtado, *How on Earth Did Jesus Become God? Historical Questions About Earliest Devotion to Jesus* (Grand Rapids: Eerdmans, 2005); Richard Bauckham, *God Crucified: Monotheism and Christology* (Grand Rapids: Eerdmans,1998) and James D.G. Dunn, *Did the First Christians Worship Jesus? The New Testament Evidence* (Louisville: Westminster/John Knox, 2010).

Yet in the light of these elevated Christological statements and confessions of assurance, humans are faced with a very vexing question: How can one then understand Paul's assertion that he "emptied" (*ekenōsen*) himself (Phil 2:7)? It is at the heart of the great tension in the Christian understanding of the Incarnation.

Tensions in Formulating the Early Perceptions of Jesus

So, it is not difficult to recognize why these and other texts became the basis or raw materials from which the scholars and leaders of the early church wrestled in their debates over several centuries as they sought to formulate their early confessions about Jesus. Grasping the task of formulating the early Christian confessions is exceedingly crucial for contemporary Christians to understand.[21]

The Task of Developing the Early Confessions of Faith about Jesus

The history of the early church's struggles to define this Jesus as both God and human is witnessed in the repeated reformulations of their confessional statements.[22] The task was a painstaking one that involved disagreements and debates that were not settled for several hundred years. Was there complete unanimity? Hardly! Indeed, various groups of Christians condemned each other as heretics in the process.

Our problem is that we are frail, fallible humans who find it difficult to comprehend the infinite God let alone the divine-human Son, whom Christians confess as the Lord Jesus Christ. We often make statements about God and God's attributes, but our statements do not mean that we understand what we have said. Many of our cherished theological statements about God are conclusions from wrestling with mystery and attempting to say something meaningful about the God who does not fit into our human categories.

But this problem did not stop the Church Fathers from trying, and it should not stop us from our endeavors at attempting to understand and articulate who

---

[21]For an excellent outline of Christological developments. see the classic work by J.N.D Kelly, *Early Christian Doctrines*, rev. ed. (New York: Harper & Row, 1960), 138–162, especially 138–142. For select sources, see Cyril C. Richardson, *Early Christian Fathers*, vol. 1, LCC (Philadelphia: Westminster Press, 1953) and Edward Rochie Hardy, *Christology of the Later Fathers*, vol. 3, LCC (Philadelphia: Westminster Press, 1954). For a helpful review of reflections on who Jesus is, see also Raymond Brown, *Jesus, God and Man: Modern Biblical Reflections* (New York: McMillan, 1967).

[22]See Henry Bettenson, ed., *Documents of the Christian Church* (London: Oxford University Press, 1943). For an interesting account of the debates in the church over the formulations of Christian beliefs and confessions, see Philip Jenkins, *Jesus Wars: How Four Patriarchs, Three Queens and Two Emperors Decided What Christians Would Believe for the Next 1500 Years* (New York: HarperCollins, 2010).

Jesus is and what Jesus has done for us in coming into the world, in dying on the cross for us, in being raised from the dead, in providing the authentic pattern of life for us, and in coming again to receive us into his eternal realm. These ideas are crucial to Christians, which means that we will struggle to understand Jesus and his divine mystery.[23] But as humans we need to adopt a sense of humility before God and before others because we must admit our proximate understanding. And we need to avoid condemning others with whom we may disagree. Sadly, Christians are not always very successful in being "Christian" and loving others as Jesus instructed (cf. John 13:34–35)—especially when we make our formulations.

The Early Confessions/Creeds about Jesus Christ

Are most contemporary Christians interested in confessions and creed today? Perhaps. But we need to recognize that persecution as well as denials by some Christians concerning the two natures of Jesus in the post-first-century church inevitably led to these fairly precise, articulated statements concerning Jesus.

The Old Roman Creed. In the early fourth century the Old Roman Creed was finally formulated and codified, having seven specific affirmations concerning Christ Jesus, namely that:

1. Jesus was God's "only son, our Lord."
2. He "was born of the Holy Spirit and the Virgin Mary."
3. He "was crucified under Pontius Pilate and was buried."
4. On "the third day" he "rose from the dead."
5. He "ascended into heaven."
6. He now "sits on the right hand of the Father."
7. From there "he shall come to judge the living and the dead."[24]

This Old Roman Creed was later expanded slightly and became known as the Apostles Creed. It is now regarded by many as the universal confession of Christianity concerning Jesus.

---

[23]See the classic work of C.H. Dodd, *The Apostolic Preaching and Its Development* (London: Hodder & Stoughton, 1936).

[24]Bettenson, *Documents of the Christian Church*, 33.

The Nicene Creed and the Context. The early Roman creed, however, did not satisfy many in the church because it did not deal sufficiently with a number of the tensions that troubled the early Church Fathers. As a result, in AD 325, the Council of Nicea met at the prompting of Emperor Constantine (who wanted "uniformity" in the church) and the church leaders began the process of reformulation. Eusebius then suggested a much more detailed modification for countering disputes and deviations of theological statements in the church.

Christians during these early centuries wrestled with the tensions concerning the two natures of Christ, but deviants sought to remove the tension concerning these two natures by reducing the significance of either the human or the divine: The Adoptionists or Docetists argued that Jesus was truly God and that God adopted the body of Jesus at the baptism or that Jesus was simply throughout his life a mere phantom human being. The Arians contrarily denied the eternal nature of Jesus as a divine person and chose to emphasize his humanity.

After much debating and amending, the amended proposal of Eusebius was submitted to the Council of Constantinople in 381. Then after further debate and the acceptance of additions, it was finally adopted at the Council of Chalcedon in 451 and has since been known as the Nicene Creed (or Confession) since the reformulation began much earlier. The section about believing in Jesus reads as follows:

> And in one Lord Jesus Christ, the [*only begotten*] Son of God, begotten of the Father [*before all ages*] Light of Light, true God of true God, begotten not made, of one substance with the Father, through whom all things were made, (*things in heaven and things on earth;*) who for us men and for our salvation came down [*from the heavens*] and was made flesh [*of the Holy Spirit and the Virgin Mary*], and became man, [*and was crucified for us under Pontius Pilate, and*] suffered [*and was buried,*] and rose on the third day [*according to the Scriptures and*], ascended into the heavens, [*and sits on the right hand of the Father and*] is coming [*again with glory*] to judge living and dead [*of whose kingdom there shall be no end*].[25]

---

[25]Bettenson, *Documents of the Christian Church*, 35 and 36–37. I have attempted here to bring the two texts together. The text in the parentheses and italicized "(*things in heaven and things on earth*)" was omitted at Chalcedon, and the text in the square brackets and identified in italics was added at Constantinople and approved at Chalcedon.

When this confession or creed was adopted, those who refused to agree with its formulation were summarily declared to be out of conformity with the historic Church, and thereby labeled as heretics and dismissed from the Church.

Although Church scholars sought painstakingly to refine their understanding of the so-called two natures of Jesus—God's incarnate messenger and the redeemer on earth, in their efforts they refused to minimize either the divinity or the humanity of Jesus. They stoutly retained the tension of these two natures in the one person known as Jesus Christ, and they denounced all forms of Docetism and Arianism.

Did they actually understand how those two natures coexisted in one person? I seriously doubt it. But they accepted this tension-filled mystery, believing that no one else was or would be like Jesus. Did they always act in the spirit of Jesus? Unfortunately, not. Yet for them and for all Christians who follow them, the unequivocal confession of the Church is that: "Jesus is unique!"

A Postscript to the Nicene Creed on the Holy Spirit. It would not be judicious to conclude this discussion on the Nicene Creed without a further note on the section related to the Holy Spirit because of the extremely important dispute that arose concerning that section in the confession. The paragraph of the creed in its briefest form reads that Christians assert their belief in: "the Holy Spirit, the Lord and Life-giver, who proceeds from the Father [*and the Son*], who with the Father and the Son is worshiped together and glorified together. . ."

This reading without the italicized insert is affirmed by the Eastern Church, but the Western Church's version includes "and the Son." This addition of "and the Son" is known in Latin as the *filioque* clause.

For many contemporary Christians, this argument may seem insignificant. But it has been at the center of a longstanding controversy and of the division between the Eastern Orthodox and Roman Catholic churches—and has not been settled even today. Yet this tension actually grows out of two statements in the Gospel of John at 15:26 where Jesus is cited as saying "I will send (*ego pempsō*) the Spirit to you from the Father. . . who proceeds from the Father" (*ho para tou petros ekporeuetai*) and John 16:7 "I will send him to you."[26]

While both sides firmly maintain that they are verbally correct, I would argue that both parties are reading the texts as Western logicians. But while the evangelist wrote in Greek, he was a Semite and his thought pattern was Eastern "picture-thinking," He did not have a Western, deductive Hellenistic mindset that

---

[26]Ibid.

argues by making distinctions. The tension between the two views would have been viewed by the evangelist as unnecessary. The real issue is not "how" the Spirit came but that it was given by God—and the Son was involved in that giving.

Do you see that biblical words do not always convey clarity to us? Some readers may consider the issue to be a chasing after the wind. But as a former lawyer, a case can be made for both views from the Greek or the later Latin. For a Semitic writer, I doubt John would see much of a tension. But, for you, when you think of the Father, the Son, and the Holy Spirit, the question before you is this: Would he separate the purposes of the Father, Son, and Holy Spirit? Some may answer "Yes" and others "No." But I tell you that it all depends on how you view the Godhead functions. Yet in the end we are dealing with mystery!

Relating the Jesus of the Bible to Our Creeds

Theological disputes and fights will obviously continue to take place among Christians. Some will focus primarily on a Jesus identified in creedal statements and/or biblical texts. But great care must be taken to avoid a pattern of thinking like the rabbis who isolated 613 rules from the Torah and identifying their espoused views with "God's self." In their process they in fact made God subject to Sabbath. Jesus condemned that type of thinking (cf. Mark 2:23–3:5, John 5:17–24). Torah or rules are not the equivalent of God any more than the New Testament and creeds are the equivalent of Jesus. Christians are not worshipers of the Bible or creeds but worshipers of the Triune God. The Bible and creeds—just as the Torah—are very important to our faith and life, but they are not ends in themselves. They are meant to be instruments to lead us to Christ. Paul made that fact very clear when he said that the Law or his Bible was "the tutor (*paidagōgos*) to lead us to Christ" (Gal 3:24).

I emphasize this last idea because of its significance. Statements of faith, the Bible, and our Christian institutions are not ends in themselves. These biblical words, constructed statements, and institutions are instruments that support faith and keep us on the correct path of "walking with God." But if they become, for us, ultimate determiners in our lives, they can become cold and harsh and can lead to fights about words, institutions, or patterns of worship and thus fail in their purposes. God is not the equivalent of words, processes, programs, or institutions.

Instead, God is the most powerful spiritual reality in the universe, and Jesus embodied that spiritual reality when he was on earth. As with Scripture, the purpose of all our instruments is to bring people to Christ. Moreover, these instruments are intended to assist Christians in their walking with God and in doing good works (cf. 2 Tim 3:16–17). Furthermore, Jesus made it clear that the key characteristic of Christians is "to love one another" (cf. John 13:34, 15:12). When Statements of Faith become more than instruments leading us to Christ and serving him, then they can become for us idolatrous vehicles.

The Bible provides a number of examples that warn us about substituting biblical-like vehicles for the great God of creation and salvation. The bronze serpent had been kept in the Ark of the Covenant as a reminder that God saved the people of Israel after they had been bitten by deadly snakes (Num 21:9). But Hezekiah was forced to destroy this important historical symbol because the people started to revere or worship it as a substitute for God (2 Kgs 18:4). In another account the sons of Eli carried the Ark of the Covenant into the battle with the Philistines as a magical emblem against their enemies because they thought it was divine and had magical powers to protect them. But God allowed the Ark to be captured and the sons of Eli to be killed (1 Sam 4:1–11). Yet for the magic-believing Philistines, the Ark was a horrible curse and they finally sent it back to the Israelites in order to end their plagues (5:1–6:16). Later, the Ark was captured when the Temple was destroyed by the Babylonians. Of course, it has never since been found—in spite of contemporary movies such as the *Raiders of the Lost Ark*. Similarly, in spite of Jewish theories that it will be miraculously revealed when the Messiah will appear, such now seems highly unlikely.

The temptations of substituting vehicles such as statements of faith for the divine presence are never far from Christians. Idolatry is not just an ancient phenomenon. Our confessions, our Bibles, and our churches are important instruments in our Christian pilgrimages, but they are not Jesus or the Triune God. Let us never forget the shocking reply of Jesus to the disciples when they were extolling the wonderful glories of the Temple buildings: "Not one stone will be left on another!" (cf. Mark 13:2). The summons to all Christians as we move into the future era is: Let us not settle for the idolatry of our vehicles of faith, even though they are crucial to our faith, but let us keep Jesus as the focus of our Christian lives. Our future as the people of God depends on our clarity concerning this issue.

… With this pertinent warning in mind, we turn next to our understanding of the coming of a new covenant through Jesus and the tensions that are present for us related to the significant subject of human salvation or wholeness.

Chapter 6

New Covenant Wholeness

Tensions over Grace and Faith, Relationship and "Thingification,"
Walking with God, and the Stages of Salvation

The Significance of Covenant

Before turning to the subject of salvation or wholeness in the New Testament, it is imperative to deal with the biblical subject of covenant. Unfortunately, in many New Testament studies the subject is often avoided or perhaps assumed. An example is the classic *New Testament Theology* by Donald Guthrie, the text of which runs to nearly a thousand pages yet only a few paltry pages are given to mentioning the subject of either covenant or the new covenant.[1] An additional problem occurs from the fact that the Greek term *diathēkē* has often been rendered in English as "testament" in addition to "covenant," which has caused confusion in the minds of many in the laity.

Now, like me, most New Testament scholars have undoubtedly studied the Old Testament and the concept of covenant. So, I assume they are quite aware of its importance to the Old Testament.[2] But for some reason, that knowledge does not carry over into many reflections on the New Testament—even though many teachers are often in some ministry and may even serve communion/the Eucharist and recite the words from Paul that "This cup is the New Covenant in my blood" (1 Cor 11:25). I ask myself as a Christian teacher and writer: Why does such an omission happen to us in our thinking? But let me turn now directly to the issue of covenant.

Defining Covenant in the Old Testament

The concept of covenant is rooted in the idea of an agreement or a "coming together" (from the Latin *convenire*), which is a translation of the Hebrew *berit* ("bond") or the Greek *diathēkē* ("arrangement"). The idea was embodied in the

---

[1]Donald Guthrie, *New Testament Theology* (Downers Grove, IL: InterVarsity, 1981), see pp. 435, 494.

[2]See for example Delbert R. Hiller, *Covenant: The Biblical Idea* (Baltimore: John Hopkins University Press, 1969); H.H. Rowley, *The Faith of Israel: Aspects of Old Testament Faith* (Philadelphia: Westminster Press, 1956); Meredith G. Kline, "The Two Tables of the Covenant," chapter 5, *Essential Writings of Meredith E Kline* (Peabody, MA: Hendrickson, 2017); and Walter Eichrodt, *Old Testament Theology*, vol. 1, trans. J.A. Baker, OTL (Philadelphia: Westminster, 1967).

well-known story of Abraham's quest for an heir and God confirming such a promise in the "cutting" or making of a covenant with him. In that event God instructed Abraham to bring a heifer, a she-goat, a ram, a turtledove, and a pigeon, then cut the animals in half—but not the birds—and place them facing each other. Then in the night God caused a smoking fire-pot to pass between the carcasses as a sign of the promised agreement or covenant made by God (Gen 15:1–16).

Binding agreements or covenants could be made between humans (cf. Josh 9:15, 1 Kgs 5:12), such as was made between David and Jonathan (1 Sam 20:3, 8), but that is not the focus of our concern here. Covenants that God makes with humans are somewhat akin to conditional promises a king makes to his subjects or those a caesar made with the people in the Roman Empire. The Romans regarded such people as caesar's "household," and they were expected to obey his rules as long as he remained the head of state. Such agreements within the ancient Semitic world of the Bible are usually designated by scholars as suzerainty treaties, and they usually involved covenant codes that must be obeyed.

In the divine-human relationship God is not beholden to humans because God is sovereign. Yet God graciously covenants with or makes promises to humans with the understanding that the covenant people will fulfill God's expectations of them. Just as God expected the man and the woman in the Garden to "walk" with their Creator (Gen 2:2–3, 8), God expects a covenant community to be obedient in response to divine blessings.[3] Thus, God blessed Abraham so that Abraham would also be a blessing to others (Gen 12:2). Later, God reaffirmed that perpetual covenantal blessing on the basis that Abraham and his offspring would "keep" God's covenant and its sign (Gen 17:1–11). But as Paul later boldly asserted, merely keeping the sign of circumcision was not the same a keeping the covenant (Rom 1:25). And to make sure his deceived, stupid, or bewitched Galatians (Gal 3:1) were clear about what he meant, Paul distinguished law from the promise and thus elevated the promised expectation that God made to Abraham above law. Keeping rules or laws was not identical to having an authentic relationship ("walking in obedience"[4]) with God (Gal 3:17).

Such covenantal promises were expected to be renewed by successive generations. Accordingly, covenantal renewals are periodically reported in the Old Testament, such as the one with Jacob who had repeatedly sought to twist things

---

[3]For the expectations or code within the Old Covenant, see the cooperative work of Bruce C. Birch, Walter Brueggemann, Terence Fretheim, and David L. Petersen in *A Theological Introduction to the Old Testament*, 2nd ed. (Nashville: Abingdon, 1999, 2005), especially chapter 5 for "The Structures of Covenant Life."

[4]See my further explanation of the importance of "walking" with God as a theme later in this chapter.

for his benefit. When he was returning to Israel and fearful of being destroyed by Esau, he tried to gain his brother's acceptance by sending all his belongings and family across the Jabbok River before daring to cross it himself. Then, as he waited uneasily to let his gifts impress Esau, he was forced to wrestle with God in his sleep. In that wrestling, he gained a renewed blessing and a change of name. After that encounter, he was "Israel" and willing to face his brother (Gen 32:3–33:17).

Following their escape from Egypt, the motley descendants of Jacob were led through the dessert to Mount Sinai. On the third new moon the people were confronted by the fearful presence of God, who called them to a renewal of "my covenant" and of being "my own possession among all people" (Exod 19:5). Then, after capturing the land from the Canaanites, at the end of the book that is called by his name, Joshua (the successor of Moses) gathered the people of Israel on behalf of God to a renewal of the covenant at the sanctuary of Shechem. To mark their covenant renewal, the people promised to "serve the Lord" (Josh 24:21). But Joshua understood their frailties and set up a great stone—a testimonial sign—to remind them of their covenant reaffirmation (24:25–26). But such a sign was no guarantee of faithfulness. So, God had to send a periodic reminder to the people of Israel that the Lord would "never break [God's] covenant" with them (Judg 2:1). Yet the pathetic summation at the end of the Book of Judges is that "everyone did what was right in his own eyes" (21:25)—a scathing condemnation!

Briefly I would remind you that such a pattern hardly changed in the succeeding books of Samuel and Kings, as another theme from the period of the judges continued—namely, that "the word of the Lord was rare in those days" (1 Sam 3:1). When the young Samuel entered the scene, he became God's witness to the shocking disintegration of the priesthood, the defeat of Israel, and the capture of the ark. This ark, remember, was the primary symbol of the people's covenant with God and was treated as a "magic box" by Eli's sons (3:2–4:18). The writer of the story, however, notes that in Samuel something was different: The messenger was authentic, and God's message was "not falling to the ground" but was trustworthy (3:19). He called the people to turn away from foreign gods and turn their hearts to the Lord (7:3).

It became apparent, however, that Eli's sons would not follow in his footsteps and the people became anxious concerning their future. Instead of accepting new judges as spokespersons for God, they demanded an earthly king who would lead them "into battle" like the other nations (8:4–5). While such an idea greatly displeased Samuel, the Lord advised Samuel that he should grant their wishes because the people had not merely rejected him but actually had rejected God

(8:7). So. in his farewell address, Samuel rehearsed Israel's history—as was done in the earlier patterns of covenant renewal. When he finished, the people realized their sin and begged Samuel to "Pray for your servants ... that we might not die [because we asked] for ... a king" (12:19).

The story of the kingship in Israel was hardly any better because almost immediately Saul, Israel's first king, foolishly almost assumed the role of a priest at Gilgal when Samuel was delayed. In defense of his action, Saul argued that he "forced himself" to do so because of the immanence of a battle with the Philistines (13:8-12). Saul's response reminds us of the Garden of Eden and the excuses the man and the woman made to God. But we should also recall the devious excuse of Aaron when he was confronted with making the golden calf and replied that he simply threw the gold into the fire and "out came the calf" (Exod 32:24)! Although Saul continued as king, God removed his blessing and indicated to Samuel that he would replace Saul with "a man after [God's] own heart" (1 Sam 13:14).

That later king was, of course, David (16:1–13) who went on to become a fairly consistent model of following the ways of God and of God's desire to establish a covenant people. Yet readers of Scripture know that even David and his son, the wise Solomon, were not perfect models of integrity. And as one reads through the list of kings, one can generally write off as failures the kings of Israel and most of the kings of Judah. Exceptions may include Jehoshaphat, Hezekiah, and particularly Josiah who sought quite consistently to clean up the state with respect to idolatrous worship and the groves that promoted immorality in their fertility rites (2 Chron 34:1–7). The effort of Josiah reminds us that immorality and idolatry are the two major sins that Paul challenged the Corinthians to "flee" (*pheugete*; see 1 Cor 6:18, 10:14).

Indeed, immorality and idolatry are the two major sins that the decision of the Council of Jerusalem highlighted for rejection (besides drinking blood and eating bloody flesh) when it agreed to accept the Gentiles as members of Christian churches without the need for being circumcised (Acts 15:20, 29). These two sinful patterns of life are also the same two sins listed in the condemnations of the churches of Pergamum and Thyatira in the Book of Revelation (cf. Rev 2:14, 2:20). The Bible is consistent that idolatry and immorality are sins that must not be tolerated by the covenant people of God!

The Coming of the New Covenant

Although the prophets warned the people of Israel frequently that their sins and their faithlessness would not be tolerated by God, it was not until the emergence of the great "weeping prophet" Jeremiah (probably meaning "the Lord hurls") that there is the promise of a new covenant with God's people.[5] Following the reigns of the nefarious Manasseh and Amon, the young Josiah came to the throne of Judah (639–609 BC) with a great reforming spirit that was evidenced by the destruction of the high places (the groves of the Asherim and the centers of the Baals). Indeed, Josiah even had the bones of the priests who served these idolatrous gods burned on their altars as he attempted to purge the land of Israel of its idolatry (cf. 2 Chron 34:1–7). Then in the eighteenth year of Josiah's reign, a Book of the Law (perhaps Deuteronomy) was rediscovered and read to him. The king repented of Israel's sins and sought to recall the people to a serious renewal of the covenant (2 Kings 23–24, 2 Chron 34:8–35:19).

While Jeremiah observed these reforms of Josiah, the prophet was not convinced that a real reform was being achieved. So, Jeremiah called the people to remember that the heart is exceedingly deceitful (Jer 17:9). And in response to the Lord's summons, he took his stance at the gates of Jerusalem to call for keeping the Sabbath holy because he was certain that judgment was coming to Judah and its palaces (17:19–27)! As we can imagine, this message did not sit well with the defenders of the king, and they sought to silence the prophet. But not long thereafter Josiah was killed at Megiddo by the forces of Pharaoh Necho, who supported the weakened Assyrians against the rising Babylonians. The death of Josiah in 609 brought his reforms to a screeching halt, which elicited a mournful lament from the prophet and the people (2 Chron 35:25). From that relatively high point, the situation again degenerated under the kings to Zedekiah and the destruction of Jerusalem by the Babylonians in 586 BC.

Yet it was during this period of the disintegration of Judah's religious life that Jeremiah repeatedly and forcefully proclaimed his warning messages that Judah was doomed to exile—even though he was continually reviled and tormented for his message. But although he promised a harsh period of weeping for the people of Israel, it was during this period that he also announced an amazing "hope for [the people's] future" and a return to their homeland (Jer 31:15–17). In this context Jeremiah proclaimed the surprising message that "the day is coming, says the Lord, when I will make a new covenant" (31:31). And in this new time there

---

[5]For a review of the painful prophetic work of Jeremiah, see Thomas W. Overholt, The Threat of Falsehood: A Study in Jeremiah, SBT (Naperville, IL: Allenson-Breckinridge, 1971).

would be a significant change because the Lord promised to "put my law [instructions] deep within them and I will write it[them] on their hearts." Moreover, the Lord promised, "I will be their God and they shall be my people" (31:33).[6] The result would be that the people "will not need to teach their neighbor ... [and tell them] 'You should know the Lord' because they will all know me from the least to the greatest." And God also promised: "I will forgive their evil ways and not remember their sins" (31:34).

This phenomenal text of Jeremiah 31:31–34 is one of the great promises or predictions in the Bible and stands in Hebrews 8:8–11 as the longest single quotation of an Old Testament text in the New Testament.[7]

This promised New Covenant was realized with the coming of Jesus and in both his sacrificial death and awe-inspiring resurrection. This New Covenant is encapsulated in the Christian celebration of the Lord's Supper and the Christian expectation of Christ's *parousia* (coming/return). In that final meal with his disciples Jesus declared that he would "not drink again of the fruit of the vine until the day when [he would] drink it again in the kingdom of God" (Mark 14:25, Matt 26:29, cf. Luke 22:30). This celebration of the Supper has a threefold perspective that is foundational to our understanding of the New Covenant—namely:

1. It points back to its inauguration by Christ.
2. It points to the present and our participation of Christ working in the lives of Christians.
3. It points to the future and the wonderful hope of a promised resurrection life and table fellowship with Christ in heaven (cf. 1 Cor 11:23–26).

But there is also another crucial perspective to which this celebration of the Supper points and that is sometimes sadly overlooked. The Supper also reminds us, as with the New Covenant, that we should examine ourselves because there is in the New Covenant an age-old responsibility—a pattern of living—that goes

---

[6] In his article on "Jeremiah, Prophet of Hope," in *RevExp* 88.3 (Summer 1981): 356, Ronald Clements of Cambridge notes that "Jeremiah's new covenant is not promised to contain a new law which will replace the old laws of Moses and the Decalogue. Instead, it promises a new power and possibility of obedience to the law, made real because God will inscribe the laws on the heart ... the prophet perceives the inwardness of true religion and the necessity for a personal response to God." As Elmer A. Martins argues in Larry L. Walker and Elmer A. Martins, *Isaiah, Jeremiah and Lamentations*, vol. 8, CorBC (Wheaton, IL: Tyndale House, 2005), "the short answer" to the implied question of what guarantee there is concerning the coming of this new covenant "is that "God, the cosmic commander-in-chief (31:35), guaranteed it."

[7] For a helpful study of this theme in Hebrews, see Susanne Lehne, *The New Covenant in Hebrews*, vol. 44, LNTS (Sheffield, UK: Sheffield Academic, 1990).

with being a member of the people of God for whom Christ died (11:28–29). As I have indicated elsewhere, the magnificent Book of Ephesians at 4:17–6:9 makes this way or pattern quite clear.[8] I call it the "New Morality"—it is ***not*** a new law or code that some might view as a basis for gaining salvation. Instead, it is a remarkable test or mirror to indicate whether humans are living according to the expectations of the Sovereign Christ in their lives. And with this brief review of the New Covenant as the basis for understanding the new wholeness or salvation, I turn now to the thorny tension of grace and faith.

Understanding the Tension Between Grace and Faith

Perhaps next to the security tension (see chapter 7), the grace/faith tension has caused some of the most intense arguments among Christians even to the present time. This dispute has sometimes been labeled the Calvinist (Augustinian)/Arminian conflict. Part of the reason for the intense feelings that have been engendered in this dispute arises over the legitimate starting point of one's thinking. So, let me turn to a brief consideration of the starting point.

The Importance of the Starting Point

Let me begin by seeking to demonstrate how we sometimes arrive at our theological presuppositions.

Calvinists/Augustinians usually begin their theological formulations with the doctrine of God, arguing that God has definable qualities such as omnipotence, omniscience, omnipresence, immortality, invisibility, etc.[9] When we define God in this manner, it means that according to our assumed definitions, God is either "all" (*omni-*) something or "not" (*in-/im-*) something. In reality, this group is saying that whatever we can conclude concerning ourselves and our phenomenal world, the definition does not apply to God.

As a result, we need to admit that we do not know as much about the nature and attributes of God as we presume to know, except that God has revealed God's self to us most clearly in the incarnation of Jesus. But even then, God did not provide a full understanding of God's self because, as the brilliant Paul has indicated, Jesus "emptied" himself (*ekenōsen;* Phil 2:7) of much of what we would term to be his divine transcendence (which we do not really understand).

---

[8]Pamela Scalise and Gerald L. Borchert, "The Bible and the Spiritual Pilgrimage" in *Becoming Christian,* ed. Bill J. Leonard (Louisville: Westminster/John Knox, 1990), 31–45, especially 40–42.

[9]For example, the way we can describe the length of God's life is to say that God cannot die (i.e. God is immortal). Yet the term "immortal" hardly says anything about what God's life is; it only addresses what God is not—namely not terminal!

Accordingly, when we talk about God, we do so only in proximate speculations. Again, we are reminded that in his wrenching discussion concerning the Jewish rejection of Jesus, Paul asserted: "How completely unknowable are [God's] judgments and untraceable are his footprints," He followed that assertion by asking the unanswerable question: "Who can actually know the mind of the Lord or who can be his adviser?" (Rom 11:33–34; cf. Ps 92:5–6).

The real problem is that as soon as we try to formulate our presuppositions about God, we limit our subsequent arguments and propositions by the interplay between those propositions about God's divine *persona*.[10] So, when we apply our terms such as "*omni*-science" and "*omni*-potence" to God, they are foundational assumptions that can easily collide in our thinking and leave us with an unresolved tension. While that does not stop our assumptions concerning God, we may be tempted to ask: Can the "Almighty" change the divine mind? Such a thought may seem irrational or non-godlike, but such a view would then fly in the face of what Jeremiah 18 asserts: that God can change the way the Lord promises to deal with humans in any given circumstance, depending on human responses. So perhaps those of us who propose to be of this Calvinistic or Augustinian mindset need to be careful in supposing that we possess an adequate starting point or that we can actually define God's characteristics.

The second group in this major face-off between grace (the action of God) and faith (the action of humans) are those among us who advocate the Arminian perspective. These advocates usually begin with the doctrine of humanity (an anthropological foundation) rather than the doctrine of God. It is highly probable that, as fallible human beings, we may be somewhat enticed with this starting point because we know our frailties as mortal humans who are subject to all sorts of errors. So, the problem of adopting this starting point is that "human faith" is notoriously unstable. Accordingly, this perspective can mean that salvation is a temporary reality and that the believer can move in and out of salvation depending on the state of one's faith at any particular time. Such an unstable view is hardly attractive, yet the positive side is that it takes seriously human accountability before God. But it hardly represents an adequate picture of what God has done and is doing for us in sending Jesus.

I would suggest that we have to deal with grace and faith together in tension as a trust "relationship." But before I move to that concern, I need to mention a strange concocted view that seems to be inherent in the thinking among some

---

[10]Please note that I use the Latin persona here to designate "personal aspects" of God so as not to confuse our discussion concerning the nature of God.

Christians. It is an intriguing interweaving of these two views demonstrated in the practice of those who assert that "whosoever will can come to Jesus." But this merged view asserts that when humans of their own free will have come to Jesus, they can then never fall away or be excluded because they are then viewed as being predetermined to be saved by God. This idea is strange but is built on a concern related to a fear of losing one's eternal security, to which I will return in chapter 7. This human frustration in dealing with the tension in grace and faith then leads to another issue.

The Difference Between "Thingification" and Relationship

The basic problem at work here is our understanding of grace and faith, as derived from word studies or assumed definitions that are not recognized. Here we are faced with a major interpretational issue identified by James Barr who indicated the weakness of word studies as a foundation for developing theology. Because words can have multiple meanings depending on their context, it is impossible to explain fully the meaning of words such as grace or faith outside of their usage in specific passages. Thus, he advised interpreters to determine meanings in combination of words.[11] And that concern leads me to the problem of what we might call the "thingification" of grace and faith.

When we "thingify" grace, it is easy for us to envisage that God supplies us with a "thing" called grace that we then receive and quickly deposit in our pockets or in our personal spiritual treasuries so that we do not lose the "it." To employ a more mundane example, suppose we receive a supporting document from our church such as a baptismal or confirmation certificate and we then deposit it for safekeeping in a vault or our safety deposit box along with our personal papers and other fire-insurance documents. Although such documents are important, they are no guarantee of salvation.

A similar pattern applies to the thingification of faith. In this scenario we give God our thing called faith. God receives our faith and, since by our assumed definition God can make no mistakes, God then takes our thing and puts this faith in the divine pocket or heavenly safe.

We can then continue the pictorial argument by saying that as a result of our giving God our thing called faith, in return we now receive from God the thing called salvation! Such a thingification pattern of logic can lead in many directions. For a stark example, it led to the medieval development of Roman

---

[11]See James Barr's important work, *The Semantics of Biblical Language* (Oxford: Oxford University Press, 1961, repub. Wipf and Stock, 2004).

Catholic indulgences, a concept that was forcefully condemned by the early Protestant Reformers. In this construct, the papacy created the concept of the church treasury in which the excess good of the saints (their faith or faithfulness) was deposited in the church's treasury of excess goodness. This thing called excess goodness could then be distributed as indulgences by the church's hierarchy to those desiring special assistance in gaining heaven or forgiveness—with or without the need for contrition, repentance, and a coordinated change of life! (These indulgences then could naturally be made available for a price, especially if the Vatican or another institution was in need of repair or new construction.)

These comments may seem to be simplistic, trite, and rather harsh—certainly neither irenic nor ecumenical in this era when we seek greater harmony. But I have detailed the concept of thingification to make a strategic point: Grace, faith, and salvation are not things.

How then should we describe these realities? We are dealing with relational words. God does not give us a thing called grace. God graciously gives us a relationship with God's self. We do not give God a thing called faith. We give God ourselves. This mutual giving of selves creates the relationship that we refer to as a saving relationship. But notice that since it is a relationship, it is an ongoing reality.

Such an explanation may help us recognize why the patriarchs and kings of Israel were each expected by God to reaffirm the covenant with God on behalf of the people. That such reaffirmations or renewals were not always done goes without saying. But neither was the covenant a thing. It was a continual recommitment or reaffirmation of a relationship between God and God's people. The important fact to recognize is that God was faithful (steadfast) to the covenantal relationship, but faithfulness was hardly true of Israel. Accordingly, instead of receiving blessing, the Israelites usually experienced judgment. Do you think that in the New Testament era the relationship between God and humans was changed on this issue? Clearly, no!

For further insight into this concept of relationship as opposed to thingification, I turn now to the New Testament use of the term "faith." Paul frequently uses the Greek noun for faith (*pistis*) in his epistles. But notice that when you turn to the Gospel of John, the noun "faith" is never used. Moreover, the noun "knowledge" (*gnōsis*) is likewise never used. Only the verbs for "believe" (*pisteuein*) and "know" (*ginōskein* and *oida*) are used.[12] Even more intriguing is that after the

---

[12]See also my discussion in *John 12–21*, vol. 25B, NAC (Nashville: Broadman and Holman, 2002), 353–55.

prologue in the Gospel of John (1:14–17), the word "grace" (*charis*) does not appear in any of the Johannine writings except for the typical Christian greeting and benediction (cf. 2 John 3; Rev 1:4, 22:21).

The avoidance of these nouns in the Johannine writings is so obvious that it undoubtedly points to something that was occurring in the early church at that time. The gospel writer recognized that an unacceptable, proto-heretical tendency—later often called Gnosticism—was developing in the early Christian community, and he was intent upon forcefully counteracting it.[13] The problem was that basic terms such as faith, knowledge, and grace were being redefined and manipulated into a dualistic system that implied receiving special or secret knowledge. This belief system advocated a strange form of salvation or liberation (escape) from the bondage of this negative world to the freedom of a hidden world for those who gained the secret knowledge, But the Johannine writer clearly recognized that such thinking would destroy genuine Christianity.

Now mark me well at this point. It is not primarily the "what" (secret or special information) you believe, and it is not the "what" you know that is crucial in Christianity. The foundational factor in both Israel's faith and in Christianity is the one whom you know and the one in whom you believe that is important. And the loving God does not merely provide humans with grace in the form of information. Instead, the crucial issue is that God continually touches or impacts humans with God's self. To exchange a relationship with God for information or knowledge about God is a total misrepresentation of the Christian message.

Since grace and faith are not things but actually ways of expressing a significant aspect of an ongoing relationship between God and humans, there will be a tension in human understanding of the relationship because even Christian perceptions are unfortunately marred by sin and unfaithfulness. On the other hand, one of the repeated biblical qualities attributed to God is divine steadfastness or faithfulness (e.g., Ps 36:5, 89:2, 117:2; 1 Cor 1:9, 10:13; 1 Thess 5:24; 2 Thess 3:3). Fortunately, humans can depend on God's faithfulness so at least half of relationship remains consistent.

One of our problems in understanding the Old Testament statements concerning God is that most of us as western Christians have inherited a Greek mindset. We can easily illustrate this mind-set by examining how we understand the word for "truth" in scripture. When we read in John 1:14 that the incarnate Word [Jesus] was "full of grace and truth" (*alētheia*), we are tempted to think

---

[13]See my further discussion on Gnosticism as a background for understanding the Fourth Gospel in *John 1–11*, vol. 25A, NAC (Nashville: Broadman and Holman, 1996), 76–80.

about truth in academic or intellectual terms. But truth for writers of the New Testament such as John and Paul (who wrote in Greek but were basically Semitic in their thinking) did not mean that a word akin to truth was regarded as merely having an intellectual orientation.

The Hebrew word that stands behind truth is *emet*, which implies steadfastness, firmness, trustworthiness, or consistency in a relationship.[14] So, not only must we not thingify grace, we must also not merely intellectualize truth. God is a relational *persona*, and God is concerned about our relationships. While God may be faithful to our relationship, the tension comes because of our human unfaithfulness.

The Tension Between Walking with God and Obeying Rules

A problem occurred among the people of Israel during the rise of rabbinic thinking and the time that scholars refer to as the period of the *Tannaim*. It involves a change or a shift from emphasizing the verb *halak* (walking with God) to the noun *halakah* (obedience to the rules or the prescriptions for the walk.)

Walking with God: The Significance of *Halak*

Perhaps it will help the Christian reader to realize how catastrophically destructive are seemingly innocuous differences if we illustrate the implications from the history of Judaism. The Old Testament frequently describes the relationship between God and the faithful people of Israel by the Hebrew verb *halak* that means "to walk."

Thus, even in the brief account concerning the man called Enoch, he is described as having "walked" with God (Gen 5:22–24). Abraham is commanded to "walk with God and to be blameless" (17:1; cf. 24:40). After the people of Israel were rescued from slavery in Egypt, they were clearly instructed not to "walk" in the customs of the Gentiles but to keep the statutes of God (Lev 20:22–23, 26:3). The Lord also indicated that their God would "walk" among them and cause them to "walk" uprightly (26:12–13), but God also warned them not to walk contrary to God because all types of misfortunes would then plague them (26:21–22).

---

[14]For a helpful discussion on Hebrew and Greek mindsets, see Thorleif Boman, *Hebrew Thought Compared to Greek*, trans. Julius Moreau (London: S.C.M. Press, 1960). For the Hebrew meaning of emet(h), see Ludwig Koehler and Walter Baumgartner, *Veteris Testamenti Libros* (Leiden/Grand Rapids: E.J. Brill/Eerdmans, 1958), 66–67. Cf. also the discussion on *alētheia* by Gottfried Quell, Gerhard Kittel, and Rudolf Bultmann in Gerhard Kittel, ed. *TDNT*, vol. 1 (Grand Rapids: Eerdmans, 1964), 232–247.

The prophets of Israel likewise continually insisted that the duty of the people was to "walk" with God (e.g., Isa 2:3, 30:21; Jer 6:16–17; Ezek 11:19–20; Mic 6:8; Zech 3:17; etc.). But perhaps Amos summarizes this relational understanding best when he asks on behalf of God whether two can "walk together" unless they are in agreement (Amos 3:3).

Now while the Old Testament often refers to walking in the statutes and ordinances of the Lord, these ordinances were only a symbol of the relationship that God was to have with the people of Israel. But like so many things in life, people often substitute the symbol for the reality to which the symbol is pointing. So, humans easily develop misconceptions about relationships with God. This mention of the symbolic statutes and ordinances implies the necessity of incorporating into our discussion the second aspect of the salvation issue, the tension between law and works on the one hand and grace and faith on the other.

The Issue with *Halakah*: Obeying Rules

The rabbis referred to their walks—namely, the precise legal requirements they drew from the Torah—by the noun *halakah*. They then formulated these laws in order of priority, and their arguments/decisions on these laws were codified in the late first century AD/CE in what became known as the *Mishnah*.[15] Other statements that were thought to be merely suggestive they designated as *haggadah* (interpretations or comments). This development of a stringent legalistic perspective on the many rules/decisions based on the 613 laws that the rabbis found in the Torah (the Pentateuch) ultimately led to the period known as the age of the *Tannaim* (the rabbinic period after Ezra).[16]

These rabbis frequently referred to their newly articulated legislative decisions as the "oral law" and by clever deduction attributed its origin directly to Moses, comparable to the written Torah. This oral law (their legal deductions) was given a similar significance to that of the written Torah. This process continued after the codification of the *Mishnah* with materials collected both in Babylon and in Palestine and were finally codified in the two *Talmuds* (of which the Babylonian Talmud is considered by many Jewish scholars as more authoritative).

---

[15]For a helpful explanation and history of the formulation and development of these laws that were drawn from the 613 rules found in the Torah, see the Introduction to Herbert Danby, *The Mishnah* (London: Oxford University Press. 1933), xiii–xxxii.

[16]For a further discussion of this process, see George W.E. Nickelsburg, *Jewish Literature Between the Bible and the Mishnah* (Philadelphia: Fortress, 1981) and my further comments in chapter 2 of Gerald L. Borchert, *Jesus of Nazareth* (Macon, GA: Mercer University Press, 2011), 43–47.

The Jesus Revolution

Into the midst of this legalistic development Jesus entered the scene and "walked" with his disciples, teaching them to relate to God in a different way than through the obedience to a set of rules. But the legalistic rule-makers could not tolerate this envoy from God who particularly challenged one of their chief building blocks of legalism—namely, the Sabbath. Jesus declared that "the Sabbath was created for humanity and not humanity for the Sabbath." He even added the revolutionary statement that "the Son of Man is Lord also over the Sabbath" (Mark 2:27). The gauntlet was delivered by Jesus! The rule-makers responded quickly. They engineered the death of this God-sent challenger to their legalistic system.

But that death was not the end of the story. Not only did God raise Jesus from the dead to confirm Jesus' divine perspectives, but he also established a community of faith to carry the message of "walking with God" rather than following the way of legalism. Furthermore, after God's envoy left this earth, the risen Jesus selected a fiery rabbi Saul/Paul who was thoroughly steeped in rabbinic logic[17] and Jesus transformed Paul into a firebrand proponent of Jesus' revolutionary perspectives.

Among the chief foci of Paul's strategic message was a frontal attack on the rabbinic perspectives of the law. His repeated theme was none other than a reassertion of the summons to "walk with God!" Indeed, one of Paul's favorite words is *peripatein* ("to walk" or "conduct one's life," used thirty-two times in Paul). Failure to miss this central refrain in Paul is to truncate his proclamation of the gospel. Moreover, to treat Christianity as a new set of rules is a failure to comprehend the core message especially of Galatians but also of the entire New Testament.

So, the follow-up question is: If legalism has been abandoned, does that mean Christians are left with a perspective of libertinism? To use Paul's familiar retort in his diatribes: Absolutely not (*mē genoito*) or perhaps more vehemently, That idea is stupid! "Anything goes" is not the Christian message. Walking with God means following in the footsteps of Jesus, the Lord (cf. 1 Pet 2:21).

The Law, the Reformation, and Polarized Misunderstandings

But now it is time to return to the issue of law and the aftermath of the Diet of Worms in 1521. In that important debate, Luther relied on Paul and Eck (the Vatican spokesman) relied on the Epistle of James. The issue of faith/grace vs.

---

[17]For further insights into several opinions concerning Paul's relationship to the rabbinic process, see W.D. Davies, *Paul and Rabbinic Judaism: Some Rabbinic Elements in Pauline Theology*, 4th ed. (Minneapolis: Fortress, 1980) and E.P. Sanders, *Paul and Palestinian Judaism*, 40th ann. ed. (Minneapolis: Fortress, 2017).

the works of the law became an unfortunate and major dividing point between Protestantism and Roman Catholicism in the sixteenth century. While there were many more issues at stake in this arguement,[18] the division of Western Christianity was sealed in the emergence of the faith and grace message as the clarion call of the Reformation.

A number of inappropriate results, however, were attached to this division. The first was the unfortunate designation of the Book of James as a secondary level text in the New Testament canon by Luther who apparently viewed it as not much more than an epistle of "straw." But that designation grew out of his defensive reaction in the crucial struggle against the concept of works as means for gaining salvation. It is hardly a fair assessment of the Book of James. For example, the statement in James concerning the deadness of faith without works (2:17) is in fact an attack on so-called Christians who parade a non-transforming faith, or who talk about faith without evidencing an actual change in life, or who fall under Bonheoffer's expression of reflecting "cheap grace."[19] James is not really an attack on Paul's concept of justification, but his work is an aggressive assault on those who misunderstand Paul and justification by faith.

Luther's emphasis on "justification by faith" also led later scholars to posit that this theme was to be regarded as the identifying mark of authentic Pauline writings. Accordingly, the Lutheran scholar F.C. Baur argued that those works that did not emphasize this basic theme were to be regarded as non-Pauline and probably written by a minor figure in the Pauline camp. As a result, only Romans, Galatians, and the two Corinthian letters were ascribed to Paul by Baur.[20] Since that time, scholars have agreed that Paul clearly wrote more letters than his first four epistles in our canon, although the debate continues especially over the Pastoral Epistles.

But there is a much more serious tangential result of this face-off. It was the re-emergence of an earlier unqualified antithesis between law and gospel or law and grace. The dissident Marcion,[21] in an effort to free Christianity from what

---

[18]Among the side issues involved at the time were the politics of Emperor Charles V, his love-hate relationship with the papacy (who feared the emperor's interference in Italy), and the growing political strength of the German Elector Frederick III of Saxony.

[19]See Dietrich Bonhoeffer, *The Cost of Discipleship* (London: S.C.M., 1959).

[20]See for example the discussion on F.C. Baur and the Tübingen hypothesis in Johannes Munck, *Paul and the Salvation of Mankind* (Richmond: John Knox, 1959).

[21]For easy access to annotated quotations from Marcion and responses from Irenaeus and Tertullian, as well as Adolf von Harnack's analysis of Marcion, see Wayne A. Meeks, ed., *The Writings of St. Paul* (New York: W.W. Norton, 1972), 185–198. See also chapter 2, "The Internal Crisis: The Gnostic and other Heretical Sects" for the classic analysis of Joseph Cullen Ayer, Jr., *A Source Book for Ancient Church History: From the Apostolic Age to the Close of the Conciliar Period* (New York: Scribners, 1913, [Paulist, 2015]).

he viewed as a Jewish hangover, completely separated the teachings of the gospel/ new covenant from its Jewish roots. Anything Jewish was sloughed off from his version of the Christian canon as a holdover from its legalistic past. Indeed, like Sethians and other Gnostics, Marcion regarded the Old Testament God as an enemy who was antagonistic to the God represented by Jesus. Marcion deleted not only the Old Testament from his canon, but also much of the New Testament—with the exception of the Pauline epistles and an expurgated edition of Luke's gospel.

Accordingly, while Marcion viewed Paul as a patron saint, he completely misunderstood Paul. The apostle did not despise the law, and he certainly did not regard the law negatively akin to sin. Indeed, Paul patently stated that he delighted in the law of God in his innermost being (Rom 7:22), and he stoutly refused to call the law sin with his forceful *mē genoito* (7:7). For Paul the law was a gracious gift of God to help people recognize that they needed God in their lives. When the Torah is correctly understood, it serves as a way one should live. But when one does not live appropriately with God, the law operates as a stern judge on sinful living (7:10–12).

The Importance and Function of the Law

We can sense, then, that what on the surface might appear to be a rigid alternative of law against grace/faith becomes a completely false dichotomy. Law is a God-given gracious gift! Christians should not regard law negatively but as a reminder that God expects people, who are related to the Son of God, to live wholesome, temperate lives. It is precisely at this point that the classic text of Galatians 3:23–24 should be central in our discussion of faith and law. That text involves Paul's designation of the law prior to the age of faith as a *paidagōgos* (a guardian, disciplinarian, tutor, or teacher) for the specific purpose of leading humans to knowing they need Jesus. But since Jesus has now come and the way of faith has been established, the *paidagōgos* should not be primary (3:25–26).[22] I often state this idea as follows: "You will need rules, if you do not know and follow the Ruler!" The pertinent question is: Do you and I know and follow the Ruler?

To sum up, Paul forcefully rejected legalism and the works of the law as a way of life because it was an attempt to gain status with God. But instead of status, it brought a curse (Gal 3:10–14). Paul never rejected the basic role of the law.

For Marcion, see 102–105.

[22]For my further explication of this text, see "Galatians" in Roger Mohrlang and Gerald L. Borchert, *Romans and Galatians*, vol. 14, CorBC (Carol Stream, IL: Tyndale House, 2007), 297–298.

Instead, he clearly affirmed its value. Yet he wanted Christians to move beyond their reliance on law and walk with God. Law, for him, was an interim way of relating to God. But Jesus has offered Christians a new way to "walk" with their Lord through the Holy Spirit in their lives (Gal 5:16–24; cf. the Paraclete sayings in John 14:15–16:15).

The Tension of Time and the Three Stages of Salvation

I turn briefly here to the tension in time, another major issue that I shall treat again later (see chapter 9). In the present context, humans are bound by the created phenomenon of time. But how does such an idea relate to God and salvation or wholeness? The statement of Jesus in John's gospel that "before Abraham was, I am" (John 8:58) is pertinent, yet it causes us confusion as it did for the Jews.

In reflecting on this matter, I refer to a favorite illustration I heard while I was teaching Greek and studying at Princeton and which I love to retell. As the supposed story goes, two well-known Scottish theologians were walking the streets in Edinburgh when a Salvation Army officer approached them and asked, "Brothers, are you saved?" One of the theologians replied, "Yes, partly, and no." The officer in shock responded, "What?" To which the theologian answered, "Yes, I am justified! Partly, I am in the process of being sanctified! And No, I am not glorified!" While that little story is probably apocryphal, it does raise the important tension concerning time and salvation.

Thus, it is imperative for us to be clear on what the focus is in any discussion related to salvation. The reason is that there are past, present, and future aspects to this subject. All of these dimensions are clearly present in the classic text of Romans 6 that deals with baptism. In verse 5 of that chapter Paul refers to both the past and future when he states that "we have been joined to [Christ] in a death like his," and he continues by indicating "we shall be joined to him in a resurrection like his." Then in verse 11 he employs the present and advises his readers that we "ought to consider [ourselves] dead to sin and alive to God in Christ Jesus." In the first section of this epistle to the Romans (particularly chapters 1–4) Paul treats the subject of justification (e.g., 3:21–26, 5:1). But in chapter 6 his primary focus has moved to sanctification or the life of holiness, and his concern is with our "walk in newness of life" (6:4). In this walk he counseled his readers to yield their bodies "to righteousness for sanctification" (6:19). The end result he quickly asserted would be "eternal life" (6:22–23), or the third stage of salvation.

So, do you see how we need to deal with the salvation tension? When we speak of salvation or wholeness and we are meaning the initial stage—technically justification—we would be referencing salvation as the faithful officer in our story. But do we then have the full realization of salvation now in the form of "eternal life" as the best-known verse in the Bible (John 3:16) promises? The adequate answer is: yes, partly, and not really (at least we do not experience it in its entirety)!

Can anything change between the first stage of salvation and the final stage? That tension is what I will discuss later in dealing with living with Christ. It is an ongoing reality (a relationship between God and humans), and not everything is finalized at the initial stage. God has a will for us, but God has also given us a will and has not removed freedom from us. Can we disobey God? Of course. Does God want to give us the final stage of salvation? Unequivocally, yes. Does God promise to protect us? Again, yes. At least, that is what God wills for us. Do we deserve it? Absolutely not. Will we receive the final goal for our lives? That answer depends upon how we handle the tension in our relationship with God. We would like to have everything solved now, but we have an important role to play in the final outcome because salvation or wholeness is not a certificate we can put in our safety deposit boxes. Therefore, it is necessary that we take the stern warnings of the Bible seriously and not play games in our commitments with God.

The resolution of the salvation tension does not simply depend on God. God has done, is doing, and will do the divine part. The outcome depends on whether or not we take the gracious relationship with the presence of God seriously. Remember that God is faithful. The question is: Will we be faithful and return to God—renew our covenant with God—when we err or stray from God's loving care?

… So, now we turn to the touchy issue of the believer's security.

Chapter 7

New Covenant Security

Tensions in the Message of Assurance and Warning

The Uneasy Tension in Christian Security

Scarcely is there a tension among Christians that evokes a more visceral feeling than the issue concerning the security of the believer. Many assert that "If one has believed in Jesus, surely that belief is sufficient to guarantee one's position with God and an eternal place in the divine realm"—or is it? Let us ponder that query further because it raises the crucial question of believing and what believing implies. Moreover, one cannot help but recall the somewhat disturbing summary in the second chapter of John's gospel that reads: "Now during the time [Jesus] was in Jerusalem at the Passover festival many people believed (*episteusan*) in his name when they saw the signs which he was doing. Jesus, however, did not believe (*episteuen*) in them because he understood *at a deep level* (*ginōskein*) all people" (John 2:23–24).[1]

Can you imagine the possibility that Jesus might not "believe" our believing? Is that idea not a little disturbing to us? So, we ask: Are we not in control of the salvation process? Since we have already discussed believing in the previous chapter on salvation and wholeness, maybe we need to take a second look at what security of the believer actually means. We are quite aware that Jesus understood the frailties and inconsistencies in our living. Now perhaps it is appropriate that we focus particularly on the subject of security or what I have labeled elsewhere as the important tension between assurance and warning.[2] Howard Marshall earlier wrestled with the same problem, but he named the tension as "perseverance and falling away." Judith Gundry Wolf reviewed the arguments in her published doctoral dissertation under the intriguing title *Paul and Perseverance: Staying In and Falling Away*—which revels the complexity of the issue. [3]

---

[1]Some scholars seek to make a change in the meaning of the word "believe" here, but that is a manipulative style of exegesis. I will not here cite those commentaries, but see my further comments in Gerald L. Borchert, *John 1-11*, vol. 25A, NAC (Nashville: Broadman and Holman, 1996), 167–168.

[2]Gerald L. Borchert, *Assurance and Warning* (Nashville: Broadman, 1997; Singapore: Word N Works, 2006).

[3]See the important discussions of I. Howard Marshall, *Kept by the Power of God* (Minneapolis: Bethany Fellowship, 1969) and Judith M. Gundry Volf, *Paul and Perseverance: Staying In and Falling Away*

The Human Quest for Security

By our very nature of living in what we perceive to be an unfriendly world, we humans seem to be insecure. We may put on false faces and muster courage in an effort to appear secure, but essentially from birth we are thrust into a world that seems exceedingly unfriendly and unwelcoming. Since we cannot climb back into our mother's womb (cf. Nicodemus' question in John 3:4), we long for someone such as a parent or a nurse to caress and love us. Hopefully those who care for us can help us look out at the world and see that it is not a totally fearful place. But sometimes it is very hard for us to understand the biblical statement that God saw all that was made and declared that "it was very good" (Gen 1:31)!

As we grow a little older, we are thrust into the world of school and we discover it is not always the affirming place we had hoped. Most of us, however, learn not merely the academic lessons in school but also important patterns of independence that assist us in making our way in a fear-inspiring society. And the lessons continue throughout out our school days and into the university or college of our or our parents' choosing. Having been a professor in various colleges, universities, seminaries and graduate schools, I am always intrigued to watch for students who seem to be ready to leave the wombs of our academic institutions and find a place in society as wage earners and people on a mission. But we always have some who would rather continue in the womb of school.

Some young people, however, never make it very far in education and become "drop-outs." Some enter the workplace, but others find another womb such as a gang where they can gain some acceptance, even if it leads to negative behavior and perhaps to prison. But for those who have been involved with prisoners, we also recognize the same phenomenon often continues so that when prisoners are freed and are once again cast out into an unfriendly world, many even long to return to the security of prison where the rules offer them some sense of security.

Disaster and Hope in the Biblical Message

It is precisely at the point of security that the church is supposed to have a message. But this message is often badly misunderstood. The God of creation and salvation did not intend the biblical message to be one that has God's people remaining babies in the faith. That point is how the so-called unsettling text of Hebrew 6 begins. The call of the Preacher of Hebrews is for his readers to go on

---

(Louisville: Westminster/John Knox, 1990). Compare Donald A. Carson, who focuses his thinking more on the sovereignty of God and entitles his work *Divine Sovereignty and Human Responsibility* (Atlanta: John Knox, 1981).

to maturity (6:1). It is in fact a call to accept responsibility and to live a consist life directed by God. But turning back from the commitment to God is to court disaster (6:6) and is a sure recipe for rejection (6:4, 8).

Disaster is what happened several times to the Israelites in the desert when they grumbled against God and Moses after God had miraculously rescued them from Egypt. They made a golden calf and called it "god." As a consequence, many died in the wilderness (Exod 32:1–35). They rebelled against God and Moses, and they were killed by serpents (Num 21:4–6). Then they were led to the promised land, but after they sent spies to give them a report of their task, they refused to enter because they thought the God who rescued them from mighty Egypt would be unable to help them enter because of the "giants" in their new promised land (Numbers 13–14). The reason of course was that they paid more attention to the powers in the world than to God (cf. the disciples' reaction to Jesus' announcement that he was returning to hostile Judea to deal with the death of Lazarus in John 11:8–16). And so, God forced the Israelites to wander for forty years until those who had rejected God's leading had died in the desert.

We do not like to imagine that God might give up on us. That scenario hardly fits our view of a caring God who surely would not punish us but would always seek to restore us. But be careful here! It is true that God is one who is in the business of restoration, as Richard Rohr has so ably articulated. God's justice is restorative.[4] and Rohr carefully supports his thesis by citing patterns from prophets such as Moses, Isaiah, Jeremiah, Ezekiel, and Hosea. But that theme is not the whole story. Yet God does not remove free will from his human creatures. God was willing to allow the Israelites to wander for forty years in the wilderness following their own free wills, even if it meant they would die in the wilderness and not reach the promised land. You see: God's justice is not retributive; it is more permissive and allows humans to reap punishment for disobedient and evil actions.

Do you wonder then why the Apostle Paul used Israel as an illustration to warn Christians about not meeting their commitments (1 Cor 10:6–10)? In that Corinthian passage he briefly detailed for his inconsistent children a few failures of the Israelites in the desert, and he employed the harsh judgments of God through the work of the "Destroyer" (*tou olothreutou*) as a sharp wake-up call to the deviants among them not to test God. But Paul did more than warn the

---

[4]Richard Rohr, who has learned much from Francis of Assisi, provides some helpful insights into living positively as Christians, but we must take care not to extend his views of restorative justice to the point of neglecting to recognize the equally significant issue of assuming responsibility for one's actions. See his *Eager to Love: The Alternative Way of Francis of Assisi* (Cincinnati: Franciscan Media, 2014) and *Breathing Under Water and the Twelve Steps* (Cincinnati: Franciscan Media 2011).

Christians not to be like Israel, and herein lies the tension. He also highlighted the fact that no temptation would come to them without the divine provision of an escape hatch—namely, God would make a way for his children to resist (*hypenegkein*) temptation (10:13).[5] Yes, I would agree with Rohr that God is in the business of restoration and God will even make ways for us to avoid tragedy, but God does not consign us to the blessed state of acceptance in spite of our rebellion or disobedience and against our free will. The Bible is quite clear that God loves us but that God also expects us to be responsible.

A somewhat similar tension is present in the passage from Hebrews 6 that I briefly introduced above. The Preacher of Hebrews 6:1–6 informs his readers that it would be "impossible" to restore those who turned away from God after they had been integrated into the Christian faith if they had been enlightened, received God's gracious gift of God's self (God's gracious presence), become a recipient of the Holy Spirit, loved God's word, and become eschatologically oriented to the future hope of the Christian.[6]

Yet the Preacher actually had another message. The latter part of Hebrews 6 seems to be at odds with the beginning, but it is crucial for understanding the tension that is present in the text. In verses 17–20 the Preacher reminds his stunned readers of another "impossible" in the equation: it is impossible for God to be proven a liar. The tension emerges because God swore with an oath to be a refuge for the people in a time of trauma. Thus, God's presence is pictured here as a firm anchor. Can you envision this united symbol? The God of the Cross (6:6) is also the God of the Anchor (6:19)? I suggest that you begin to visualize the Cross in the Anchor. [7] It may change the way you look at reality and the full importance of the Preacher's argument in the sixth chapter of Hebrews.

---

[5] See my comments on this central section of 1 Corinthians in G. Borchert, *Assurance and Warning* (1997), 45–60.

[6] I have often told my students and laypeople that this passage actually provides the best statement of what it means to be a Christian found in the New Testament. If it were not in this context of a warning, it would be quoted widely by most preachers, evangelists, and missionaries who are searching for a brief definition of an authentic Christian. But it is shunned by many because of the severity of the warning. So, the significance of Hebrews 6 is often missed. For a further discussion of this issue, see Gerald L. Borchert, *Christ and Chaos: Biblical Keys to Ethical Questions* (Macon, GA: Nurturing Faith, 2020), 63–71.

[7] For some excellent studies on Hebrews, see Gareth Lee Cockerill, *The Epistle to the Hebrews*, NICNT (Grand Rapids: Eerdmans, 2012); Harold W. Attridge, *Hebrews: A Commentary on the Epistle to the Hebrews in Herm* (Minneapolis: Fortress, 1989); William L. Lane, *Hebrews 1–8, Hebrews 9–1*, WBC (Dallas: Word Books, 1991) and Craig R. Koeter, *Hebrews* , vol. 36, AB (New Haven: Yale University Press, 2001). For contrasting views of warnings in Hebrews, see Herbert W. Bateman IV ed., *Four Views on the Warning Passages in Hebrews* (Grand Rapids: Kregel, 2007).

Promise and Responsibility

Christians must understand at this point that God does not give promises to people without demanding that we assume responsibility for our lives and actions. In such contexts all statements of assurance concerning our relationship to God are made. It is God, not a human, who is the judge of authenticity. Moreover, it is imperative to recognize that conditions are laid down for the people of God that coordinate with divine promises. I always remind students and others that all promises of God whether stated or unstated are in fact conditional! Jeremiah provides confirmation of this fact in his famous sermon at the potter's house[8] when he told Israel that God's judgment was coming to the nation. Indeed, he thundered:

> If at any time I solemnly state concerning a nation or a kingdom, that I will pull it up, break it down and destroy it, and if that nation of which I have made the declaration turns around from its evil pattern, then I will turn away from [reject] the destructive evil which I had planned [promised] to do to it. Moreover, if at any time I solemnly state concerning a nation or a kingdom that I will establish [construct] and plant it, but if I see that it does evil and does not listen to my voice [instructions] then I will turn away from [reject] the prosperity [good] which I had planned [promised] for it. (Jer 18:7–10)

The point is that all assurance texts in the Bible must be coordinated with the warning texts of Scripture. It is only in the tension between these two types of inspired texts that one can really understand the purposes of God with humans.

If you have difficulty understanding this fact, ask yourself: Why was Israel repeatedly punished? Then ask yourself: Why did Paul in Romans 9–11 wrestle so hard with Israel's rejection of Jesus?[9] Paul knew that Jesus was Israel's Messiah and that Israel had been given strategic historical blessings and instructions by God, such as their special relationship to God, their covenants, their patterns of

---

[8]For helpful discussions on this text, see Walter Brueggemann, *Commentary on Jeremiah: Exile and Homecoming* (Grand Rapids: Eerdmans, 1998) and R.E. Clements. *Jeremiah* in Int (Louisville: Westminster/John Knox, 1988).

[9]For helpful discussions on Paul's attempt to understand the Jewish rejection of Jesus in Romans, see James D.G. Dunn, *Romans 9–16*, vol. 38B, WBC (Dallas: Word Books, 1988); Douglas Moo, *The Letter to the Romans*, 2nd ed., NICNT (Grand Rapids: Eerdmans, 2018); and John R.W. Stott, *The Message of Romans: God's Good News for the World* (Downers Grove, IL: InterVarsity, 1994). For a helpful dialog on Romans 9–11, see David Compton and Andrew David Naselli, eds., *Three Views on Israel and the Church Perspectives in Romans 9–11* (Grand Rapids: Kregel/Zondervan, 2018).

worship, their promises, their heritage, and their historic relationship to Jesus (9:4–5).

Why then did most of the Jews reject Jesus? The answer was difficult for Paul to comprehend. It was clear to him that some Jews had indeed accepted the message. But why did most of them turn their backs on God's chosen envoy? The only answer for Paul seemed to be that not all of the Jewish descendants had turned out to be among the true children of God. Yet he was certain that he was one of God's true children (9:6–29). Nevertheless, he would have been willing to sacrifice himself if he could convince the rest of the Jews to accept Jesus (9:3). Still, the failure of most of Israel to accept their Messiah (they stumbled over Zion's chosen stone) meant that the promise to Abraham was also being fulfilled because not only would Abraham's seed (Israel) be blessed by Jesus, but Abraham's seed (Jesus) also would be the blessing to the nations (9:30–33; cf. Gen 12:1–2).

Understanding Assurance and Warning

Here is the important point: Those who respond positively to God's chosen agent do so because they have heard the message and are obedient (Rom 10:5–13). They in fact have been given the divine assurance by being inserted into the historic "olive tree" (a symbol of God's people). But there is also a corresponding warning because these new branches need to be careful and not assume that they have no responsibility to God. If God could cut out natural branches (Israel) from the olive tree because of disobedience and rejection of God's intentions, God would have no difficulty doing likewise with the non-natural (Gentiles) inserted branches (11:13–24). Do you see the interplaying tension of both assurance and warning in this important text from Paul? The Apostle's letters literally ooze with confidence concerning the power of God to hold the believer. But Paul also warns his readers repeatedly that they must not take God's graciousness for granted and assume that they are so secure that they do not have to be responsible and obedient to God.

Now, to be representative of the full range of the biblical perspectives, we should also turn to the Gospel of John and determine if a similar tension is present in that work since John is often used to support the idea of total security. Before we look at a few texts from that gospel, however, we should recall that the Johannine books come from a time and situation that is very different from the time of the texts just quoted. John's gospel was written late in the first century. The stellar figure who stands behind it and the other Johannine works was by that time an old man who was still with the community of faith but who soon would face death (John 21:22–23).

The church and Christians had experienced hostility in the Roman Empire. Not only had the mad tyrant Nero (ruled 54–68 CE/AD) come and gone, but the Johannine books were probably written during the reign of the more ruthless tyrant Emperor Domitian (81–96), who, from the Johannine perspective, was hardly friendly to Christians. So readers should immediately sense the different perspectives concerning the Roman state in Romans 12 and in the later Revelation 12. Here of course is another tension in the New Testament, namely our understanding of the Christian's relationship to the state (see chapter 12 on Dual Citizenship). Here I would briefly note that in the Romans text the state was regarded rather positively while in Revelation it was regarded as very negative toward Christians. Bible interpreters should recognize this difference in perspectives and the tension that is created in our theologies concerning the state.[10]

By the time of the Johannine writings many Christians including Paul and Peter had already suffered martyrdom (e.g., John 21:18, 24). Understanding this context is essential when reading the Johannine gospel and related documents. The question then was: Would Christians be sustained by God in the midst of such hostility? Or, would they be abandoned by God and collapse under persecution? That question was crucial for the early Christian community, to say nothing concerning many Christians today. We in the Western world may not live in a setting of persecution, but there are many contemporary Christians who live in such contexts. So when you read these texts, never forget their hostile context.

Now many biblical readers freely cite John 10 as a basis for their understanding of security of the believer. This chapter involves the first of the two magnificent *mashals* (extended parables[11]). The first is the *Mashal* of the Good Shepherd,[12] and the hostile discussion that follows takes place in a conflict setting during the Festival of *Hanukkah* (Dedication[13]).

---

[10]For a helpful overview of some of the issues related to the New Testament teaching on the state, see the classic work of Oscar Cullmann, *The State in the New Testament* (New York: Charles Scribner, 1956).

[11]These two Johannine mashals of the Good Shepherd (John 10) and the Vine and the Branches (John 15) differ from the brief parables that are like pointed illustrations in the Synoptic Gospels. These Johannine mashals are more like counterpoint illustrations within the overall argument of the gospel.

[12]See my further comments in G. Borchert, *John 1–11*, 327–44. See also Raymond E. Brown, *The Gospel According to John i–xii*, vol. 29, AB (Garden City, NY: Doubleday, 1966), 383–412; cf. Rudolph Schnackenburg, *The Gospel According to St. John*, vol.2 (New York: Crossroad, 1987); and D.A. Carson, *The Gospel According to John* (Grand Rapids: Eerdmans, 1991).

[13]This festival of Hanukkah celebrated more precisely the cleansing and rededication of the Second Temple under Judas Maccabeus after the Syrians under Antiochus IV [Epiphanes] had desecrated the temple by slaughtering a pig on the altar of sacrifice and setting up a statute of Zeus in the Most Holy Place.

No doubt, this passage offered Christians assurance because Christ's sheep hear his voice and follow him (note the context of obedience). Accordingly, Jesus here declares to the faithless, conspiring Jews that they were not his sheep but that he was the one who would give to his faithful sheep (those who follow him) "eternal life and they will never perish." Then, he announces that "no one can wrench them out of my hand." Indeed, he adds "my Father's hand." The reason for their great sense of security is because Jesus and the Father were to be understood as one (John 10:22–30). No hostile force—not the emperor nor any other enemy—could separate them from the protecting hands of God and God's Son (cf. also Paul's affirmation that nothing can "separate us from the love of God in Christ Jesus" in Rom 8:31–38). In the midst of such conflict and persecution his followers could be assured that the power and authority of the Godhead (which we do not fully comprehend) would hold and preserve them. The issue at that point was one of divine protection (cf. John 17:12): Jesus promised to guard his followers. The issue here was not one of a relationship between Jesus' followers and their God: they were already said to be following the shepherd. The question of relationship would be answered in the next passage that we will now discuss.

The other side of the issue involves the second magnificent *Mashal* of the Vine and the Branches in John 15. This text is positioned at the heart of what I call the "bull's eye" of the Farewell Cycle in my commentary on John. Jesus was giving his closing advice to his disciples in the context of the five Paraclete (Holy Spirit) sayings (14:15–18, 25–30; 15:26–16:1, 7–11, 12–13),[14] offering them assurance that God would be in their midst through the personal presence of the Holy Spirit. In this context, the divine presence would not merely be with them (like Jesus, their tangible "human" companion) but the Spirit—his substitute ("another") Paraclete (Supporter)—would actually be within them, actively counseling them in every difficult situation (John 14:15–17). But here again the passage emphasizes the precondition of obedience—namely, loving Jesus and keeping his commandments.

With these preliminary comments in mind, we turn to this second well-known *mashal*.[15] The focus of this text is upon the relationship between believers and God, who is here likened to a vineyard farmer, and Jesus is compared to the

---

[14]For an extended discussion on the nature of John 13–17 as the third of the Johannine cycles and the five Paraclete sayings, see Gerald L. Borchert, *John 12–21*, vol. 25B, NAC (Nashville: Broadman and Holman, 2002), 71–211. For this issue see especially 73–75.

[15]For my further interpretation of this mashal, see G. Borchert, *John 12–21*, 137–52. See also Brown, *The Gospel According to John xiii–xxi*, 658–702; cf. the perspective of D.A. Carson, *The Gospel According to John*, 511–24.

vine who replaces Israel as God's servant or agent (John 15:1; cf. Isa 5:1–7, Ezek 19:10). Believers are then represented as branches, and they are warned not to regard themselves presumptuously as the vine (John 15:5; cf. the temptation of Adam and Eve to be like God in Gen 3:5). Their cleansing, acceptability, and effective service should not be viewed as the result of their own effort, but rather because of their attachment to the vine (John 15:3–5).

So, what would happen if a branch thought it could function apart from the vine? The answer is obvious. It would be useless, and the branch would die. It would be fit for nothing except to be burned (15:6). Assurance comes as a result of abiding in the vine—namely, Jesus. Believers, therefore, are stoutly warned that failure to remain attached to the vine and receiving the divine sustenance means destruction. Now let me forewarn you as you read both of these two extended parables in John not to try and over-read them, such as asking: How can the branches become unattached? These are parables. Read them as illustrations and not as answering all your questions.

But, do you see how these two *mashals* (*meshalim*) actually function as two sides of a single coin or argument? Yes, there is assurance. Yes, there is security in Jesus. But no, this security is not absolute, because the human will is also involved. The human will can change the equation because God has never eliminated human freedom or choice. Humans can choose to disobey God, but the results are catastrophic.

There is tension here! The tension between assurance and warning is clearly present in John's gospel. Security is provided but not without obedience. The same tension is present in chapter 12 (the crucial introduction to the second half of this gospel). There, many Jewish leaders were said to believe, but they refused to confess Jesus because they feared being excommunicated from the synagogue. They made a choice, and their choice was not for God but for human acceptance (12:42–43; cf. 6:66). Such an alternative is the tension that always faces humans, no matter their situation.

Clues to Authentic Christianity in 1 John

To treat the Johannine perspectives on assurance and warning adequately in this discussion, we must briefly consider the so-called epistle known as First John and consider its perspective.[16] As I have detailed elsewhere, this work of 1 John is not

---

[16]For my further views on these Johannine treaties, see Gerald L. Borchert, *Worship in the New Testament: Divine Mystery and Human Response* (St. Louis: Chalice Press, 2008), 203–211. For a slightly different perspective, see Gary M. Burge, *Letter of John*, NIVAC (Grand Rapids: Zondervan, 1996), 24–28, 124–141. Also see the study of John Painter, *1, 2, 3 John*, SP (Collegeville, MN: Liturgical Press, 2002).

really an epistle or a letter. It is instead more like a term paper on theology that a student might write in an advanced class in New Testament theology. Moreover, when it was delivered to the churches in the Roman provinces of modern Turkey, it was probably accompanied by the short covering letters known as Second and Third John.[17] In this treatise the Johannine writer is wrestling with a topic similar to Paul's discussion in Romans 9–11, but the context and the conclusion are very different.

In Paul's discussion the question is how can he explain the Jewish rejection of Jesus, while in 1 John the writer is trying to explain why some Christians left the Christian community. He asks how could people become followers of Jesus and then turn their backs on the community. His simple answer could be that they must never have been a genuine part of our community, because if they had been a true part of us, then they would have (*memenēkeisan*) stayed with us (1 John 2:19). The use of the verb *menein* at this point reminds us that in the *Mashal* of the vine and branches the same Greek verb *menein* ("remain," or "stay") is used as the crux of his gospel argument, indicating a person's willful choice to continue in a relationship. Like Paul's conclusion, the Johannine conclusion is that persons who do not "remain" cannot be counted as legitimate children of God. "Staying" or "remaining" is the key to membership.

Now this conclusion may satisfy us academically, but it is hardly an adequate response to those who would ask the question in the context of turmoil and persecution: How can we tell if we or other Christians are true children of God? In times of persecution, this question becomes very significant, because faithfulness in fact is the real test of legitimate believing—not mere words or confessions. Do you want to know who is a legitimate Christian? Words are not the test; people's lives are the test! With this understanding in mind, now read First John again and it may become a very different book for you. Here are some of the elder John's concerns:

• Do you think you are a Christian model, but say that you don't sin? You are nothing but a deceiver and truth is not in you (1 John 1:8). You need to repent.
• Do you say that you are a follower of Jesus, but disobey the Lord's instructions? You are actually a liar (2:4). Faithfulness or walking (conducting one's life) like Jesus is in fact the test (2:6).

---

[17]For a further explication of the relationship between these documents, please see G. Borchert, *Worship in the New Testament*, 203–11. For Raymond E. Brown's changed views on the authorship and relationship of the epistles to the Fourth Gospel, see his *The Epistles of John*, AB (New York: Doubleday, 1982), 14–35.

- Do you think you have been enlightened, but still hate your brother or sister? You are pathetically still in the darkness (2:9).
- Do you say you are a member of the community, but deny that Jesus is the Christ? You are a falsifier and have the spirit of the antichrist (2:22).
- Do you think you belong to God, but commit all kinds of sins? You are guilty of being an outlaw (3:4).
- Do you consider yourself okay with God, but hate your brothers and sisters? You are no better than a murderer (3:15).
- Do you say that you love God, but close your heart to those who are in need? God's love can hardly be at home in you (3:17).
- Do you think the Spirit of God is in you, but deny the Incarnation? You have the spirit of the antichrist (4:3).
- Do you lack confidence in God, and are you afraid? You have hardly discovered what perfect love is all about (4:17–18).

John concludes: Those who are born of God have a very different mindset than that of the world because they have learned what believing in Jesus Christ really means (5:4–5).

As a contemporary reader, do you now understand what the Johannine writer was attempting to do? He was trying to provide his children in the faith with some easy ways to determine authentic Christianity. They were under siege, and they needed advice and direction to determine what Christian integrity looks like. He knew their lives were filled with fuzzy thinking and uncertainty, and while his statements appear to reduce Christian behavior to simple either/or alternatives, he did not reduce the basic tension between God and humanity in his message. He clearly desired for them to recognize the difference between what is true and what is false. Or, to put it another way, he sought to distinguish what is authentic living from what is merely a charade of integrity.

But the readers were still forced to integrate their faith and God's presence in their lives. They still had to face their traumas without yielding to fear. They were a community of Christians who were living in a tumultuous world, and they needed confidence that they were a genuine part of God's eschatological purpose (2:8). The day of judgment was coming, and they had to face the stark reality of that ultimate day (4:17). They were like many of us who are living on the edge of a conflicted world while seeking and trusting to be true children of God.

Conclusion

Similar to the early Christians, we long for the assurance that God cares for us (1 Pet 5:7) and will be with us through all our turmoil and difficult testing situations. We can be certain of God's undiminished love and faithful concern for us currently and provision of ultimate security, because God sent Jesus into the world to clarify the divine intentions (John 3:16–17). Not only did God's Son die for us in order to institute the new covenant, but Jesus also rose victorious over death to assure us of our reconciliation with God, provided we commit ourselves to the new covenant pattern of living (Rom 5:8–11).

This living Jesus has returned to the Godhead to prepare for us an eternal inheritance among God's people (John 14:1–2). But this sacrificial love of God in Christ demands the response of authentic life from God's children. Otherwise, we may experience condemnation (John 3:18). So, as humans and recipients of God's priceless love, we ought to live boldly! Yet we still live in the uneasy context of the tension between divine assurance and divine warning.

As we face the future, we must recognize that simplistic concepts of security without responsibility will hardly supply us with an adequate sense of assurance. Instead, God in Christ calls us to an obedient pattern of living with the Holy Spirit. The Spirit's leading is not to be confused with having a set of rules but is an authentic presence that leads us to embody the empowering Spirit of the living, loving Jesus in our world.

… And these reflections lead us naturally to the next chapter that deals with the foundational characteristic of New Covenant living—love!

Chapter 8

The New Covenant Characteristic

Tensions in Living the Way of Love

Seeking to Understand Love

Have you ever encountered Christian people who tell you that they love and respect you and then unfortunately add "but..." to their previous statement? Those people know that their lives should evidence love, yet their words betray another reality at work in them. Frankly, their actual lives sometimes indicate a clear lack of love, but reveal a sense of coolness, dislike, alienation, disgust, and perhaps even an outright rejection of those they are addressing. Of course, there are patterns of life that violate Christian integrity, but that issue is not our focus here. We are referring to the integrity and consistency between our words and life. Words can be very cheap because they are not the real test of love.

Actions and attitudes usually speak much louder than words. The New Testament indicates that both Jesus and Paul understood such a tension between words and actions, between outward communications and our inward feelings. We will, of course, discuss John 3 and 13 and 1 Corinthians 13 later, but we humans find it is very easy to hide behind slogans of love that can conceal different attitudes than the idea of love. For example, in Christian circles one can encounter the slogan, "I love the sinner but not the sin." That slogan certainly expresses an important concept—if it actually represents a true perspective of a person. But often a critical, condemning spirit can use such a slogan as a convenient mask to cloak a different spirit. The mind can easily shroud genuine feelings of rejection and pretend acceptance and love. So, let us be forewarned that good words such as "I love you" may indeed be sheltering the opposite realities.

The Starting Point for Understanding Love

By placing this discussion under the heading of the New Covenant, there is in this approach an implied presupposition that our interpretation of love grows out of a relationship to Christ and the New Covenant with God. This relationship should be exemplified in our new communities we call churches. These communities are to be built upon the redemptive work of Jesus, who came to the world as God's self-embodiment in an authentic human and gave himself to assure our ultimate wholeness or salvation. To know and follow the redemptive pattern of the Lord Jesus when he was on earth and to demonstrate the implications of his self-giving crucifixion and marvelous resurrection is the foundation for gaining a correct perception of Christian love.[1]

But our context of humanity in the world is not a loving one. So, like Jesus, we are in the world that basically does not know God and rejects genuine collegiality, unity, cooperation, and partnership. Instead, humans tend to use relationships if they can profit by them. The world's way is "me first," the "law of the claw," and "survival" in a hostile and unfriendly context.

Understanding our context is crucial because the natural fallen way of humans is to distrust anyone except our self—and maybe we are not always sure about that person! If we understand who we are in our context, then perhaps we also will recognize that even Christians often evidence the me first, uncooperative spirit. Not all of our attitudes and actions are transformed when we become Christians. We are works in progress, learning and experiencing the wonderful transforming power of Christ. Perhaps for this reason, in reflecting on the world, Paul concluded that the creation itself was marked by "futility" and inner "groaning." Yet he looked forward in hope to the time of redemption for the creation—and even "ourselves"—which was promised to the people of God at the *parousia* (the coming/return) of the Lord (see Rom 8:19–25).

Love and the Great Antitheses of Matthew

At this point it is probably helpful to turn to the antitheses—the great alternatives of Jesus—in the so-called Sermon on the Mount that are preserved in Matthew 5.[2] The fifth antithesis (5:38–42) deals with the rabbinic rules of retaliation or the "eye for an eye" justice pattern that developed from texts such as Exodus 21:23–25 and Leviticus 24:19–20. The question was: When is vengeance satisfied? Seemingly, justice would mean at least equal vengeance, but common wisdom would argue not to go too far with vengeance—for example, Lamech

---

[1] See my further explanation of these verses in Gerald L. Borchert, *John 1–11*, vol. 25A, NAC (Nashville: Broadman and Holman, 1996), 99–121. See also R. Jackson Painter, *The Gospel of John: A Thematic Approach* (Eugene, OR: Wipf and Stock, 2010).

[2] For an excellent analysis of the antitheses in Matthew 5, see Robert Guelich, *The Sermon on the Mount: A Foundation for Understanding* (Waco, TX; Word, 1982), 175–271. See also John Stott, *Christian Counter-Culture: The Message of the Sermon on the Mount* (Downers Grove, IL: InterVarsity,1978); Glenn Stassen, *Just Peace Making: Transforming Initiatives for Peace and Justice* (Cleveland, OH: Pilgrim, 2004) and Charles H. Talbert, *Reading the Sermon on the Mount: Character Formation and Decision Making in Matthew 5–7* (Grand Rapids: Baker Academic, 2006).

who boasted that while Cain avenged seven times, he would avenge seventy times seven (Gen 4:23).

Jesus, however, enunciated what seems to be an odd idea of "no vengeance" and non-resistance instead. What kind of justice is that? The bully gets double benefit! Actually, Jesus was saying: Show the ruthless person a new way, and do not become unglued by the loss of things and by unfair practices. Yet, we might wonder: How do I get ahead in the world if I let people take advantage of me? So the question is: Was Jesus establishing a new set of laws, or was he doing something else in these antitheses?

The answer to that question resides in the sixth and final antithesis and the text of Matthew 5:43–48. The rabbis and the Qumran covenanters had developed interpretations that advocated loving your neighbor (the Jewish people/the members of the community) and hating your enemy (the Gentiles/those outside the community).[3] This concept is actually not enunciated in the Old Testament—even though the rabbis had determined that some people were acceptable and they made distinctions they thought were appropriate. Indeed, as I indicated in chapter 3, they even thanked God in the old Jewish prayer for these distinctions. But Jesus called his followers to "love" others, including "your enemies" and to "pray for those who persecute you" (5:44). Accordingly, Jesus' disciples were instructed to follow the model of God who does not make such distinctions but instead gives sun and rain and thus harvest not only to the good/just people but also to those who are evil/unjust (5:44–45).

I must note that this old rabbinic view is not the view of many contemporary Jews, as in Rabbi Joseph Telushkin's monumental work.[4] In spite of human rebellion, God still loves humanity and is in the business of re-creation and reclamation. God in Christ Jesus wants all people to be transformed so they will recognize that petty practices such as making distinctions, seeking retribution, and focusing on "me first" and personal gain are hardly God's intention in the world. Rather, God intends for humans to follow the model of Jesus and demonstrate authentic love. Such love is not spineless, just as God's will for authentic truth and justice is not weak or self-oriented.[5]

---

[3]For quick access to understanding the rational of such thinking concerning one's neighbor, see Guelich, *The Sermon on the Mount*, 225–227. See also Donald A. Hagner, *Matthew 1–13*, vol. 33B, WBC (Dallas: Word Books, 1993), 134 and Gerald L. Borchert, "Matthew 5:48—Perfection and the Sermon," *RevExp* 89 (1992), 235–52.

[4]Rabbi Joseph Telushkin, *A Code of Jewish Ethics: Vol. 2: Love Your Neighbor as Yourself* (New York: Bell Tower/Harmony [Random House], 2009).

[5]See for example Nicholas Wolsterstorff, *Justice in Love* (Grand Rapids: Eerdmans, 2015).

God's people are called to recognize that God's pattern has always been amazingly bold because God is slow to get angry and very patient with human frailties and rebellion, and stands ready to forgive when there is genuine repentance (e.g., Ps. 103:8, 145:8–9; Joel 2:12–14; Jon 4:2). Jesus' followers are summoned to embody that model of integrity (the biblical idea of perfection, Matt 5:48). At the heart of that commission to perfection stands love.

The Words for "Love" and Misconceptions in Meaning

I turn now to some common misconceptions concerning the words for love that were introduced by the work of Andres Nygren.[6] His "motif analysis" has unfortunately been exploited by well-meaning preachers who have perhaps studied a little Greek in their education but who have passed on their ill-understood ideas to their accepting congregations. Their recipients in turn have "taken the bait," in an inappropriate understanding of the post-resurrection fishing story of John 21. But let me offer two illustrations in pursuing this matter.

Greek Words for "Love". I once encountered a situation in which a pastor was waxing long on his understanding of John 21, proclaiming different meanings for the Greek words *agapaō* and *phileō* that appear in John 21. He argued that Jesus asked Peter twice, "Do you love (*agapas*) me?" In response Peter answered twice, "Yes Lord ... I love (*philō*) you." Then the third time, he indicated that Jesus came down to Peter's level and asked, "Do you love (*phileis*) me?" and sensing the Lord's critique, Peter replied, "I love (*philō*) you." Not long thereafter my granddaughter, who is very bright, asked me to explain the biblical words for "love" that her teacher was using and how *agapē* differs from other forms of love. These two illustrations indicate how widespread is this misconception concerning the Greek words for "love."

"Love" in John. As I indicated previously, the connected stories in John 21 of the large catch of fish and the reinstatement of Peter after his denial of Jesus form the heart of the common misunderstanding of love. First, let me clear up one basic

---

[6]In his work, *Agape and Eros* (Philadelphia: Muhlenberg, 1953), Andres Nygren set out a motif analysis in which he sought to distinguish patterns in society—the Christian pattern and the selfish one. In talking with him many years ago, he said his point was not to do a philological or linguistic study of the Greek words for love. However, the book sparked an immediate response by those who carried his ideas far beyond anything Nygren intended. For an excellent study of linguistic patterns in biblical studies and their inadequate uses, see the important work of James Barr, *The Semantics of Biblical Language* (Oxford: University Press, 1961), especially 216–17. See also Leon Morris, *Studies in the Fourth Gospel* (London: Paternoster, 1969), 293–319.

fact related to Andres Nygren's "motif study." The Greek word *eros* is absent from the New Testament. But does that absence mean the New Testament does not deal with sexual love? Of course not!

Second, the text tells us why Peter was grieved: Jesus asked him a "third time" if Peter loved him (John 21:17). Peter's sense of being "exposed" came from his recognition of the "third time." It does not hinge on the change of the Greek words, although the Johannine author clearly highlighted the exposure by the change. But Peter was forcefully reminded of another "charcoal fire" experience where he denied Jesus three times. [Note: there are only two places in the New Testament where the Greek word *anthrakian* (charcoal fire) appears (John 18:18, 21:9).] But there is a previous question that must be asked concerning this conversation. Did it take place in Aramaic/Hebrew or in Greek? If it was in the former, the argument is tenuous!

Third, there is a far more serious problem that must be faced by those who attempt to make such a distinction between these two Greek verbs (*agapaō* and *phileō*) for "love." It has to do with the fact that the Johannine writer does not make such a strict distinction in Greek between "brotherly love" and "self-giving love," as is supposed by many interpreters. John 5:20 states that "the Father loves the Son." The Greek verb used in this verse is *philei*. Do you think that the Father's love for the Son is a lower class of love than the so-called higher form of self-giving love that *agapaō* is supposed to mean later?

This argument is another case of James Barr's misuse of word studies to make theological distinctions. In this case it involves Greek rather than English words. In his significant critique of Kittel's massive *Theological Dictionary of the New Testament*, Barr argued cogently that single words have multiple meanings and the best studies are those that involve a combination of words.[7] While I do not wish to denounce the use of dictionaries—especially those related to other languages—I recognize that the meaning of a single word may not carry the distinction we wish. But let us return briefly to John 21.

Do I think that the writer was trying to say something in the change of the Greek words? I would answer that the evangelist was probably trying to indicate that Peter was not taking Jesus' questions seriously because Peter tended to speak from the top of his head. His misunderstandings are legion. Did the probing of Jesus succeed in making him face the reality of his denial and his future? Absolutely! Did the facing of reality arise from the use of two "Greek" words for love? I doubt that was the main point! The issue was much deeper. Words, of

---

[7]See previous footnote.

course, are important signals of deeper realities. Love is a crucial word for John, especially in his gospel and in his first epistle (which is a treatise on love). But remember, the conversation was probably not in Greek!

So, when the evangelist changed the Greek words in John 21, he was probably signaling that something important took place. I believe that Peter finally recognized that Jesus was absolutely serious in Peter's reinstatement. We should concentrate on the strategic "third time," as the text tells us (21:17). And remember that the word *philein* is also significant in John 5:20.

Love as the Identifying Characteristic of the Christian Life

The Johannine gospel identifies what Jesus considered to be the crucial characteristic of the Christian life: to "love one another." This characteristic should be evidenced in all of our relationships, especially in the Christian community that we call the church. It is by love that the world would recognize Christians are authentic disciples of Jesus (John 13:34–35; cf. 15:12).

Moreover, Jesus indicated the crucial nature of this command by establishing it as the Christian model of self-giving at the strategic Last Supper on the night he was betrayed by Judas. Jesus wrapped a towel around himself, poured out water in a basin, and began to wash the feet of his disciples (13:1–5). He made good progress until he came to Peter who resisted being washed. Why did Peter resist? I usually tell my students that a rabbi could ask his students to do most slave chores, but he could not ask them to touch his feet. Peter realized Jesus was acting the part of a slave, and it was demeaning.[8]

Do you understand the response of John the Baptist to the Sanhedrin's investigating committee when he said that he was "unworthy to untie the thongs of the sandals of the one who … was coming" (John 1:26–27)? John clearly recognized what his relation to the coming Messiah should be, and he was willing to be the lowest imaginable slave. Indeed, he was willing to be a mere "voice" of witness calling Israel to repentance (1:23).[9] But even more astounding is that Jesus, the Son of God, washed the feet of his disciples—and he called his followers to "follow" his example (13:13–14)! Do you want to know what love is all about? Look at Jesus! His stories demonstrate love.

---

[8]See my further discussion and the implications of the command of Jesus in Gerald L. Borchert, *John 12–21*, vol. 25B, NAC (Nashville: Broadman and Holman, 2002), 75–87

[9]See my further comments on the text in G. Borchert, *John 1–11*, 125–133.

The Seriousness of "Love" in John 3:16–18

I turn now to what may be considered the most crucial verse in the New Testament. Obviously, I must give attention to John 3:16. But in doing so, we must realize that the full meaning of John's message here is not contained in one verse but in a minimum of three verses: 16, 17, and 18. Verse 16 functions as the statement of fact concerning God's amazing love in sending the Son of God to bring salvation/wholeness to the world. Then, verse 17 indicates that God's purpose in sending the Son was not to condemn but to save the people of the world. Finally, verse 18 recognizes the sad reality that those who do not believe are condemned—not in some distant future but "already" (*ēdē*), for we humans are already under condemnation for our disobedience to God.[10]

Many people think of the Gospel of John as the Gospel of Love. But actually, it is also the severest book of judgment in the New Testament—with perhaps the exception of the Johannine Apocalypse (Revelation). Clearly, God sent Jesus into the world to bring about wholeness to humans, but in this action God was not playing games with us. God was absolutely serious in the divine mission. Accordingly, the rejection of God's love has dire consequences. Human toying with God's love has resulted in condemnation and judgment— already! Far too many people think that God will not judge them, but such is not the message of this gospel. Playing at Christian faith means disaster.

There is no question that God loves humans in spite of all our warts, error-prone ways, misconceptions, and sin. The divine love is the reason why God sent Jesus to change the focus of our living and ways of acting. To be precise, Jesus became human to rescue us from our rebellious ways. His love expressed in his self-giving life, his death, and his resurrection fulfilled God's purpose. But God has never been spineless and unable to punish.

Reading the Old Testament should remind us of the countless times God judged Israel. Jesus is no different. He did not give his life without expecting us to be responsible for our lives. Instead, John 5:22 makes it clear that the Father does not need to pass judgment on people: that task has been given to Jesus who is in charge of both the resurrection to life and the resurrection to judgment (5:29). We humans should not think that Jesus, who became human, does not understand the ways of our insincerities, pretenses, manipulations, hostilities, and refusals to honor God. Jesus came and loved humanity, but we must take that coming very seriously.[11]

---

[10]G. Borchert, *John 1–11*, 183–86

[11]G. Borchert, *John 1–11*, 237–242. See also the brief but helpful comments of Ben Witherington III

Masquerading Patterns in Religious Life

Jesus knew that humans evidenced many patterns that masqueraded as religious life and love. His severest criticisms were leveled at those who pretended to be religious. He cleared out cheaters at the Temple tables (*trapezas* is the Greek word for bank; John 2:15) and whipped their livestock out of the Temple precincts (John 2:14–16, cf. Mark 11:15–16, etc.).[12] But there is perhaps no more caustic chapter in the Bible than Matthew 23 and the scathing condemnations of the Pharisees whose pretense of pious religion was identified by Jesus as whitewashed tombs filled with decaying bones (v. 27). [13]

Paul's Triadic Thinking and the Role of Love

I turn briefly in closing this section to an important clue in Pauline thinking: his use of triads. Paul loved to think in threes. Just read 1 Thessalonians and you will discover a number of triads. The triad most recognized by Christians is "faith, hope, and love" (1 Cor 13:13). That triad, in a different order, represents the three stages of the salvation process—justification, sanctification, and glorification. When Paul uses those three words in a verse or context, the last word in the triad usually indicates where the emphasis of Paul falls in the discussion.

For example, 1 Corinthians 13 focuses on growing with Christ in the life of love. The same is true of Romans 5:1, 2, and 5 where the words faith, hope, and love appear in the same order. When we turn to 1 Thessalonians, the concern of Paul is very different and therefore the triad is used differently as faith, love, and hope (1:3). Indeed, in that same chapter Paul makes his point clear by defining that triad more precisely as: 1) they "turned to God from idols," 2) in order "to serve the authentic and living God," and 3) they "await the Son from heaven" (1:9–10). Understanding the significance of this triadic thinking in Paul can, therefore, assist the reader in perceiving the point in Paul's arguments. There is a similar outline in the magnificent handbook for Christian living in Ephesians 1:13–14, which we shall discuss in the next chapter. Authentic living is a major goal of the Pauline corpus.

---

in "What 'God is Love' Actually Means," *BAR*, 46.4 (Fall 2020): 60–61.

[12]See G. Borchert, *John 1–11*, 160–167.

[13]For a helpful interpretation on this caustic attack on the Pharisees and their legalistic companions in Matthew 23:13–33, see Donald A. Hagner, *Matthew 14–28*, vol. 33B, WBC (Dallas: Word Books, 1995), 662–678. See also R.T. France, *The Gospel of Matthew*, NICNT (Grand Rapids: Eerdmans, 2007), section IV.D.2.

A Closing Question on Love

If a Christian is interested in living a growing relationship with God, then that life should be marked by the clear evidence of love. I must confess, however, that in this era of so many church battles I fear that the living Jesus must be shaking the divine head and wondering if Christians really understand the new dominical command concerning love (John 13:34–35). I also wonder why so many Christians condemn others who think differently than they do? Do we not realize that we are not the measure of authenticity? Do we not understand that we are not God? Perhaps it is time for Christians to fall on our knees and confess that we have not loved as Christ commanded. The church that is emerging in our world today will have to find the better way of love if we are to produce authentic followers of Christ. The future is open to us.

… Will we follow the model of Jesus as part of the New Covenant?

Chapter 9

New Covenant Living

Tensions in Living with the Spirit, a Commitment to Prayer,
and a Respect for Time

Seeking to Understand and Live in the Way of the Spirit

With the Lord's imperative of love as the Christian characteristic in mind, I turn now to reflect on the way of the Spirit in understanding the transformed life. Historically, there have been great tensions among Christians, strong opinions, and not a few hostile conflicts and condemnations related to the issue of the Spirit. Indeed, Paul placed his classic interpretation on love (1 Corinthians 13) to the Corinthian misfits at the center of his advice concerning the way of the Spirit (1 Corinthians 12–14).

Doing the Will of God and Following the Way of the Spirit

The issue of understanding the will of God is also one that has created considerable consternation for Christians who struggle to gain a sense of certainty in following the leading of God. Indeed, many Christian young people as they move through the stages toward adulthood and the possibility of an uncertain future often attend classes or seminars on the subject of "knowing the will of God." For anyone who has taught such classes, that person knows the difficulties in helping others discover meaningful Christlike patterns for living that do not reintroduce old styles of legalism.[1]

An Old Testament Reflection. The Old Testament stories are replete with figures such as Abraham, Joseph, Moses, Joshua, and Daniel who seemingly knew the will of God for them and yet so many others failed even to recognize God's intentions for the people of Israel. Instead of following the will and purposes of God, the theme of the Exodus for the Israelites could easily be categorized as "grumble, grumble" or, as the theme of Judges indicates, "the people did what was right in their own eyes" (Judg 21:25). Both are hardly commendations but

---

[1]I have dealt with the subject of the will of God at greater length in "The Will of God and Christian Freedom" in Gerald L. Borchert, *Christ and Chaos: Biblical Keys to Ethical Questions* (Macon, GA: Nurturing Faith, 2020), 83–94.

are harsh condemnations of a people who were called to be followers of God. But they chose doing things their own way and complaining when they entered new swamps of trouble.

Jesus, Paul, and the Spirit. Jesus knew that Christians would have a difficult task of finding their way in the world, so that is the reason he gave the Holy Spirit or the "other Paraclete" (from the Greek *paraklētos* meaning "the one alongside," "Supporter," "Advisor," etc.) to be "in" us, to "teach" us, to keep us from becoming a "scandal," to "judge" error, and to "guide" us into all truth (John 14:12–16:15).[2] Paul likewise provided a fairly clear indication of what a life led by the Holy Spirit would resemble when he outlined that the fruit of the Spirit would be: love, joy, peace, patience, kindness, faithfulness, gentleness, and self-control (Gal 5:23).[3] Now this list was hardly meant to be a new set of rules we can attain on our own. But it can provide a thermometer or reminder of our necessary dependence upon God's Spirit for direction.

The Magnificent Christian Handbook: Ephesians

We turn now to the circular letter generally known as Ephesians[4] for some further insights into the pattern for living an authentic life with God. I believe that this work resembles something akin to an early catechetical book written in magnificent Greek prose that flows almost like free verse.[5]

This catechetical epistle begins with the forceful statement that Paul was an apostle by "the will of God" (1:1), and it continues with the conviction that

---

[2]The above statements are a brief summary of the five Holy Spirit/Paraclete sayings in John 14:15–17, 26–27; 15:26–16:1, 7–11, 13–15. For my further elaboration on these verses in John, see Gerald L. Borchert, *John 12–21*, vol. 25B, NAC (Nashville: Broadman and Holman, 2002), 119–136, 158–171. See also Raymond E. Brown, *John xii–xxi*, vol. 29A, AB (Garden City, NY: Doubleday, 1979), 643–647, 652–654, 698–702, 709–716.

[3]For my views on this Pauline text, see "Galatians" in Roger Mohrlang and Gerald L. Borchert, *Romans and Galatians*, vol. 14, CorBC (Carol Stream, IL: Tyndale House, 2007), 320–327. See also Scot McKnight, *Galatians*, NIVAC (Grand Rapids: Zondervan, 1995), 270–281.

[4]The circular nature is attested by the missing of *en ephesō* in most early manuscripts. While some scholars question Paul's authorship of Ephesians, I will not pursue this matter except to indicate the intriguing relationship that Ephesians has with Luke's works. The expression "filled with" the Holy Spirit occurs only in Ephesians 5:18 and in Luke's gospel and the Book of Acts. Also, the concept of the wall separating the Gentiles in Ephesians 2:11–22 may reflect the separating temple wall important in Acts 21:27–22:29 and 15:1–35. While Luke was not the author of Ephesians, was he the amanuensis?

[5]For my discussions on Ephesians, see Pamela Scalise and Gerald Borchert, "The Bible and the Spiritual Pilgrimage" in *Becoming Christian*, ed. Bill J. Leonard (Louisville: Westminster/John Knox, 1990), 37–46 and Gerald L. Borchert, *Worship in the New Testament: Divine Mystery and Human Response* (St. Louis: Chalice Press, 2008), 130–139. See also Lynn H. Cohick, *The Epistle to Ephesians*, NICNT (Grand Rapids: Eerdmans, 2020) and Frank Thielman's *Ephesians*, BECNT (Grand Rapids: Baker, 2010).

Christians are blessed, chosen, and destined in Christ to fulfill the purpose of the divine will for the glory and praise of God (1:3–6). To fulfill that divine will, Christians have been graciously redeemed and been given knowledge and wisdom to understand the "mystery of his will" that is to bring together all things in heaven and on earth (1:7–10). In Christ rests the divine purpose, and he is accomplishing in Christians what he intended for his glory (1:11–12). Paul then outlines again the three stages of salvation so that we understand clearly what is the will of God, namely: People will have heard and believed (justification), will be sealed by the Holy Spirit for living authentically on earth (sanctification), until they gain their ultimate inheritance (glorification) that will resound to the ultimate praise of God (1:13–14).[6]

The focus for understanding God's purposes should not be on us as humans and our personal desires, but must be on God's purposes for us. Jesus summarized this point poignantly with "Seek first the Kingdom [of God] and his righteousness and all the rest will be given" (Matt 6:33). Our problem with the will of God usually comes with where we place the emphasis—God or us!

The rest of Ephesians then is aimed at supporting the outworking of God's purposes in us.[7] But I pause briefly to mention several additional matters in this remarkable Christian Handbook. At Ephesians 4:11–16 our writer indicates that God in Christ has gifted his church with persons who should assist them in carrying out the divine purposes of building up the body of Christ in love, namely: apostles, prophets/spokes persons, evangelists, pastors, and teachers.

Then at 4:17–5:20 he outlines what the new morality of a Christian should look like in 5:21–6:9. Using baptismal imagery, he instructs his readers to put off the old ways of living and to put on the model of Christ (4:20, 22, 24, 25, 31; 5:1). That model was none other than to walk in love as Christ did (5:2) and to banish from one's life the non-productive ways of darkness (5:8-11). The writer of Ephesians concludes this new morality by directing his readers to reject substance abuse as debauchery and instead "to be filled with the Spirit" and to heartily praise and thank God in the name of Jesus.

Thereafter, he sets forth how Christians in their household life should relate to one another. Finally, even as a prisoner (6:20), he expresses his confidence in concluding this marvelous document by indicating that God will supply Christ's followers with the needed armament to overcome the tensions and frustrations

---

[6]See my reflections here on Paul's triadic thinking in chapter 6.

[7]See Scalise and Borchert, "The Bible and the Spiritual Pilgrimage," 37–46, and G. Borchert, *Worship in the New Testament*, 133–136. For a helpful study on discipleship, see Richard H. Longenecker, *Patterns of Discipleship in the New Testament* (Grand Rapids: Eerdmans, 1996).

they experience in society and overcome the attacks of spiritual forces that seek to destroy them and their witness for Christ (6:10–20).

I am increasingly convinced that Christians will have to become more clearly oriented to the leading of the Holy Spirit if we are going to counter the growing secularization in our culture. Programs and buildings will not convince our society of the transforming power of the gospel. Christians living with the creative Holy Spirit that directs their lives in every circumstance is the only answer. Will we fail to represent God's intentions and lack the resolve needed in our efforts? Of course! But we still can be used by God in this transforming process.

Pondering the Gifts of the Spirit

Having briefly introduced this subject of our need for the presence of the Holy Spirit in our lives, I turn now to the tension-filled subject of the gifts of the Spirit, especially in 1 Corinthians 12–14.[8]

The Nature and Purpose of the Gifts. Before proceeding too far into this minefield of strong opinions, there are several matters that I should highlight in connection with the gifted persons introduced above in Ephesians 4, namely: These persons are gifted for service by God; the goal of these gifted persons is to create unity in the body of Christ; and the undergirding characteristic of these spiritually directed persons is to be love.

But I ask myself what is usually encountered among Christians in dialogues about the "gifts of the Spirit." I have found that: the emphasis usually falls upon the gift and not on service; division is encountered rather than unity; and the characteristic present is usually discord and one-upmanship rather than love.

So, as we reflect on 1 Corinthians 12–14, we might ponder seriously why Paul placed chapter 13 on "love" at the heart of his discussion on spiritual gifts. Then ask: Why did he insert a similar section on love and care at Romans 12:9–21 after providing a different list of gifts in that text? Do you think that Paul might have understood that Christians do not really comprehend what is the actual purpose of the gifts of the Spirit? Perhaps reflecting on that reality might provide help in dealing with tensions over the gifts of the Spirit that Christians often face.

---

[8]Please see the carefully nuanced study of these chapters in Gordon Fee, *God's Empowering Presence: The Holy Spirit in the Letters of Paul* (Peabody, MA; Hendrickson, 1994), 146–271 as well as the Excursus, 272–281. See also Max Turner, *The Holy Spirit and Spiritual Gifts: In the New Testament Church Today*, rev. ed. (Peabody, MA: Hendrickson, 2005, Zondervan 1996) as well as my reflections on "Church Worship Practices" in the section on Paul in Gerald L. Borchert, *Worship in the New Testament: Divine Mystery and Human Response* (St. Louis: Chalice Press), 109–114.

The Framework of 1 Corinthians 12–14. As we review this extended Pauline dialog that has been the subject of myriads of debates among Christians, let us first consider the context to see if we can gain any insights that will help us cope better with disagreements that are often evident in relating to the gifts of the Spirit.[9]

Paul opened his response to his proud Corinthian children who regarded themselves as intellectual "knowers" but who were short on love (cf. 1 Cor 8:1) with a reality check. He reminded them that in the matter of spiritual gifts he did not want them "to be ignorant" (*agnoein*, 12:1). Then he promptly pointed out to them that they had recently come out of paganism where in their worship practices they were seduced (*apagomenoi*) by idols that could not even speak (12:2).[10] Instead of recognizing their past, the Corinthians had instead begun to make distinctions among believers by thinking they were superior Christians, not realizing that it was the Spirit who was responsible for their new lives as Christians, and even for helping them to speak/confess that "Jesus is Lord" (12:3). So, instruction was necessary for these "know-it-all" Corinthians.

Accordingly, he began his subsequent counsel to them by asserting that in the church there are various spiritual gifts (*charismatōn*) and various patterns of service (*diakoniōn*) and actions (*energematōn*) but that there is only one triune God (Spirit, Lord, and God). And he insisted that not everyone is blessed in the same way but that all blessings are meant to enhance everyone in the faith community (12:4–7). Since we are all different, the gifts are different. The church, as a body, needs all the parts working together to function properly. Mutual support, not self-assertive individualism, is the goal (12:12–26).

Then Paul identified several gifts such as: wise advice, brilliant communication, model faith, a healing ability, miraculous power, prophetic proclamation, insight into the spiritual realms, incomprehensible speech, and comprehensible interpretive ability (12:8–10; cf. Rom 12: 4–8). Is this list exhaustive? Hardly! But it was provided to make the Corinthians aware of the wide range of the gifts and that none of them are personal possessions. But their presence is an indication of the Spirit's presence and they are not for personal enhancement but for the work of ministry (12: 7–11). And in case they focused on the gifts per se, Paul emphasized the functionality of the gifts by identifying the persons who would

---

[9]For my further thoughts on 1 Corinthians, see Gerald L. Borchert, *Portraits of Jesus for an Age of Biblical Illiteracy* (Macon, GA: Smyth & Helwys, 2016), 103–127.

[10]For the contextual background to these statements in 1 Corinthian, see Gordon Fee, *God's Empowering Presence*, 146–158. See also C.K. Barrett, *The First Epistle to the Corinthians* (New York: Harper & Row,1968), 278–280. For the background to the Corinthian letter, see Wayne E. Meeks, *The First Urban Christians: The Social World of the Apostle Paul*, 2nd ed. (New Haven: Yale University, 2003), 9–50, 140-162.

use those gifts such as apostles, prophets, teachers, miracle workers, healers, assistants, administrators, and tongues speakers (12: 27–29)—a list somewhat similar to the shorter list in Ephesians 4:11–16.

And before he inserted the important role of "love," Paul added an important caveat that prepares the reader for chapter 14. He stated unequivocally that in understanding the gifts, Christians should "fervently strive [struggle] for the better gifts" (12:31). Why did Paul make such a statement? The reason for his warning becomes clear in chapter 14: it was speaking in tongues!

Speaking in Tongues. The Corinthians had forgotten that the purpose of the gifts was to enhance their common ministry in the world, especially prophecy or proclamation. Instead, they had focused on self-gratification and experiences of speaking in tongues (14:1–4). It was just another case of Satan bending God's provisions into self-centeredness.

Now, Paul did not condemn speaking in tongues. He even affirmed it by stating that he spoke in tongues more than they did (14:18). But he set tongues speaking in its proper role among human spiritual exercises (14:5, 13–17). For any gift to be helpful in the public, communication of God's purposes had to be central. In the use of the mouth, therefore, proclamation or instruction had to be primary. Speaking in tongues was a low priority at merely .05 percent (5 to 10,000) in effectiveness (14:19). The gift could certainly be regarded as a sign for unbelievers (14:22), but what was it communicating? Without an authentic interpretation, it would communicate that Christians must be mad or crazy (14:23)!

Madness in the First-Century Context. To understand Paul's designation of speaking in tongues as madness, one needs to recognize the first century context for that statement. As I turn to this discussion, I do so with a degree of hesitancy because I do not wish my readers to think that I am charging anyone with madness today. But on advice I have greatly moderated the force of my presentation because the pagan activity was really ghastly and hardly a topic for polite discourse. Indeed, it is rather sickening!

Briefly, we should remember that besides the fact that Aphrodite, the goddess of love, was honored in Corinth, the citizens there revered Dionysus, the mad Reveler, also called Bacchus (Plutarch, *Moralia* 671). Because this area was known for grapes and wine production, the worship patterns of Dionysus easily became associated with debauchery. The Dionysiac celebration held in December at the time of the winter solstice was a drunken festival in that men and women dressed in garments resembling deer became highly "inspired" by imbibing the "nectar of the god" and at a given signal rushed off into the woods to engage in sexual orgies and other despicable carousing.

But some of the worship patterns of the women devotees were far worse. Pausanius described the Pythian women who danced nearly nude around the two wooden statues of Dionysus (the Reveler) and Lysia that were painted in gaudy colors to remind them of an earlier mythical orgy in which a man climbed a tree to watch the women revelers. When they spotted him, they dragged him out of the tree and tore him apart while he was still living (*Description of Greece*, II. ii). Some have even suggested the revolting idea that the cult tradition included the women tearing apart dedicated animals and eating them while the blood was still pumping so that they could receive the power and life of the god.

Strabo indicated that the noise and frenzy of these women in worship was very intense and that they used various instruments such as drums and cymbals to enhance the sound of their worship (*Geographica*, X. 3.7; cf, 1 Cor 13:1). Moreover, Aristophanes identified the strange confusing speech (babbling) of the worshipers as the "tongue of Bacchus" (*Frogs*, 356–57).

To conclude this brief excursus into worship madness in the period of the early church, it is important to realize that even the Roman Senate became involved over the Bacchic practices. Livy stated that these women were the instigators of all sorts of mischief and that there were males who were driven senseless and engaged in nocturnal confusion as the result of wine (XXXIX. 15). Cicero reported that the Senate finally acted to curtail Bacchic activity by prohibiting in perpetuity these nocturnal orgies and punishing those who engaged in them with the support of the consular armies (Laws, II. xv).

Is it any wonder why the Apostle Paul tool pains in 1 Corinthians to curtail his deviant children in the faith from engaging in any activity that suggested public madness might be present in the community and degrading to the name of Christ. The proper use of the gifts of the Spirit, however, was hardly condemned by Paul. But their public use of some were carefully monitored.

Illustrations Concerning Speaking in Tongues. I have often pointed out in interchurch discussions that during the Marxist period in Russia, Soviet leaders thrust the Baptists, Pentecostals, and other Evangelical Christians together in a unified church structure. In that structure the parties agreed that speaking in tongues was allowed in personal piety and devotion, but that it would not be practiced in public worship. The groups worked together quite well under the domination of an outside force. But as soon as the Marxist heavy hand diminished, the groups would no longer work together in the cause of Christ. Now, because of outside pressures, it is quite possible in the future that Christians of various types may be forced to discover they can actually work together in the Spirit of Christ. Secularism and outright hostility to anything representing Jesus is today gaining strength, as it did in Nazi Germany. Do not think it cannot come to your region of the world. (I will deal with this concern in chapter 12, but new types of dictatorship are clearly emerging.)

My second illustration involves my experiences of speaking in a variety of charismatic churches. Frequently I am asked: "Do you speak in tongues?" I have never answered that question because of its implications: it draws a line of separation in the sand. I am usually intrigued to listen to the prayers of people after I have spoken and hear them say: "Thank you God for sending Dr. Borchert to us who has the gift of teaching." Let us be known by what we do for God in the Spirit and not by what we assert about ourselves.

Summation

In concluding this section, let me say that we need to be irenic and Christlike in our understanding of the role of the Holy Spirit. Many will be adamant in their views, but let us as followers of Jesus attempt to evidence the spirit of Jesus. Let us remember that our fallible opinions may not be the measure of divine reality. So as members of Christ's body, let us move forward into the future, evidencing the loving attitude of the Apostle Paul in dealing with our differing views. In pursuing our dependence on the leading of the Holy Spirit, let us not allow the devil to divide us from one another.

Finally, this concern for dependence upon divine direction leads quite naturally to the next subject, a topic that involves personal tension as we face our commitment as Christians to prayer.

The Significance of Prayer for the Christian

The subject of prayer is a strategic one for Christians who are committed to new covenant living. Prayer follows quite naturally after the subject of the Christian's understanding of the Holy Spirit because prayer involves the human side of our relationship to God. While prayer has spawned many fine devotional books that encourage Christians in their daily lives and their walk with God, it carries with it tensions and some poorly understood ideas. While I could write another volume on the necessity of prayer and our dependence on God, I will mention here only a few of these concerns that pertain to the Lord's Prayer.[11]

Asking "in the Name of Jesus"

In his life on earth, Jesus seems to have risen early to pray and retreated from people even late into the night to do the same (e.g., Mark 1:35, 6:46; Luke 5:16, 11:1). And during crucial times he prayed even in the midst of people (e.g., Luke 3:21; 6:12; 9:28, 28; 22:41–44; John 11:41–42; 12:27–28). The Gospels provide a portrait of Jesus who modeled for his followers the patterns of keeping in close touch with the Father through prayer and also directed them to make their requests known to God (cf. Mark 11:24, Luke 11:9, Matt 7:7; cf. also Jas 1:5–8, 1 John 5:14–15). Clearly Christians are enjoined to bring their cares to God in prayer (e.g., Mark 11:24–25; 13:18, 33; Matt 5:44; 6:5–6; Jas 5:16; 1 Pet 5:7), and the Book of Acts is filled with accounts of the Christians praying as they followed the pattern of Jesus and the earlier prophets (Acts 1:24, 6:6, 8:15, 9:40, 10:9, etc.).

But when in John 14:13 and 15:16 Jesus is reported to have said "I will do" or the "the Father will give" "whatever you ask in my name," the question in many minds often is: What does it mean to ask or pray in the name of Jesus? Can it actually mean that if we make a series of requests and append or introduce the list with the words "in the name of Jesus" that these requests will automatically be fulfilled? Of course not! To comprehend this Johannine concept of asking in the name of Jesus,[12] one must remember that "name" in the Hebrew or Semitic context implies "nature."

Names were very important in that culture so that a change of name implied a change of nature. Remember the names of Abraham, Sarah, and Israel are all changed names, implying an important change in those people. And the task of Adam was to give names to the animals, which meant to the early Semites that the human was defining the nature of those creatures (Gen 2:20). To ask "in the name of Jesus" then means to ask as Jesus would ask. With such a perception in the meaning of "in Jesus' name," the entire base system of prayer has thus been radically shifted from self-centeredness to a Jesus-orientation.

---

[11]For further insights into the Lord's Prayer, see for example C. Clifton Black, The Lord's Prayer in *Interpretation: Resources for Use of Scripture in the Church* (Louisville: Westminster/John Knox, 2018); Robert A. Guelich, *The Sermon on the Mount: A Foundation for Understanding* (Waco, TX: Word Books, 1982); Charles H. Talbert, *Reading the Sermon on the Mount* (Grand Rapids: Baker, 2006).

[12]For my further discussion on the Johannine texts, see Gerald L. Borchert, *John 12–21*, vol. 25B, NAC (Nashville: Broadman and Holman, 1992), 115–119, 150–151.

The Jesus-orientation in prayer is far from expecting that God will be like a spineless Santa Claus who gives us anything we want. Indeed, when we remember that Jesus prayed in the Garden to have the cup of suffering removed from him, he nevertheless agreed to accept the will of God (Luke 22:42; cf. John 12:27–28). In that petition we recognize a model in which prayer becomes very serious for humans in determining the will of God for them in their circumstance. Our praying, therefore, can even mean that we will accept suffering, turmoil and bad things happening to us. Moreover, Eduard Schweizer reminded us that in Luke's version of the Lord's Prayer the first three petitions of Jesus (Luke 11:2–4) actually counter his earlier three temptations in the wilderness (4:1–12).[13] To put this idea in its proper context, we should remember that if anyone should have had the right to be granted his desire and not to die his cruel death, it should have been Jesus. Yet the witness of Jesus is contrary to self-centered praying.

Recognizing the tension involved in praying "in the name of Jesus" is thus an important task with which humans are called to wrestle. Attempting to discover what might be God's will for humans in any specific circumstance may indeed involve a great deal of sacrifice—a prospect that is not usually easy to accept.

Prayer can also be fraught with possible misunderstandings and with potential manipulations by human desire. It involves the delicate and tricky tension of perceiving how God and humans are in fact related in this created world. Given this tension, Christians now and in the future need to develop a genuine sensitivity to our divine-human relationship if we are to be effective in carrying the transforming message of Christ to our narcissistic world.

Praying for Forgiveness

We introduced the subject of forgiveness in chapter 1, but here I am concerned with the crucial question of actually praying for forgiveness. When the early disciples asked Jesus to teach them to pray, Luke provided a brief response that included a model of praying for forgiveness (Luke 11:2–4).[14] Matthew in the section of his gospel that is generally known as "the Sermon on the Mount" included an expanded version of that model prayer in which Jesus advised brevity and the eschewing of long-winded prayers (Matt 6:7–14). In that model prayer, Jesus instructed his disciples to pray for forgiveness. In the Lucan version,

---

[13]See Eduard Schweizer, *The Good News According to Luke*, trans. David E. Green (Atlanta: John Knox Press, 1984), 191.

[14]For a helpful discussion on this concept in the Lucan version of the Lord's Prayer, see I. Howard Marshall, *The Gospel of Luke: A Commentary on the Greek Text*, NIGTC (Grand Rapids: Eerdmans, 1978), 454–462. See also John Noland, *Luke 9:21–18:34*, vol. 35B, WBC (Dallas: Word Books, 1993), 607–621.

however, this petition contains a significant caveat. Praying for forgiveness—which is needed by everyone—is patently circumscribed by the petitioner's own pattern of forgiving others (6:12). Thus, we are encouraged in the fifth petition to pray for forgiveness, but in doing so we could easily be calling for a condemnation upon ourselves if we fail to forgive.[15]

That petition with its caveat is further enhanced by Matthew's reasserting the warning to those who fail to forgive (6:14–15). This two-dimensional petition is forcefully illustrated by Jesus' parable of the unforgiving servant who was treated graciously by his master but when he did not treat his fellow servant graciously, the master reversed his forgiveness and condemned the unforgiving servant to a long-term imprisonment (cf. Matt 18:23–35). Our praying, therefore, could actually turn out to be a cursing of ourselves!

So, we are faced with a tension-filled dilemma. We are instructed to pray for forgiveness, but we are also told to measure up to God's expectations of the Lord's gracious response by demonstrating forgiveness to others. I have often wondered how many people in our church services actually realize what they may be asking of God when they pray the Lord's Prayer. But just in case some might think it would be wise not to pray that particular petition, I would also add that failure to include that petition in one's mouthing of the Lord's Prayer is no golden parachute of escaping the warning concerning potential judgment. That petition is our model for praying to God, and God is not a fool who can be manipulated. So, the warning stands whether we like it or not. We need forgiveness, but we also need to forgive others. Authentic prayer is in fact an admission of our own weakness.

But such praying is not to be understood in terms of making a bargain with God or earning the right to be forgiven as though our forgiving of others is a *quid pro quo* for our own forgiveness. We can do nothing to earn God's forgiveness since we are helpless sinners (cf. Rom 3:23–24, 5:6). But our willingness to forgive others is a demonstration of our seriousness in requesting God's forgiveness for ourselves. Moreover, our forgiving represents our acceptance of God's graciousness in sending Jesus to forgive not only our sins and rebellion but also those of others (cf. Paul's advice in 2 Cor 2:5–11).

Finally, the forgiving pattern of Jesus on the cross quickly became a model for the church as Stephen is said to have followed the Lord's response when he

---

[15]See Guelich, *The Sermon on the Mount*, 293–294, 298, 315–316 and Donald A. Hagner, *Matthew 1–13*, WBC (Dallas: Word Books, 1993), 150–152.

was martyred (see Luke 23:34, Acts 7:60). It remains the appropriate model for all Christians today and in the future.

Expecting the "Kingdom to Come"

Jesus embodied the kingdom of God. As George Beasley-Murray asserts, this petition is a "request for God to act in his power and love to bring about judgment and salvation in his creation."[16] When we make this petition, we meet another tension. Are we sure that we want the Lord's kingdom to come on earth—now? Would it not make a radical difference in the way we live? It would mean that:

• We would not be the center of our attention.
• Competition as we know it would end.
• Everyone would be treated fairly.
• We would lose our special privileges.
• We would have to be responsible for pulling our own weight in everything.
• Color and other differences would not really matter.
• We would rejoice in the achievements of those whom we may not consider worthy of honor.
• We would not boast of our importance over against someone else.
• We would be expected to be servants to others.

So, we need to ask: Do we really want the Kingdom to come on earth, or are those words just pretty, unrealistic ideas that we pray because Jesus instructed us to do so?

Do you see how present-oriented is this petition? Please do not forget that those who listened to Jesus were living with a very different sense of time than we who now read our Bibles and pray for the return of the Lord!

Perhaps what we actually do in our prayers today is just put our minds in neutral because we feel sure there is no chance for the eschatological reign of God in our time. Maybe we live with a sense that ultimately there will be a time when everything evil will be eliminated. But do we really hope and pray today for the coming kingdom of God on earth (Rev 5:13–14)? Would that kind of kingdom get rid of all our opponents and leave us in a euphoric state? Would we actually be rejoicing if the kingdom of God came today? Do we actually spend time praying for the coming Kingdom? Perhaps we take such thoughts more seriously

---

[16]For a classic interpretation of the kingdom of God in the gospels, see G.R. Beasley-Murray, *Jesus and the Kingdom of God* (Grand Rapids: Eerdmans,1986). See also Hagner, *Matthew* 1–13, 148–150.

in periods of illness or pandemics when we are forced to slow down and reflect on reality. But what would the coming Kingdom really mean for us today? Could we tolerate God's perspectives being present in every aspect of our contexts? Would we be ready and willing to accept such radical changes? Perhaps we just mouth such a petition and live as if it doesn't really matter anyway!

Of course, if we are getting old and feeble, that is a pretty great thought. But as long as things are going fairly well for us here on earth, why should we not live in moderate enjoyment and then wait for an even better life in the next dimension?[17]

Many of us in the contemporary Western world do not understand the world to which Jesus lived and ministered. Have you wondered why the huge, helpless crowds followed him so readily? Have you visited contemporary places that are ravished by poverty, rampant marginalization, extreme disillusionment, and death—places where hope seems to be lost? Such is the plight of millions of people in the developing world. Have we asked why Muslim radicals can recruit people to be suicide bombers? Perhaps it makes more sense if one has almost nothing of this world's goods and privileges and is promised a financial endowment for one's family after one's sacrificial death and can also expect an immediate entrance into a great future paradise. Maybe such promises are appealing, especially if they are encompassed with the recognition of being a hero.

So, do not wonder why some of these people would do anything to cross an American or a European border! Some of the poor among us in the Western world may be well off in comparison to many people in the rest of the world. We in the West are blessed. We have goods and opportunities that would frankly be contained in the eschatological dreams and prayers of countless people elsewhere.

I am not trying to render a judgment on our Western society. I am grateful, even though I know what a Depression is, that I am now living in relative comfort. Thus, I try to remind myself and others why an eschatological prayer for the coming kingdom of God might be appealing. But I can assure you, it was exceedingly meaningful to many in days of Jesus. So, I am inviting us as Christians to take very seriously God's call upon us to consider the needs of those outside our spheres of existence who live without much—scarcely any food, virtually no shelter and no medical assistance. Praying for the coming of Christ's kingdom involves having "a Jesus perspective" on our current world. To be a

---

[17]See for example some important critiques on the economic situation in the world and in America: Ron J. Sider, *Rich Christians in an Age of Hunger: Moving from Affluence to Generosity*, 6th ed. (Grand Rapids: Thomas Nelson/HarperCollins, 2015, rev. of 1977) and his *The Scandal of the Evangelical Conscience: Why are Christians Living Just Like the Rest of the World?* (Grand Rapids: Baker, 2005). See also Craig Blomberg, *Christians in an Age of Wealth* (Grand Rapids: Zondervan, 2013).

Christ follower means to have the mind of Christ (cf. Phil 2:5–7)—which brings me to another aspect of the Lord's Prayer.

Trusting for Our Daily Bread

I doubt that most of us who read this book are really hungry and thirsty. Do we comprehend what is real hunger and thirst? Instead of praying for our daily bread, is it not more likely that we thank God for the abundant food we have before us?[18] Are we not more inclined to thank God for the jobs that allow us to purchase the kind of foods we prefer? Do we even stop in the grocery store and consider the abundant choices that are available to us? Comprehending radical dependence upon God for daily sustenance is not easy. Yet the coming of a pandemic or economic catastrophe with job losses can give us a partial taste of what is a perennial concern in many places. The supplying of daily food for many people in the days of Jesus was a constant problem. You should not be surprised then that, when Jesus fed the huge multitude of five thousand men in addition to their families, people were determined to install him as their king—even by force if necessary (cf. Matt 14:31, John 6:15)!

So, when we think about the blessings that have been given to us and as we enter into prayer at the dinner table, perhaps we can reflect more on what dependence upon God entails. The situation for most of us is hardly the same as in the days of Jesus, and it is scarcely the same for multitudes in our world today. Dependence upon God can bring great tension for us because in our blessed state we scarcely can sense our continual need for God to supply our "daily" (*epiousion*) bread (Matt 6:11).

Prayer in John 17 and Its Significance

In concluding this brief review of tensions in prayer, let me pause here and consider some important insights into the perspectives of Jesus for Christians that are presented in John 17. This magnificent composite prayer of Jesus provides a significant reflection on John's recognition of who Jesus really was. It also offers us a special thermometer to evaluate our own prayers and spiritual lives. As I have indicated in my commentary on this chapter, Jesus voiced seven distinct petitions that are worthy of close study.[19] In John we can usually identify a petition or

---

[18]For a Christian perspective on hunger in our world, see Jeremy K. Everett, *I was Hungry: Cultivating Common Ground to End an American Crisis* (Grand Rapids: Baker, 2019); Ron Sider and Heidi Unruh, eds., *Hope for Children in Poverty: Profiles and Possibilities* (Philadelphia: Judson Press, 2007); and Leslie Hoppe, OMF, *There Shall Be No Poor Among You* (Nashville: Abingdon, 2004).

[19]G. Borchert, *John 12–21*, 185–211. The Greek of chapter 17 reminds one of the poetic qualities

prayer by the fact that Jesus directly addressed God as "Father" (cf. John 11:41; 12:27, 28), a formula used six times in John 17 (v. 1, 5, 11, 20, 24, 25) and implied a seventh time in verse 17.

The initial petition of Jesus (17:1) occurs in the context of his appointed "hour" and involves his prayer that he should be glorified in order to bring glory to God and give eternal life to those who believe in him because of his sacrificial death. This petition reflects the purpose statement for the entire gospel that concerns the fact that one needs to believe in order to gain life (cf. 20:30–31). The second petition is built on the first and reflects the main point in the prologue: namely, that the *logos* existed from the beginning and his very nature was divine (1:1–4). When taken together, these two petitions focus on the Cana cycle (John 2–4) and emphasize the importance of correctly identifying and believing in Jesus as the one and only son of God.

The next two petitions (17:11, 17) involve Jesus' concern for the protection of his followers in the face of hostility and his desire for them to be holy. For that perspective of holiness to be evidenced in them, Jesus prayed that his own life would be completely enveloped in the holiness of the Father so that he might be their model of holiness on earth. These two petitions, therefore, reflect the focus of the Festival Cycle with its emphasis on the Jewish hostility against Jesus but highlight the integrity of Jesus in dealing with human coldhearted enmity (chs. 5–11). He was indeed the authentic bread from heaven that provided his people with life (ch. 6); the true light in the midst of a dark world (chs. 8–9); the protecting shepherd who was willing to lay down his life for the security of God's trusting sheep (ch.10); and the guarantee of the resurrection and life with God (ch. 11).

Then the last three petitions involve the longing of Jesus for the spirit of oneness to be evident among Christians so that God's mission to the world might be achieved (17:20–21); that his followers might reach their eschatological goal of being with him and seeing his divine glory (17:24); and that believers might manifest genuine love that is the mark of true discipleship (17:25–26). As one might expect, these petitions reflect the focus of the Farewell Cycle (chs. 13–16). The emphases of these chapters fall on providing the followers of Jesus with a

---

of the prologue (cf. John 1:1–18). B.F. Westcott argued for three divisions in Jesus' petitions: concerning himself (vv. 1–5); concerning his disciples (vv. 6–9); and concerning the later community (vv. 20–26). R.E. Brown also chose a three-part division. C.H. Dodd and R. Schnackenburg chose a four-part division. A. Loisy in *Le quartrieme evangile* (Paris: Emile, 1921), 441, chose a seven-part division. Some have sought to combine the lines into Greek strophes. While I affirm the seven petitions (cf. Borchert, *John 12–21*, 185–186), I find it difficult to view this prayer in parallel Greek stanzas or strophes.

model of genuine love and service (ch. 13); confidence in the face of loneliness and abandonment (ch. 14); support and guidance through the Holy Spirit (chs. 14–16); and a sense of divinely supplied integrity, fruitfulness, and joy because his followers are firmly attached to God as their source of nourishment (ch. 15).

This prayer thus encompasses the full purpose of God's divine-human messenger in coming to earth. But notice something very significant. These petitions are directed not to a self-serving purpose but to enhancing the purposes of God and to the protection and spiritual development of Jesus' followers. So, the question that should be obvious to the readers of this prayer is this: What is the focus of our praying? Is our concern primarily about ourselves, our families, and our personal interests, or is it about God and God's purposes in the world? As we seek to define and attain our purposes for God, we must bear in mind that self-centered praying will not enable us to achieve Christ's goal for us. Perhaps, in this tension between self and God lies an important key to true new covenant living. Comparing our petitions to those of Jesus might assist Christians and their faith communities to refocus and become more like Jesus in the way they establish their purposes, employ their resources, and use their time—the latter of which is a crucial subject when considering New Covenant living.

The Importance of Time in the Christian Life

There is among humans a fundamental presupposition that time is a constant or immutable factor of reality. Upon this assumption rests most other human assumptions.[20] The above assumption is a basic day-to-day working hypothesis. As a result, even if one believes in God, then that believer would likely assume that in the beginning there was God and time. Yet such a conclusion is not the biblical perspective. The first chapter of Genesis is built on a very different understanding. In the Bible, God alone stands at the beginning and God was and is ultimately responsible for the ordering of or bringing order to all things— and that would include time itself. So, in reading Genesis we should, as Walter Brueggemann reminds us, be "freed from mechanistic notions of reality."[21] And, in response to the issue of time, one of my colleagues observed, "The Christian view of time encompasses an ontology that is revelatory of God."

Now, granted that creation in Genesis 1 is described phenomenologically rather than scientifically (familiar to contemporary readers), nevertheless time

---

[20]For an intriguing perspective, see Oliver O'Donovan, *Self, World and Time: Ethics as Theology* (Grand Rapids: Eerdmans, 2013).

[21]See Walter Brueggemann, *Genesis*, Int (Atlanta: John Knox Press, 1982), 27.

is clearly identified as having a beginning and therefore subject to the creative power of God. It is also assumed in the Bible that time is subject to alteration by God. Such a view, however, generally violates our scientific understanding of reality.[22] Thus, when we read that the great warrior Joshua told the sun to "stand still" in Gibeon and the result was a much longer than usual day (Josh 19:12–14) or that the righteous king Hezekiah received a divine sign by the retreating of the sun dial by 10 points (2 Kgs 20:8–11), we probably shake our contemporary heads and say: *scientifically impossible!* But as I stated at the beginning of this book, the issue of science and the Bible usually comes down to the way in which we humans read the messages of God. Yet one thing seems certain for Christians: time is subject to God, and time will end when God decides. Time is not God, and it is not immutable. But time is a created entity, given by God for a divine purpose.

Yet for some people, time seems to pass them by. Others refer to their activities as a "waste of time." Still others consider their labors as "taking too much time." But Christians should understand time not as a natural possession but as "a gift of God" to be used appropriately for the purposes of God. Such a perspective can help us deal with the frustrations and tensions of both life and time that come to everyone. We Westerners are busy people. In fact, we are usually too busy for our own good. We have difficulty juggling all the demands that are placed upon us. Many of us are so busy that when we "take time" to relax, we usually work at relaxing. So, as frustrated humans, we sometimes need pills so that we can take the time to relax, and our children pick up our tensions and also need medication to concentrate. What is the matter with us—especially in this time (era) when we have the intelligence to put a man on the moon, develop micro-computers, I-pods, and to isolate segments in the genetic code—when we have become like gods?

Here lies the problem: we are not gods! I would assert that we did not create the universe and we have forgotten that it was God who created the world, the vast stretches of the heavens, and even us humans. But God also gave humans the special gift of time. Yet in time God also gave humans a time period called "*Shabbat*" or Sabbath (Gen 2:2–3). The gift of this one day in seven was a time for regeneration, renewal, refreshment, and honoring God—the giver of creation and time. Recognizing the role of God in all we undertake, puts everything in the correct perspective.

---

[22]For a creative discussion of the symbolism in the Genesis accounts, see Conrad Hyers, *The Meaning of Creation: Genesis and Modern Science* (Atlanta: John Knox Press, 1984).

Unfortunately, humans seem to have assumed they do not need a day of rest, a Sabbath, or a Lord's Day in which they not only can recuperate but also a day to honor the one who gave them time. So, we compress our honoring of God on the Lord's Day into an hour or two and then we get on with the "job" of working at relaxing. Most of us basically know that our organizational patterns for our time are misconceived. Still, we excuse ourselves and blame others, our circumstances, or our priorities for our problems. But when we accuse someone or something as the cause of our failure to relax and take God into account, we need to remember that next to the pointing index finger is a thumb that points back at ourselves. So, let's take a closer look at time and the calendar since most of us carry date books or handheld computers that organize our time.

The Ancients and Time

When Jesus was on earth most early Christians were of the peasant class, and even the elite Roman class had little concern for the future (see the Introduction). They lived in the present or in relationship to the past. What future they recognized was embodied in their sense of an extended present. They had little understanding of clock time because, as Sorokin indicates,[23] mechanical clocks did not emerge until the fourteenth and fifteenth centuries, and time pieces continued to be perfected in the Industrial Revolution and forward through the development of the computers that can be worn on the wrists of humans.

Before the Renaissance, all time perspectives were viewed as local time. Abstract time categories—such as past, present, and future—as Malina attests, did not exist in the first century.[24] Indeed, Zerubavel argues that, our contemporary concepts of calendars by which we today organize our lives were non-existent.[25] I would note, however, that such a statement does not mean that the ancients were ignorant of how to mark out important events.

Our Western or Northern European linear clock time is indebted to the rise of monasteries and their commitment to scheduling that involves an understanding of linear time.[26] This view of linear time can then be divided into separate segments and can also be extended into the future and back into the past. Moreover, as Edward Hall indicates, it may be viewed as "tangible" and can then

---

[23]Pitirim A. Sorokin, *Sociocultural Causality, Space, Time: A Study of Referential Principles of Sociology and Social Science* (Durham, NC: Duke University Press, 1943), 169.

[24]Bruce J. Malina, *The Social World of Jesus and the Gospels* (London: Routledge,1996), 187.

[25]See Eviatar Zerubavel, *Hidden Rhythms: Schedules and Calendars in Social Life* (Chicago: University of Chicago Press, 1981).

[26]Ibid., 31–39.

"be saved, spent, lost, made up … [and] slowed down," which are "metaphors [that] should be taken very seriously because they express … an unconscious determinant" in our lives.[27]

Having lived and taught in the bush country of Africa, I learned a little from those who live by a personal sense of time. As missionaries, we would often ask each other "Is that appointment on African time?"—by which we were attempting to determine whether it meant clock-time or not. But when one lives without the importance of watches, then one soon learns more clearly the implications of "rainy season" over against "dry season" or of viewing time as the biblical writer did when he stated "there was evening and there was morning, day one" (Gen 1:5) or the organic unity of springtime and harvest.

The "forthcoming" as Malina argues, is understood in the unfolding of the present or in the already known.[28] Thus, he would posit that the early Christians in their present thinking perspective would have viewed the appearance of the Messiah, the end, and the picture of Paradise as the completion of a great cycle.[29] A present orientation is quite different than our future-oriented time where expectations are based upon the extension of divided periods that exist in the present. Ancient Hebrew time was a combination of the linear and cyclical, but the important factor was that it was basically present-oriented. With these comments in mind, I turn to the early Jewish festival calendar that is based on their community understanding of how God was in charge of their time.

Time and the Jewish Festival Calendar

Have you ever wondered why the Jewish year was divided into a series of feasts or festivals? Yes, I realize that even the pagans had their yearly cycles as the earth revolved around the sun. Although most ancients did not understand much of the earth's rotation, they divided their year and particularly celebrated the winter equinox (the dead of winter) with looking forward to the coming of spring and new life on the earth. But at the heart of the Jewish calendar there was more than a series of celebrations related to the weather and agriculture such as the festivals of Dionysus or the cult patterns of Baal and Ashtaroth. The Jewish calendar was established as a constant reminder to the people of God's actions in rescuing and preserving Israel. These experiences were branded into the history of Israel not only by their documents of faith but also by their major festivals.[30]

---

[27]Edward T. Hall, *Beyond Culture* (Garden City, NJ: Doubleday, 1976), 16.

[28]See Malina, *The Social World*, 194–195.

[29]Ibid., 198–199. See my later discussion about heaven in chapter 13.

[30]Some see the three major Jewish festivals of Passover, Pentecost, and Tabernacles as being reflected

The Mosaic Feasts. In the first month, Nisan (our March–April), the Jews celebrate the feast of Unleavened Bread or Passover (*Pesach*, Nisan 14–21) that is a reminder of Israel's liberation from slavery in Egypt with Moses. Then in the third month of Sivan comes the feast of Weeks (Pentecost/*Shavu'ot*) that is celebrated about fifty days after Passover and is focused on the dedication of the first and best of the harvest. It was joined to Passover in the giving of the law and reminder that all firstborn belonged to the Lord.

The seventh month of Tishri (our September–October) is the most popular month in the Jewish year. It begins with Rosh Hashanah and the Feast of Trumpets (the Jewish New Year on the first and second days) and is followed by Yom Kippur (the Day of Atonement on the tenth day), the most holy day in the Jewish Year that reminds Israel of sin and the need of God's forgiveness. The last of the major Mosaic feasts is Booths (Tabernacles/*Sukkot*, 15th–22th) that looks back to God's preservation in the wilderness. In Jesus' day it was a festive time because it occurred after the final harvest when the Jews packed their tents and took vacations. But the city-dwelling Pharisees were hardly concerned with harvest celebrations, and so in gratitude for preservation they added a water festival with prayers for rain because their cisterns would be dry after a hot summer.

Alexander Jannaeus, the Sadducean high priest (103–76 BC/BCE), however, desecrated this urban rite by dropping the sacred water pan at his feet. When the urban-oriented Pharisees pelted him with citrons, Jannaeus called out his troops and killed many Pharisees within the Temple precincts. A longstanding hostility followed between the rural-oriented Sadducees and the urban-oriented Pharisees. After Jannaeus' death, however, and the growth of urban centers the Pharisees gained power and the water festival was firmly ensconced in the Feast of Tabernacles (cf. John 7:37–38).[31]

The Later Feasts. Beyond the Mosaic festivals, two more important feasts were added. *Hanukkah* (Dedication) is celebrated on the 25th of Kislev (in our December) and commemorates the Jewish victory over the ruthless Syrian king, Antiochus IV (Epiphanes) by Judas Maccabeus. He then expelled the foreigners and cleansed (rededicated) the Temple after it had been desecrated by the killing a pig on the altar of sacrifice and enshrining a statue of Zeus in the Most Holy

---

in the original understandings of the three cycles of the Christian year that are discussed on pp. 149–153.

[31]For more details on the festivals and Jewish parties and their theological and social orientations, see Gerald L. Borchert, *Jesus of Nazareth: Background, Witnesses and Significance* (Macon, GA: Mercer University Press, 2011), 19–21 and 51–65. See also Louis Finkelstein, *The Pharisees: The Sociological Background of their Faith* (Philadelphia: The Jewish Publication Society of America, 1962).

Place. The later feast (7), *Purim*, occurs in the last month of Adar (our February–March). It is a three-day (13th–15th) festival that remembers God's preservation of the Jews during the time of Queen Esther.

The Jewish Feasts and the Gospel of John. A list of the Mosaic feasts is given in Leviticus 23 and an abbreviated account of Jesus and the feasts can be found in John 5–11(including Passover, Tabernacles, and Dedication). In spite of what scholars such as Bultmann tried to do in identifying the feast in John 5 with one of the other Jewish feasts and shifting chapters of John around, I am convinced the text refers to Sabbath as the key to the feasts.[32] Our task as interpreters is to try and understand what the biblical writer meant and not to rearrange texts so as to eliminate what we perceived to be historical mistakes in the arrangement of the chapters. What John sought to do is to show that Jesus assumed to himself every aspect of Jewish worship that includes the Jewish calendar. Jesus, as the special agent of God, is the focus of Sabbath (John 5:15–18), the true point of Passover (1:29; 2:13; 6:4; 11:55; 12:1; 13:1; 19:14, 31), the authentic meaning of Tabernacles and the Water Festival (7:2, 37–38), and the genuine embodiment of Dedication in the midst of our feelings of desolation (10:22). He is the very Word of God who was in the beginning before time and creation existed (1:1–5).

Time and the Christian Calendar

With this Jewish perspective of the calendar in mind, I turn now to the reasons for understanding and celebrating the Christian calendar. I do so quite aware of the fact that a large segment of Protestantism rejects the subject of a Christian calendar as being "too high church." My genuine response to my friends who take this approach is that I once took such a posture but that after study and teaching scores of worship students, I believe there is value in viewing each year from the perspective of Jesus' life rather than merely using a "Hallmark calendar." We should not reject the historic Christian calendar because of misuse, misunderstanding, or misinterpretation by misguided Christians.

---

[32]See my extended explanation for John's use of the festivals and their relation to Sabbath in G.Borchert, *John 1–11*, 228–230.

A Christian Perspective and Contemporary Calendars. There is little doubt that most of our generation is organized either by that "Hallmark" calendar or by our national calendars, depending on the country in which we live. Accordingly, we often focus our attention on occasions such as New Year's Day, Valentine's Day, St. Patrick's Day, April Fool's Day, Mother's Day, Memorial Day, Father's Day, Labor Day, Halloween, Thanksgiving Day, the First or the Fourth of July —depending on whether we are Canadians or Americans—(or other days if we live elsewhere such as Victoria Day and Bastille Day), Veterans' Day, President's Day, Martin Luther King Day, even Secretaries Day, and of course we should not forget all those sports days such as Super Bowl Sunday. In addition, we should mention Easter and Christmas! Do you sense where I am going? For many people, Jesus is just tacked on to their lives. The world fills our year so full that we really do not have much time for God.

I am grateful to my colleague, the late Robert E. Webber, for his work on ancient-future time[33] and the Institute for Worship Studies for a setting in which to clarify my mind on this issue and for the opportunity to assist students in becoming more aware that their time belongs to God.

From my perspective there is an important tension in life between the way the world infects our lives with busyness and activity and the way God purposefully seeks to direct us in the use of time and our lives. Failing to understand the purpose-driven life is a recipe for frustration, irritation, anxiety, emptiness, anger, and breakdown. Of course, a calendar whether secular or religious will not correct our confused lives, but seeking to follow the will of God for one's life is a step in the direction of healing and wholeness. The Christian calendar is not a program or a cure-all for a confused life, but it can be a vehicle in helping us realize that the Christian life is not primarily about "me"! A purposeful order to a life can confront the meaninglessness of many lives today and can direct our attention away from ourselves to focus on God's work.

Christians, like the Jews, are basically a pilgrim people who should know that their life today is not an end in itself. Even though this life may be hard, and the journey may be difficult, indeed sometimes very lonely, God is always close to us even when we may not sense the divine presence. But Christ will never abandon his followers (John 14:18) and has provided a covenant community to be a support. Unfortunately, sometimes the community does not truly represent the loving spirit of Jesus (cf. John 13:34–35), because it is also frail and forgets its

---

[33]See Robert E. Webber, *Ancient-Future Time, Forming Spirituality through the Christian Year* (Grand Rapids: Baker, 2004).

role. So, the church also must be reminded throughout the year that it is a crucial part of God's continuing story.

For many Christians, the Christian calendar may seem to be a system that was invented by the church to organize its liturgy. But the Christian calendar is not first and foremost a liturgical tool. It is rather a strategic reminder that God has called us in Christ Jesus and is sustaining us during each part of the year. Thus, it can be fruitful for our personal health and wellness to be recalled to an orderly patterning of our lives on God's acts in Christ.

The Cycle of Light. The Christian calendar begins with Advent and what some refer to as the "Cycle of Light" that anticipates not merely Christmas and the coming of Jesus who is "the light of the world" and the revelation of God (John 1:5, 3:19, 8:12, 9:5; cf. Matt 4:16, Luke 2:32) but concerns the encompassing significance of the Incarnation and its meaning for our lives as Christians. Naturally there should be reflection on personal preparation for Jesus in one's life, just as God prepared Israel for the coming of the Christ. But this time of celebration does not focus only on his first coming because Christians expect the *parousia*, the return of Jesus in power and glory. As a result, the focus of this time in the year brings together the entire sense of time from the beginning of God's creative activity to the end of time. In it we are to consider not only the concerns of Advent, but also the meaning of the Christmas story itself and the fact that Jesus came with a divine purpose to save the world from the destructive nature of sin and evil. This period also includes Ephiphany, the baptism of Jesus, and Jesus' miracles such as at Cana that remind us of all the revelations of Jesus as God's divine manifestations on earth. And it points us beyond the coming of the wise men and the baptism to the temptations of Jesus, and then to the experience of the Transfiguration and the resurrection appearances while reminding us that we are to "manifest" the living Jesus in our own lives.

The Cycle of Life. Next, the "Cycle of Life" reminds us to face the difficulties of life and seek to understand in the period of Lent (forty days excluding Sundays) the reasons why Jesus had to suffer for our transformation. While some people focus on denying themselves their favorite food(s), such acts can be very superficial. The point here is not simply a denial of something but a serious contemplation of our unworthiness before our great God and Savior and of our joining Jesus in his conscious march to the cross and his humbling (*ekenōsen*) of himself (cf. Phil 2:7) by offering his life for our salvation. Likewise, at this time we should remember and reaffirm our baptism and also renounce the way of evil in our lives. We should rededicate our lives to follow the way of Jesus and accept the new life that he assured to us by his marvelous resurrection.

When we take seriously the *Pascha* (from the Greek *paschein*) or "suffering" of our Lord and the road to Calvary, we recognize with John's gospel that the so-called "triumphal" entry into Jerusalem (Palm Sunday) and the people shouting "Hosanna" did not confuse Jesus and it should not confuse us (John 12:23-26) as we seek to embody the great sacrificial journey of Jesus. Those shouts of praise soon turned to cries of "Crucify him!"[34] The Great Triduum that follows involves the three days from Maundy (from the Latin *mandari* or "command") Thursday and Good (Black) Friday through to the Paschal Vigil (Saturday evening to early Sunday morning) should be a staunch reminder of Christ's command to love others and of our passing from the darkness of sin and death into the dawning light of hope and life.

Easter is then not just a happy fairy-tale ending to a sad story but the zenith of the Christian year and the actual signal to the forces of evil that God is the victor and that the end of the cosmic struggle or tension with the dark side is certain. Not only has Jesus been raised from the dead, but the Christian calendar also recognizes that he has ascended into heaven and has been enthroned next to the Father, confirming his triumph.

There Jesus intercedes for his followers on earth. So, while it is patently clear that the final victorious conclusion has not yet been achieved on earth and that we struggle with sin and evil, Christians nevertheless boldly seek to live for Christ because they know the conclusion is certain. Living in the context of the dark side, Christians can, therefore, witness to a very different but powerful perspective in life. But we cannot do it on our own because the evil forces are strong and harass Christians. Therefore, Christ's followers need the companionship and strength of the Holy Spirit to assist them in living in a hostile world. So, the Cycle of Life concludes with Pentecost and the joyous acceptance of the Spirit's leading in our lives. These two cycles of the Christian calendar are thus thoroughly biblical and Trinitarian in their perspective, and they lead us to Trinity Sunday that not only reminds us that God created the universe but also that God has formed us and called us to mission.

---

[34]For an excellent review of Holy Week, see the articles by Robert E. Webber, John Grabner, and Sue Lane Talley, "An Introduction to Holy Week" in *The Services of the Christian Year*, vol. 5, The Complete Library of Christian Worship, ed. Robert E. Webber (Peabody, MA: Hendrickson, 1993), 277–285.

Redeeming the Degenerated Third Cycle. The final cycle in the Christian calendar is not nearly as clearly defined and is known as "Ordinary Time" or "Kingdom-tide." The unfortunate designation "ordinary" is derived from the concept of "ordinal" or a position in a series. In this case it stands as the third and final cycle between Pentecost and the restart of the Cycle of Light. It is supposed to refer to the presence of the kingdom of God in the current time that serves as a prelude or a proleptic experience (a foretaste) of the Kingdom of Heaven/God[35] in the future (which I will discuss in chapter 13). This cycle was intended to focus on the role of Christians in their service to the world as ambassadors for Christ. This period that is focused on mission in the world was developed to end with a special celebration known as Christ the King Sunday, which affirms the reign of Christ through Christians on earth. The concept of these three cycles is certainly one that should be commended because in the ancient world such a concept of three cycles would represent the impact of the divine reality upon earth.

Unfortunately, the third cycle that was supposed to embody proclamation and mission to the world degenerated among some Christians into a "Sanctoral Cycle" that focused more on the so-called saints within the history of Christendom. This move away from mission to honoring "saints" in the third cycle is the primary reason that many Protestants have rejected the concept of a Christian calendar. Moreover, the designation of some people as "saints" over against the rest of Christians flies in the face of one of Protestantism's most revered theological affirmations: "the priesthood of all believers."

Furthermore, many people assume that the Christian calendar applies only to the church's liturgical patterns. But such an assumption reflects a tragic failure to understand that we all live with calendars and they are either secular or an integral part of our faith. Therefore, to reject the important theological idea of a Christian calendar that can bring focus to living for the Christian in this self-centered, hostile world is another sad testimony of how Satan can twist something good and anticipated as an instrument for spiritual formation into a mere shell of its intention. Christians must, therefore, always be alert to the devil's confusing patterns (cf. Gen 3:1–4) because they can easily be blindsided and deflected from their true goals of worship, evangelism, and service.

Now there is no question that the Christian Church has been blessed by many people who legitimately could be called "heroes" in the secular world. Many have

---

[35]I have purposely referred to this joint designation of the Kingdom of Heaven and the Kingdom of God in order to remind you of their interchangeable meaning in the gospels. Frequently, Matthew will use "kingdom of heaven" and Luke will use "kingdom of God" in parallel pericopes (texts).

made strategic contributions to the expansion of the Christian mission while others have been instrumental in developing new programs and institutions that have benefitted not only Christians but also humanity in general. Many have died because they were following Jesus. Love that Jesus imparts to believers is not limited to time, geography, race, or culture. So, it is quite appropriate periodically to remember and celebrate the contributions of those both from the past and from our current era who have made contributions to Christ's work and to humanity.

But there is an important tension here. For Christians, there is in reality only one ultimate hero whom we worship: the Triune God represented in the divine-human Son of God, Jesus the Christ. Nevertheless, God is glorified in the lives and work of humans who have sought to represent their Lord authentically. So, days of remembrance such as All Saints Day are important times when we as Christians can celebrate, give thanks, and recall significant contributions of all those Christians who have impacted our lives and those of others. Failing to remember them would mean that history is meaningless and Christian contributions are ineffectual. We are indebted to many, and we stand on the shoulders of those mothers and fathers in the faith who have brought transformations to our world. Remembering their deeds and accomplishments can challenge us to do likewise. But like all of us (and like the stellar figures in the Bible), they and we are only human and subject to sin and fallibility.

They may surely have left us the gifts of their service, but we cannot store up any unused grace from them and we cannot put it in some bank or treasury of the church to be dispensed in place of our shortcomings as was thought to be done in the Middle Ages and later. There is no such thing as extra grace. We are all immensely indebted to Jesus. Therefore, we must take care how we revere our saints because we must never worship them. As the seer of Revelation boldly reminded us, our worship belongs only to God (Rev 19:10, 22:9).

What then should be the focus of this third and final cycle? It should be on our mission for Christ our King who leads his people by establishing Christian footholds into the domain of the dark side. Do we do the conquering? No! It is Jesus who conquers, and we are his servants (cf. Rev 19:11–16). Yet we can thank God who works through us as humans for divine purposes (cf. Isa 26:12), which we may not even understand.

In this important cycle, then, as we move forward in mission we can look back and thank God for what many have accomplished for Christ in the past. Studying and reflecting on the accomplishments of our forefathers and foremothers in the faith can embolden us in our mission for the kingdom of God.

To remember and be inspired to faithfulness and mission by people such as Polycarp, Justin, Irenaeus, Tertullian, Egeria, Origen, Augustine, Francis of Assisi, John Wycliffe, Martin Luther, John of the Cross and Teresa of Avila, John Calvin, Meno Simons, John Smyth, William Carey, John and Charles Wesley, William Wilberforce, Pope John XXIII, Martin Luther King Jr., Mother Theresa, and many others is crucial. Their mission for Jesus Christ has been extremely important for all Christians.

Events such as All Saints Day can then become precious times of remembrance and stir our consciences to give ourselves in further service for Christ. Then the purpose of that day will conform to the driving goal of Kingdomtide—the true intention of the Ordinary Cycle.

A Conclusion Concerning Time

Time is a precious gift from God, and our duty is to use it wisely. Many pressures, however, are upon us, especially the pressure to assume that time belongs to us and therefore we can use time for our own advantage. But that assumption is a complete misconception for Christians. And that thought reminds me of an experience I had in visiting a dear Christian woman in a retirement home in North Dakota. She had been a stalwart Christian in her Church, and the pastor requested that I should visit her. It was a delightful experience, but during the visit I asked her about her devotional times and I merely said: "I suppose that you have plenty of time with the Lord now." Her response took me back when she said, "We are so busy here with activities that I do not have much time for my devotions." Too busy in retirement to have time for God! Well, I was delighted that she enjoyed life, but her response is the refrain of many people. Christians are always faced with the tension of how to use the time and resources that have been given to them. Will it be for me or for God; for my benefit or for the kingdom of God?

Jesus, too, faced such tensions: Should he use his time and power for his own advantage or for God's mission? We frequently refer to that option as the temptations of Jesus. The way he handled those constant temptations has had a great impact on us and our receiving of salvation/wholeness. Jesus stoutly refused to yield to the dark side of that tension and he relied instead upon the direction of his Father for all his activity on earth (Matt 4:1–11, Luke 4:1–12, cf. Heb 4:15).

The Gospels also indicate that he often went off by himself to pray and commune with the Father. One of the clearest indications of that directive pattern in his life is the Johannine theme of "hour." The Greek term *hora* that is used twenty-six times in the Fourth Gospel is a haunting term that reflects the driving force in his life. Jesus committed himself to the leading of the Father in all that he did (cf. John 5:19–20). That special hour was his sacrificial death on the cross when he announced "It is finished" (19:30). Those final words on the cross have echoed down through the corridors of time, and they will again be announced in their starkness at the end of time (cf. Rev 16:17, 21:6).

We, of course, are not Jesus and consistency is hardly a category that represents humans. But greater consistency is the challenge that is set before every Christian in order that we might truly follow the model of Christ (cf. Phil 2:5–11). Most people in the world are grasping for money and "stuff" as the measure of who they are as humans. Mortals measure success by their possessions, their power, and their status in the community. Contrarily, as followers of Jesus, we have been clearly commanded to "Seek first the Kingdom of God and God's righteousness and everything else [necessary] will be added" (Matt 6:33). Such a command does not mean that we will be rich and prosperous if we put the Kingdom first in our lives, but it does mean that life will take on a much fuller meaning. The question that faces each person then is: What is the motivation for our life? Is it the collection of "stuff," power, and prestige? Our valuables may be buried with us, as in the tombs of the pharaohs of Egypt and of Philip of Macedon, but it will not make it to the life hereafter. The "stuff" buried with the ancients either became the possessions of grave robbers or remained entombed until archaeologists finally found their burial chambers and put it in museums.

Time is our gift from God. The tension of time involves the way we relate to it. Are we prepared to use this important gift in the service of God or primarily for our own interests? The answer to this tension lies before us. Christians in the present and the future will have to deal with it because in the answer to the question of time lies the ultimate vitality of Christ's covenant community.

… And that question also leads me to the subject of the covenant community.

Chapter 10

The New Covenant Community— The Church

Tensions in the Church's Nature, Structure, Message, and Service

The Nature of the Church

The twentieth century was a period of writing books on the nature and mission of the church, particularly in relation to the New Testament.[1] After two world wars in Europe during that century, Christian scholars were forced to face the question of the inherent meaning of the church as a transforming community in the world—especially since both of those wars began in one of the focal countries that gave birth to the Protestant Reformation and the latter war involved the horrors of Nazism. As a young professor, even I sought to supply my earlier denomination with a small study on the church.[2]

After the First World War some people dreamed of the possibility that Christians might finally come together in a great movement in which they would set aside their differences, be a family, and focus on bringing people to Christ. Even though many did not want to join together in a single institutional structure, others welcomed a loving fellowship with fellow Christians. But by the end of that century many churches and denominations faced conflicts and even battles that far surpassed their earlier efforts at cooperation.[3]

Now in reviewing the situation, I have often told my students that in the nineteenth and early twentieth centuries the Western church leadership recognized that missionaries from various countries were encountering difficulties of overlapping missions in the same state or region of a country. So, some mission boards made comity agreements and divided the "unevangelized" two-thirds world into sectors and assigned them to various mission societies for peaceful

[1]See for example Adolf von Schlatter, *The Church in the New Testament Period*, Eng. trans. (London: S.P.C.K., 1961), Eduard Schweizer, *Church Order in the New Testament*, Eng. trans. (1961; repub. Eugene, OR: Wipf and Stock, 2006), Rudolf Schnackenburg, *The Church in the New Testament*, Eng. trans (New York: Herder & Herder, 1968), Daniel Harrington, S.J., *The Church According to the New Testament* (New York: Sheed and Ward, 2001) and Robert C. Walton, ed., *The Gathered Community* (London: Carey Press, 1946).

[2]For my early thinking on the subject, see Gerald Leo Borchert, *Today's Model Church: A Pattern from the New Testament* (Forest Park, IL: Roger Williams Press, 1971).

[3]See for example the account of Harold Lindsell and his cry in *The Battle for the Bible* (Grand Rapids: Zondervan, 1976).

mission outreach. Naturally, not all mission societies agreed to such arrangements. This peace effort seemed to work well until the twentieth century when nationals in the two thirds world became mobile and moved from region to region in the same country.

When these nationals moved, they did not find churches that were of the same orientation as earlier experienced. Missionary Bishop Lesslie Newbigin then argued: What does a political dispute over relations to the British crown between two different Scottish churches mean to Indian nationals? It was confusing for them.[4] Of course, the situation is more complicated because political differences have evolved into theological differences. But when I was in Japan some well-meaning tourists asked me where they could find the nearest Southern Baptist Church. There was a small Japanese Baptist church there, but my unspoken question was: Is it their type? Or, in the Middle East you might be fortunate to find a Protestant church in a city. These examples illustrate that Western perspectives may not fit foreign realities.

But returning to the concern of mission executives, there was s growing sense of "bringing in the Kingdom" after the First World War. In that spirit a call was issued to study differences, hoping for more cooperation in local settings. This desire inspired major conversations in the "Faith and Order" commission that ultimately inspired the World Council of Churches and the calling of Vatican II—both of which are fascinating stories.

This progressive spirit of the twentieth century has now waned or at least has been institutionalized so that cooperation is not on the front burner of most churches. Instead, churches now focus on questions of relevance in a pluralistic society, what it means to be a covenant people of God, and how to function within the postmodern, skeptical era.[5]

---

[4]For further insights into the perspectives of Lesslie Newbigin, see *The Household of God: Lectures on the Nature of the Church* (London: SCM Press, 1953), *Foolishness to the Greeks: The Gospel and Western Culture* (Grand Rapids: Eerdmans, 1986), and *The Gospel in a Pluralistic Society* (Grand Rapids: Eerdmans, 1989). For a contemporary response, see Scott W. Sundquist and Amos Yong, ed., *The Gospel and Pluralism Today: Reassessing Lesslie Newbigin in the 21ˢᵗ Century* (Downers Grove, IL: InterVarsity, 2015).

[5]There are many works that provide us with insight into what currently lies before us and that challenge us with questions for the future. I would mention only: Jonathan Merritt, *Learning to Speak God from Scratch: Why Sacred Words Are Vanishing—and How We Can Revive Them* (New York: Convergent Books/ Random House, 2018), M. Rex Miller *The Millennium Matrix: Reclaiming the Past, Reframing the Future of the Church* (San Francisco: Jossey-Bass, 2004), Anthony Thiselton, *New Horizons in Hermeneutics: The Theory and Practice of Transforming Biblical Reading* (Grand Rapids: Zondervan,1992), and among the research work of the George Barna group, I would suggest at least David Kinnaman and Gabe Lyons, *Unchristian: What a New Generation Really Thinks About Christianity ... And Why It Matters* (Grand Rapid: Baker, 2007), and George Barna, *Generation Next* (Ventura, CA: Regal Books, 1996).

Misconceptions of the Church

The little finger-play that many of us learned as children brings to focus the subject of one of the tensions related to the church. When we interlace our fingers correctly and move the first fingers up and together, then open the thumbs, we can proceed as follows: "This is the church. This is the steeple. Open the doors and see all the people." But by simply changing the position of the interlaced fingers above the knuckles and repeating the exercise, a different result is created: "This is the church. This is the steeple. Open the doors and see *no people!*" While this exercise is simplistic, it can be profound. The second example suggests that the church is a building, while the first implies that the church is people meeting in a building.

The Church as Building

Many people view the church primarily as a building, yet the building is merely a convenient place for the gathering of a church. The misconception probably reached its zenith in the late Middle Ages when people viewed church buildings as "holy places" in the territory of heaven. The misnomer was likely enhanced because of "consecration." The clergy, after consecrating the "host" (the elements of Eucharist), would lift and carry the host out the front door of the church building, march around the building and perform liturgical acts, then reenter by the same door. The building had been surrounded by the host (or Christ's presence) and thereby had been rendered holy. The basis for such thinking undoubtedly had its roots in the consecration of the Jewish Tabernacle (Exod 40:34–38) and Temple built by Solomon (1 Kgs 8:11; 2 Chron 6:13–14, 7:2–3).[6] Justinian magnified the idea when after building Hagia Sophia declared he had outdone Solomon.

A question, however, arises: Was this pattern intended with Jesus? Does Paul's address to the Athenians on the Areopagus (Mars Hill) help? While pointing to the Parthenon and the Erectheion, Paul declared that God who made "the cosmos ... does not live in shrines constructed by humans" (Acts 17: 24–25).

---

[6]For a discussion on holiness, see Rudolf Otto's classic work *The Idea of the Holy*, trans. J.W. Harvey (London: Oxford University Press, 1923). See also N.T. Wright in *The New Testament and the People of God* in vol. 1 of *Christian Origins and the Question of God* (Minneapolis: Fortress, 1992) who argues that the Temple "was regarded as the place where YHWH lived and ruled in the midst of Israel, and through the sacrificial system ... he lived in grace, forgiving them, restoring them, and enabling them to be cleansed of defilement and so to continue as his people." Moreover, Wright continues, "the Temple was not simply the 'religious' center of Israel ... [it] combined in itself the functions of ... religion, national figurehead and government ... and also included in what we think of as the City, the financial and economic world" (224–225).

A New Testament Perspective

As further perspective, I mention three passages from the Fourth Gospel. In the Prologue, John asserts that "the [divine] Word (*logos*) became flesh and tented ("tabernacled," *eskenōsen*) among us" (John 1:14). The late philologist, Cyrus Gordon, might here see an example of language migration. Semitic words focus on consonants. So, taking the Greek verb *skēnoō* ("to dwell in a tent") and removing the vowels leaves *skn*, which is the Hebrew root for *shikinah* or God's presence. It is thus a brilliant word picture of Jesus as the dwelling or embodiment of God as suggested by the KJV translation.[7]

In the cleansing of the Temple (John 2:13–22) there is a play on words for "temple" that has a similar implication. When Jesus cleared the Temple (*hieron*) precincts of merchants, he told the hostile Jews that after they destroyed this "sanctuary" (*naos.* i.e., his body), he would "raise it again in three days." *Naos* in contrast to *hieron* refers to the central part (the sanctuary), where God was said to dwell. The Jews naturally thought Jesus was referring to the magnificent complex that was not be completed until AD/CE 65–66 but was destroyed in AD/CE 70 and never "raised up!" John knew about the destruction and knew Jesus was referring to himself (2:21)![8]

Finally, in John 4 and the conversation with the Samaritan woman, the woman asks for the right/best place to worship—by which she meant either the temple complex on Mount Gerazim or the one in Jerusalem. Jesus affirmed the Jewish tradition, not Samaritan syncretistic worship, but he pointed her beyond earthly temples to correct worship in the true Spirit of the living God (4:20–24).[9]

In this new era with Jesus, a church is hardly to be envisaged as simply a building. While it is now impossible to change the name "church" for building, perhaps Christians could be more perceptive in referring to the church as the covenant people of God.

Biblical Images of the Living Church

In 1960 Paul Minear penned a superb study on the *Images of the Church in the New Testament*. A brief review reveals that many of those nearly 100 word pictures carry a dynamic sense of the relation of God or Jesus with his people and give the sense of the church as a living organism.[10] Among the ones that seem best to represent this dynamic are the following:

---

[7]See Gerald L. Borchert, *John 1–11* (Nashville: Broadman and Holman, 1996), 118–120.

[8]G. Borchert, *John 1–11*, 160–166.

[9]G. Borchert, *John 1–11*, 206–208.

[10]See Paul S. Minear, *Images of the Church in the New Testament* (Philadelphia: Westminster, 1960,

the people of God	the household of God
the body of Christ	the fig tree
the bride of Christ	the olive tree
the elect lady	those in white robes
the branches of the vine	citizens
the communion/community	exiles
of the Holy Spirit	ambassadors
the royal priesthood	chosen race
the unity of Jews and Gentiles	a holy nation
the new humanity	the flock
the witnessing community	the remnant

The list goes on and on, and I would add "the called and gathered community of Jesus." The word synagogue from the Greek reflects a concept of "come together," and the Greek word for "church" (*ecclesia*) means a group of "called out" people—a word that implies a people with a divine commission.

The church then should be understood as a people who embody Christ's spirit—even though the members are imperfect. They have a divine calling to communicate Christ's love to humanity. If we turn away from manifesting that love, John would designate us as in darkness, pretenders, liars, and those similar to Cain who have the antichrist spirit (cf. 1 John 2:9–11, 3:11–15, etc.). But the gospel argues that believers can counteract such by relying on the Holy Spirit, the *Paraclete* (cf. John 14:15–17).[11]

Although a church is not a building, I must not leave readers thinking that Christian communities do not need buildings for worship, or for fellowship and meals together, or for studying the Bible and instruction of believers. Robert Banks reminds us in his helpful study on Paul of the importance of house churches in the early Christian community.[12] So, I must add here that Hellenistic society functioned basically on two levels: 1) the *polis* (public patterns) and 2) the *oikos* (household or family patterns). It seems clear that the early church was modeled like a family and that under the guidance of the Holy Spirit it offered a sense of both freedom and kinship to its members.

---

repr. in the *NLT* series in 2004).

[11]For my extended discussion on the Holy Spirit in John, see Gerald L. Borchert, *John 12–21*, vol. 25B, *NAC* (Nashville: Broadman and Holman,2002), 117–136, 158–171. See also Gerald Hawthorne, *The Presence and the Power: The Significance of the Holy Spirit in the Life and Ministry of Jesus* (Dallas: Word, 1991).

[12]See Robert Banks, *Paul's Idea of Community: The Early House Churches in their Historical Setting* (Grand Rapids: Eerdmans, 1980).

Acceptance was based not on legal requirements of the polis but on the "welcoming of Christ" into his body, his family (Rom 14:13–15:9, 1 Cor 12:12–27) in the model of Christ's reconciliation of humans to God (2 Cor 5:19–20). The early Christians met in the homes of those who provided space for their gatherings (e.g., Rom 16:3–5, 23; Acts 20:7–9 and perhaps 16:15; Col 4;15; Phlm 2). This household or family perspective of the church led Paul to call Christians *adelpoi* or "brothers" ("my brothers" in Rom 15:14, Phil 3:1; "my beloved brothers"—*adelphoi mou agapetae*—in 1 Cor 15:58, cf. Eph 6:21), which I should add meant both "brothers and sisters" as we translated the term in the NLT Version of the Bible.

Two crucial observations are needed here. The first is a sociological one. In the combined argument of Luke-Acts, John Elliot notes that the Gospel of Luke begins and ends in the Temple but the Book of Acts begins and ends in houses where the followers of Jesus are meeting. Elliot argues cogently that the concept of purity or acceptability has moved from a place (the Temple) to a people (the disciples meeting in houses),[13] which means that God's personal presence likewise focuses on a people rather than a place.

The second point is that birth into this new Christian family is rooted in the resurrection of Jesus Christ (Col 3:1–15, Rom 6:3–4). As Peter asserted, we are born anew to a living hope by the resurrection (1 Pet 1:3). Indeed, it was the resurrection and the power of the Holy Spirit that turned the cowardly disciples into bold witnesses for Jesus (Acts 3:15) and it was the resurrection that convinced the proof-seeking, realist Thomas that Jesus is God (John 20:26–28) and the fiery persecutor Paul that Jesus is the Lord (Acts 9:5, 17; Rom 1:4). As I have stated many times, the resurrection is "the hinge point of Christianity."[14] Without the resurrection there would be no church.

The Tension of Individual and Community Christianity

Another great tension that often confronts the person who wrestles with the nature of becoming and living as a Christian concerns the issue of whether Christianity is focused on the individual or the community. A simple answer is: "both!" This tension is highlighted in the question of how one lives an authentic Christian life.

---

[13]See John H. Elliott, "Temple Versus Household in Luke-Acts: A Contrast in Social Institutions," in Jerome H. Neyrey, ed., *The Social World of Luke-Acts* (Peabody, MA: Hendrickson, 1991), 211–240, 227–228.

[14]See for example Gerald L. Borchert, "The Resurrection: 1 Corinthians 15," in *RevExp* 80.3 (Winter 1983): 401–415. See also the important work N.T. Wright, *Surprised by Hope: Rethinking Heaven, Resurrection and the Mission of the Church* (New York HarperCollins, 2008).

Toleration and the Growth of Monasticism

By the third and fourth centuries, hundreds of people were flooding into small groups of Christians and even the persecutions hardly stalled that growth for long. With the move of Constantine toward Christianity in AD/CE 312 and the influence of his mother Queen Helena, the flood gates of the church were swung open and thousands joined the little Christian communities. Soon Christian cathedrals began to appear and holy sites in Roman *Palestina* were marked by Helena for shrines. The authenticity of Christians then became a concern as differences emerged between the so-called "common Christians" and the "committed." Lax patterns grew and a new desire for holiness arose.

The earlier declarations against elitism in movements such as Gnosticism and Marcion's rejection of ordinary life actually became a new option.[15] While the disciples of Jesus (including Peter) had been married, the issue of celibacy suggested by Paul (1 Cor 7) became an enamored pattern to holy life—over against the immorality in society. The arid lands of the Fertile Crescent and the mountain regions in Greece became attractive to the life of a hermit and to various forms of mysticism and contemplative life.

In the mid-fourth century a rich Egyptian named Anthony responded to the gospel proclamation of the "rich young ruler" and after employing his money to help the needy, he adopted the pattern of other hermits and attracted many to his austere life.[16] His theological opposition to the Arian denial of the humanity-divinity combination in Jesus gained the approval of Athanasius and even Constantine that encouraged many people to single hermitage and monastic community life. The way of the hermit can be highlighted by Simeon Stylitis (d. 459), a monk who lived on a tall pedestal for thirty-six years near Antioch in Syria.[17] These two types of recluse living (single and community) spread to

[15]The Greek pattern of thinking that divided the flesh and the spirit gave rise in Gnostic and related philosophic constructs to two different patterns of practice. On the one hand, it encouraged libertinism that basically asserted that one could do whatever one wanted in the flesh because it did not affect the spirit. Thus, some thought they could have sexual relations with a host of devotees in order to advance further to the *pleroma* or ultimate sphere of the godhead. On the other hand, the Greek dichotomy led to an asceticism that encouraged the subjection of the flesh in order to promote the well-being of the spirit. While there seems to be hints at both types of thinking in the codices from Nag Hammadi, the latter type was likely preferred by the desert dwellers of Egypt. The heresiologs, like Irenaeus and Tertullian, attacked both types. See further the classic work of Hans Jonas in *The Gnostic Religion: The Message of the Alien God and the Beginnings of Early Christianity*. 3rd ed. (Boston: Beacon Press, 2001 [1958]).

[16]For a further discussion of Anthony and the rise of Monasticism, see Kenneth Scott Latourette, *A History of Christianity* (New York: Harper and Brothers, 1953), 224–228. See my earlier discussions in chapter 5 on the tension over Jesus in early Christianity.

[17]For brief comments on the early Christian monks such as Simeon Stylites, Pachomius, and especially Basil (the Great) of Caesarea who was influenced by Clement, and particularly by Origen in formulating

various parts of the Empire and are evident side by side today on the cliffs of Meteora (Greece).

Individual Piety and the Need for Community

The individual emphasis on piety of both the hermit and the monk, however, was not attractive to many early Christians who questioned such patterns as the meaning of a "holy" or "perfected" life and it is usually eschewed today— especially in our contemporary narcissistic culture with its "me first" tendencies. Nevertheless, patterns of individual piety are flourishing in the Western world with self-help programs of Oriental mysticism and transcendental meditation. The question still remains: Can a person be a Christian without being part of a community of believers? That issue presents a genuine tension for some. The quick answer again is: Yes! Some people have found Christ by simply reading the New Testament. Early Protestant missionaries such as William Carey and Adoniram Judson lived rather lonely lives as Christians even though surrounded by multitudes of non-Christians in their new cultures. The same was true of the earlier Greek and Latin missionaries. Yet God has usually touched those around them and new believers have been formed.

But from the beginning of humanity, God knew that "it was not good for the human to be alone" (Gen 2:18, 21–22, 24–25). People were created for relationship and community. The church was intended to represent in the world both an outreaching and a close-knit community of Christi's followers in the pattern of a good relationship between a husband and a wife (cf. Eph 5:32–33). And Jesus knew that Christians would need one another for support (John 13:34, 15:12–17). So, while the Scripture provides correction (cf. 1 Tim 3:16), it is important for Christians to experience community through the Spirit's presence (John 14:15–18) and to exemplify loving fellowship in the world (John 13:34–35, 15:12–17; cf. 1 Cor 13:1–14:1, Heb 13:1).

Meeting together provides strength in confronting the world's pressures and in resisting the temptations of the devil. Accordingly, the Preacher of Hebrews strongly advised Christians not to miss assembling together (Heb 10:25). To be associated with a community of believers where spiritual strength is evident can be a powerful experience for any Christian and can counter many ill effects of nineteenth-century individualism that has infected people today. A vibrant

---

the early rules for monastic life, see Latourette, *History of Christianity*, 222–230 and John Ernest Leonard Oulton and Henry Chadwick, eds., *Alexandrian Christianity: Selected Translations of Clement and Origen*, LLC (Philadelphia: Westminster Press, 1954), 38.

covenant community can—like a wholesome Christian family—encourage believers to develop effective community relationships, holistic worship patterns, and genuine self-giving service models.

The Structure or Organization of Churches

Over the years I have come to realize that almost all denominations have developed a rationale for why their people believe that their form of government is the best, supporting their views from the Bible and Christian tradition. But most Christians would agree that holiness, apostolicity, catholicity, and unity are key historic marks of the church although they may define these marks a little differently.[18] In reflecting on this issue I am grateful that I had the opportunity to study and teach in a variety of denominational schools with Baptists, Presbyterians, Methodists, Roman Catholics, Anglicans, and Lutherans and in several interdenominational institutions. Moreover, early in my theological studies, I was fortunate to read the intriguing, classic work by B.H. Streeter called *The Primitive Church* in which he traces the expansion of Christianity into various cultures. Streeter concludes that, wherever the early Christians went, they employed political structures with which the people were familiar.[19]

Wrestling with Tensions in Church Organization

Such a thesis means that the early Christians likely modified and used the organizational patterns that were familiar to them in keeping with the Spirit of Jesus. The Jewish Sanhedrin structure in Palestine may have contributed to the patterns familiar in many Reformed churches. The Greek democratic structures and the varied synagogue patterns probably gave rise to the so-called free-church patterns. The Roman imperial hierarchical system seems to have given rise to monarchical episcopal systems that became dominant by the time of Constantine. The point is that the early Christians used various structures,

Having been brought up as a Baptist, I soon came to realize that the genius of the church is not in its political structure. Church government patterns and structures are simply the means by which Christians seek to carry out the work of Jesus in the world. Now some of my readers may react rather fiercely, but I have by now taught students all the way from Orthodox, Roman Catholic, and Episcopal on the one hand to Church of God and Assemblies of God on the other hand

---

[18]See my detailed discussion in Gerald L. Borchert, "The Nature and Mission of the Church: A Baptist Perspective" *PRSt*, 20.1 (Spring 1993): 19–41.

[19]See Burnett Hillman Streeter, *The Primitive Church Studied with Special Reference to the Origins of the Christian Ministry* (London: Macmillan, 1920).

and of course the rest in between. In addition, it has become increasingly clear to me that church organizations are not really the key to their effectiveness. I have also served as the chair of the Commission on Baptist Doctrine and Interchurch Relations for the Baptist World Alliance, and in interchurch conversations I have learned that the issue of structural identity is not the clue to effective interchange among Christians. Indeed, church organization can often frustrate relationships and get in the way of Christ's work.

So let me posit an idea that has been in my mind since I wrote my first book on the church in 1971.[20] Our English word "church," the German word "*kirche*," and the Scottish word "*kirk*" are all derived from the Greek word *kuriakon* that means "belonging to the Lord." So, I would firmly argue that the church does not belong to humans; it belongs to God in Christ Jesus! Now here comes a major difference in the minds of many Christians. There are those who would argue with Augustine from the Pauline pictorial representation of Christ being the head of the body, the church (cf. Col. 1:18, 2:19; Eph 4:15, 5:23), that the church is to be so identified with Christ. Such a view would mean that the church is actually Christ's body (*verum corpus*).[21] But while pressing the picture-thinking to identify the church as Christ may be appealing to the theology of some scholars, we must remember that it is a convenient Semitic word picture—as are references to the Lord's Table and the elements thereof. We may own buildings, altars, and water containers for baptism and the elements and vessels for Communion or Eucharist, but we do not own the church and we will never become Christ—even in the *eschaton* (at the end of time)!

Therefore, although we may differ in definitions, we would probably agree that our task as members of the church is to be obedient servants of the Lord. Paul understood his task well and called himself a servant/slave (*doulos*) of Christ Jesus (Rom 1:1).It did not mean he would call himself a "slave" of anyone else—only Jesus (cf. 1 Cor 7:20–24). Yet, he learned how to serve others while being a slave of Jesus. This understanding of Paul means he learned in obedience how to give up his life to God in Christ for the sake of others (cf. Phil 2:5–8, Mark 10:43–45). It changed his entire perspective even in a

---

[20]See Gerald L. Borchert, *Today's Model Church: A Pattern from the New Testament* (Forest Park: IL: Roger Williams Press, 1971).

[21]Augustine argued, "Let us rejoice and give thanks that we have become not only Christians, but Christ himself," by which he meant, "The fullness of Christ is then the head and the members." (See St. Augustine, *In evangelium Johannis tractatus*, 21, 8: Patrologia Latina 35. 1658.) The expression *verum corpus* was used for the church until the ninth–twelfth centuries when it was transferred to the Eucharist, and the "mystical body" (*corpus mysticum*) was then used for the church instead.

hostile context.[22] This idea is crucial for understanding the nature of the church and its organizational patterns.

In the tension of structural patterns for the church, I have come to believe that the key is not to be found in deciding which structure is the best. I believe most of them can serve God effectively, but all of them can also serve the devil—if we are not careful. Indeed, I have seen all of them do the latter. What then would I propose? I suggest in this emerging era that every church should seek to be a "pneumatocracy,"[23] or a group of Christians led by the Spirit of God. Of course, such a suggestion leaves us with multiple questions and tensions: How can a church decide what is the will of God's Spirit in any circumstance? Who is in charge? Is it a bishop, or a priest, or a synod, or a board of elders, or a deacon board, or a church council?

The answer should be "the Spirit!" But for most Christians the idea of the Spirit is extremely vague. It seems so indecisive, so unpredictable, and so uncontrollable. Perhaps the reason for our discomfort is that we have divorced our dependence on the Holy Spirit from the Word of God, and we are living in a world that has virtually "demythologized" the Spirit of God. Indeed, we live in a world where people who propose to have the Spirit of God often seem to be a little crazy or misguided or even completely wrong. And any writer who would suggest the Spirit of God is needed in the decision-making process might be thought to be odd or superficial. But such a view only points out how far removed the decision-making process in many churches is from employing the Word of God in the way of love under the guidance of the Holy Spirit!

But perhaps in the midst of our fear that the Spirit might get out of control and in our attempts to standardize the role of the Spirit, we might need to ask: Did not Paul write about the Spirit of God? Were there problems then? Did Jesus talk about the Spirit? Why are we afraid to consider seriously the role of the Spirit in relation to the Word of God and the Way of Love in our churches? Do those five Paraclete/Holy Spirit sayings in John 14–16 have any significance today? You see, in many churches we have relegated the Spirit of God to the sidelines so that the mere mention of the term sends us into a panic because we fear that we might lose control and soon be rolling in the aisles. For a church to be led by the Spirit

---

[22]In today's culture, "following Jesus" can involve great anxiety and fear. For a helpful analysis of the contemporary setting, see Scott Bader-Saye's work, *Following Jesus in a Culture of Fear* (Grand Rapids: Brazos, 2007).

[23]While you may think this term begs questions concerning structure, I chose it because it places the emphasis where I believe it should be. See Borchert, *Today's Model Church*, 44.

of God means that God is really leading the bishop, the priest, the minister, the synod, the elders, the deacons, and the congregation in decision making.

Of course, there are concerns. That is the reason we have institutionalized systems with check and balances because humans can be self-centered and evil. Can we spot falseness and lack of authenticity in a leader or a group? Maybe. Are we able to sense manipulation, greed, power-seeking, immorality, and self-justification within the leadership and congregation? Maybe not. Are Christians able to come to a loving resolution of differences in opinion? I wonder.

Perhaps my hope for authenticity is just a dream. Maybe that is the reason I am not convinced there is any better organizational system. Perhaps they are all fallible. Bishops do not always represent Christ. Ministers do not always speak a word from the Lord. Synods do not always make the correct decisions. Elders or deacons do not always act in a spirit of love. And majorities do not always have the mind of Christ. Minorities can sometimes actually represent the will of God! We are still fallible humans who wrestle with tensions between truth and error, loving others and dealing with their unfaithfulness. We are humans and often do not know the way we ourselves should go!

So, when we make decisions and deal with others, perhaps we need to speak more in love with a humble spirit, using whatever church structure is ours. And let us do so with the clear understanding that we might be wrong. But let us be ready to learn that the Lord acting through the Spirit can help us modify our insensitivities and errors in perception as we operate prayerfully in our organizations and structures.

A Suggestion for Church Structure

Because the church is a covenant community, I suggest using whatever structure fits the Word of God, the way of love, and the leading of the Spirit in a particular congregation's social setting. But that congregation must be ready to judge and evaluate honestly its effectiveness in the mission of Christ. Hopefully it will demonstrate the following characteristics:

• focuses on God as the center of worship;
• employs the Scriptures in the spirit of Jesus as its foundational guide;
• witnesses to others about the need for Christ's saving power;
• supports new believers in growing into the likeness of Jesus;
• responds with genuine care for the poor, helpless, and error-prone;
• reaches authentic, peaceful decisions as a covenant community;

- treats those who disagree with decisions also as followers of Christ;
- uses discipline with grace on those who stray so that they will acknowledge their erroneous ways and turn to Christ;
- demonstrates for all to witness that the loving Spirit of Christ is present in the covenant community.

Notice in this list that I have placed the concern for authentic worship first because worship belongs first in the church's task, work, and service. Placing the humble honoring of the loving God first will change the way we view ourselves and relate to others. But we must be forewarned that we are not God and that authenticity in decision making is subject to human fallibility. You will also notice that I put acting in love as my last point because, as Paul indicates, "love does not fail" (1 Cor 13:13). Love must be central to all Christian action and decision making.

An Illustration from the Jerusalem Council in Acts 15

An example from the early church demonstrates effective church structure and decision making. According to Acts 15 when the tension over circumcision arose, here's how the church addressed the issue:

1. The parties gathered to handle the matter (v. 6).
2. They presented the issues clearly, with a sense that the Holy Spirit was present in their covenant community (vv. 7–11).
3. They listened to the new possibilities presented by Barnabas and Paul (v. 12).
4. They weighed the new situation in the light of scriptural insights from the past (vv. 15–18).
5. They made a decision and then put it in writing (v. 23).
6. They sensed the decision was made under the guidance of the Holy Spirit (v. 28).
7. They sent representatives to give oral witness of their peaceful agreement (vv. 27, 32–33).
8. Then the community rejoiced in their common understanding (v. 31).

Did the decision mean that everyone agreed with the resolution? Clearly not. But they proceeded, knowing that they had done their best in the Spirit of the Lord. With these reflections on structure, I turn briefly to the community's proclamation.

The Church's Proclamation

Due to human desire, self-centeredness, and outright rejection of some aspects of the message such as judgment, the church's proclamation is constantly in danger of being truncated. As a result, a potential for the fragmentation of the message mushrooms because of human tendencies to "choose" which aspects of the message we prefer to emphasize and which segments we minimize, overlook, or dismiss. As Peter Bergen enunciated in 1980, humans now sense freedom from the great traditional restraint against choice that once was regarded as the equivalent of committing "a sin."[24] So, in the context of our narcissistic world, where the self is the center of human thinking, there is a tendency to render God as a subpoint in human reflection and action. Dealing with "God" in a cavalier manner, however, means that the Creator/Redeemer becomes a convenient agent for human whims. Such a "God" is hardly God! And truncation of the message will create serious tensions.

The Church's Story

In spite of our self-centeredness, the God of the Bible consistently challenges human views and the story of the Bible continually confirms the reality of our erroneous perceptions. The church's hero is not someone similar to an Abraham or a Joseph, Deborah, Ruth, David, Josiah, Daniel, Peter, John, Paul, or Mary. The hero of the Bible is Jesus (or the Triune God) who patiently has sought and continues seeking to bring humanity into reconciliation with God, with other humans, and with the entire cosmos. So, when the story is correctly understood, the Bible is God's story and humans are the focus or concern of this story.

The church's task of proclamation, therefore, is primarily to get the story straight and to make certain who actually is the central player. The story of creation, accordingly, is a story about God's desire to have a proper relationship with "humans." But within that story there is the sub-plot of the continual desire of humans to think that they know better than God how the story

---

[24]See the intriguing work of Peter Berger, *The Heretical Imperative: Contemporary Possibilities of Religious Affirmation* (New York: Doubleday Mass Market Paperback, 1980). Berger saw that choice was formerly regarded as a kind of "heresy" that in the contemporary world of a greater sense of freedom is being sloughed off.

should develop. The story of salvation or of coming to wholeness is the story of how God repeatedly has attempted to return humans to the proper path that leads to blessing and not judgment. It is not the story of human effort, but rather the story of God's loving forgiveness. It is the story of holiness and the ways, methods, and media the holy God has used to demonstrate how humans can be drawn near to the holy otherness of God without suffering judgment and destruction.[25]

The question then might be: How has God's strategy been working? From the human point of view and the numbers game, we might seriously question whether God is succeeding. The sad part of the story is that only a few humans even today seem to understand the fuller implications of that story and respond appropriately with their feeble patterns of authentic responses to God, other humans, and the created order.[26] Yet God continues to be active in the story and has enabled some humans to accomplish far more than they could in their own ability. Briefly the biblical part of that story is as follows:

> The early Genesis accounts reflect that after God created humans God tried to provide for these humans but they rejected the guidelines for having an appropriate relationship with God. Yet God did not abandon them but provided care for them in spite of the fact that they shattered their relationship with God. And it has since happened repeatedly because humans do not seem to understand the story—even though God destroyed most of them in a flood and they lost their ability to communicate clearly with each other.
>
> They did not even understand when God selected a few (the people of Israel) and blessed them so that they would become models for others in order to bless them. But these few consistently turned their backs on their responsibilities and instead, they sought their own ways apart from God. And it did not get better even though they were punished many times. That situation brings us to the core of our story—the Church's message:

---

[25]In an important theological study Donald G. Bloesch demonstrates that holiness and love are actually two sides of a correct understanding of the biblical God and of an adequate perception of Jesus, God's Son as well. See his work, *God the Almighty: Power, Wisdom, Holiness, Love* (Downers Grove, IL: InterVarsity,1996), 137–164.

[26]I strongly recommend that all Christians should have their own personal summary of God's great story in mind as a reminder for life and as basis for communicating that story to others.

> *Ultimately 1) God sent his own Son, Jesus, to the Jews to fulfill God's promises and 2) to deal impartially with human sin and disobedience. 3) This Jesus followed God's directions in doing good and healing people, but 4) most of these Jews rejected the Son who was the divine embodiment in human flesh and they had him crucified. Yet the story did not end there 5) because God raised the Son from the dead and 6) this risen Son commanded his followers) to testify to his incredible resurrection and 7) God designated him to judge all who have lived on earth and 8) to call all to believe in the Son and receive the forgiveness of their sins! (cf. Acts 10:34–43) [These eight points represent the Church's "kerygma."[27]]*
>
> These Followers have become the nucleus of a growing company who are proclaiming the astounding news that God's Son can transform the way people think and act. But since God understood that humans could not live and proclaim this transforming message on their own, when the Son returned to his Father, they together sent another Companion (the Holy Spirit) to be with the followers of the Son. And while the Spirit is an unseen persona in them, those who believe in the Son recognize that this Companion will guide them in the ways of God, will remind them of the Son and give them a sense of peace, will protect them and assure them of God's care for them, will empower them to introduce others to the Son, and this Spirit will assist them in establishing New Covenant Communities that are committed to following the model of Son of God. And these Communities of the Son of God are now called "the Church."

While the biblical text of the story ended some two thousand years ago with Jesus and the early disciples, the story is an ever-growing story that involves humans in the twenty-first century. So, this story is not merely a literary account. It is a serious reality story that has been acted out on the stage of history over a period of many years.

---

[27]The italicized section represents the *kerygma* or the basic elements of the early church's preaching about Jesus that C.H. Dodd is credited with identifying in his classic work, *The Apostolic Preaching and Its Development* (London: Hodder & Stoughton, 1936). The *kerygma* is to be distinguished from the *didache* or the church's fuller teaching concerning what Christians believe and the way they should act in the world. For further discussion on the gospel and the *kerygma*, see G. Borchert, *John 1–11*, 25–30, and John B. Polhill, "Kerygma and Didache" in *Dictionary of the Later New Testament and Its Developments*, eds. R.P. Martin and P.H. Davids (Downers Grove, IL: InterVarsity, 1997), 626–629. Since Dodd's work, many writers have emphasized the story, such as N.T. Wright and his *The New Testament and the People of God* (London/Minneapolis: SPCK./Fortress, 1992), 400.

The story of God with humanity may prompt some questions, for example: Do these new covenant communities authentically represent the will of God? Sometimes. Are the followers perfect? Hardly. Are they authentic? Sometimes. When they go astray, can they be renewed as in covenant renewals? Yes, indeed. In their fallibility, can they accomplish anything for God? Under the guidance of the Spirit, the answer is unquestionably, yes! Yet a strategic question still remains: Is there usually a tension between these followers of Christ and their cultural environment in following the will of God? Oftentimes, yes.

But as you may have surmised, we have moved to the well-known tension that was aptly identified by H. Richard Niebuhr in his classic work *Christ and Culture*.[28] In that work he identifies several possible scenarios for the relationship between Christians and culture that includes views from resisting cultural patterns to conforming to societal mores, and from standing in judgment over culture to seeking to transform culture. But for most Christians who seek to follow Christ authentically, there is usually a definite sense of tension because the way of Jesus is normally not the pattern advocated by the purveyors of culture. Nevertheless, in spite of human weakness, authentic members of the covenant community can be God's agents of communicating the story of reconciliation to the world.

Human "Testimonies"

Now in response to people asking for help in witnessing and others in preparing for mission teams, some have been hazy about the content of a witness, and others have been fearful and feel a lack of having a stirring testimony. Fear of rejection is common, but the latter view is a misunderstanding because sharing the story of Jesus (a testimony) is not primarily about us humans. A testimony, akin to the gospel, is about Jesus and what God has done and is doing for humans. Remember, we are not the main focus of testimonies. We are a subpoint in our sharing of God's wonderful story in Christ Jesus. And this priority of Jesus applies to all our service for God—which is our next subject.

---

[28]See the classic work of H. Richard Niebuhr, *Christ and Culture* (New York: Harper and Row, 1951) who posited five possible relationships in relating to this tension: Christ against culture, Christ of culture, Christ above culture, Christ and culture in paradox, and Christ the transformer of culture. For a reevaluation of Niebuhr's work in the light of our contemporary secular society, see D.A. Carson, *Christ and Culture Revisited* (Grand Rapids: Eerdmans, 2008)

The Church's Service—Tensions in Worship and Mission

At the heart of the church's service or task is a frequently suggested tension between worship and mission. But correctly understood, the first is directed to God and the second is directed to humanity. Bifurcating the two develops an unnecessary tension. Neither is focused on the self. Both are centered outside of the self. A correct perception of mission is dependent on authentic worship. Failure to acknowledge what God has done in Christ means that Christian mission will ultimately fail to achieve its God-given purpose.

Focus on Worship as Service

Worship is not simply "going to church" or participating in liturgy. Worship involves all of life as Christians live in openness/obedience to God—which is the reason my late colleague, Robert Webber, referred to worship as a verb and not simply a noun.[29] Obedience to God flows from a clear recognition of what God has done for us—recognizing how God's story impacts our stories. We worship and obey God because of what God does for us.

This perspective was made evident even as early as the strategic account of God giving the Ten Commandments. Notice that the instructions in Exodus 20 do not begin with the words "You shall have no other gods before me" (v. 3) but with the words "I am the LORD your God who brought you out of ... slavery" (vv. 1–2). What follows this statement of God's action is an implied "therefore" and then come the "ten words" or commandments. Obedience to these commandments was posited on the fact that God saved Israel from slavery. As Walter Brueggemann has noted, worship in ancient Israel was an essential part of a living dialogue between humans and God.[30]

Similarly, the divine work of Jesus affects how humans respond to God's mysterious actions.[31] Crucial for worshipers to understand is that God, the primary actor, brings reconciliation to sinful humans (2 Cor 5:18–19). The result, as Paul notes, is that human boasting has been rendered illegitimate (Rom 3:27). The proper response is gratitude and worship. Forgiveness and reconciliation are not the result of human action.

The word "worship" is derived from the Anglo-Saxon *weorthscipe*. Ralph Martin argues that worship means ascribing "supreme worth" to the Lord

---

[29]See Robert E. Webber, *Worship is a Verb: Eight Principles for Transforming Worship*, 2nd ed. (Peabody, MA: Hendrickson, 1992).

[30]See Walter Brueggmann, *Worship in Ancient Israel: The Essential Guide* (Nashville: Abingdon, 2005).

[31]See especially my introduction in Gerald L. Borchert, *Worship in the New Testament: Divine Mystery and Human Response* (St. Louis: Chalice Press, 2008), 1–7.

who "alone is worthy"—"alone is worship-ful"[32] because, as G. Ernest Wright frequently reminds us, God is the "God who Acts."[33] Clearly, God acted decisively in sending Jesus! And God continues to act in providing humans with a foretaste of wholeness that we will experience in the *parousia* (final presence or return of Jesus). It is God's story of our coming to wholeness.[34]

Authentic worship is not directed to humans; it is directed to God! And this statement reminds me of what my colleague and former student Constance Cherry has artfully asserted in her introduction to *The Worship Architect* and to what, I trust, you have been perceiving in my work here: namely, that Christian worship like Christian theology and ethics is focused "on God's acts of salvation," "patterned on revelation and response," both "covenantal" and "corporate in nature," thoroughly "Trinitarian," and evidenced in the human "transformational journey" with God.[35] Such a holistic view of Christian worship is the natural foundation for Christian action and an authentic perception of tensions involved in Christian service.

Because God was very serious in sending Jesus as the divine answer to human sin and rebellion, Christian worship must be modeled on the seriousness of God's actions. We dare not play loose with the seriousness of God. Or, as Marva Dawn asserts, we must not "dumb down" our worship to meet human wims.[36] But does this seriousness mean that Christian worship is to be somber and conducted like a funeral? Christian worship should represent both the death and resurrection of Jesus—a serious reflection of the costly death and a marvelous proclamation of God's victory that anticipates the joy of Christ's *parousia*. He is coming again!

Focus on Mission as Service

For Christians authentic worship should lead to self-giving service or mission, following Christ's example.[37] In his death and resurrection, Christ initiated our

---

[32]See Ralph Martin, *Worship in the Early Church* (London: Marshall, Morgan and Scott, 1964, Reprint, Grand Rapids: Eerdmans, 1995), 10

[33]See G Earnest Wright, *The God Who Acts*, in *SBT* (London/Naperville: S.C.M. Press, 1952).

[34]For a further discussion of how God's story impacts worship see Robert E. Webber, *Ancient Future Worship: Proclaiming and Enacting God's Narrative* (Grand Rapids: Baker, 2008).

[35]See the excellent work of Constance M. Cherry, *The Worship Architect: A Blueprint for Designing Culturally Relevant and Biblically Faithful Services* (Grand Rapids: Baker Academic, 2010), 5–17, for an expansion of these ideas.

[36]See Marva J. Dawn's work *Reaching Out without Dumbing Down: A Theology of Worship for the Turn-of-the-Century Culture* (Grand Rapids: Eerdmans, 1995).

[37]See William J. Larkin, Jr. and Joel F. Williams, eds., *Mission in the New Testament: An Evangelical Approach*, vol. 27, American Society of Missiology (Maryknoll, NY: Orbis Books, 1998). See also Donald Senior, C.P. and Carroll Stuhlmueller, C.P., *The Biblical Foundations for Mission* (Maryknoll, NY: Orbis, 1991). For a critique on the church's approach to mission, see Ron Sider, *The Scandal of the Evangelical*

forgiveness from sin (Rom 8:1) so that we see the world differently. Indeed, we even see Christ differently, which in turn forces us to view ourselves differently—as servants (2 Cor 5:16–18). This new vision provides us with an understanding of reconciliation because God intends for everyone to be reconciled to God through Christ as the God-ordained bridge of reconciliation (2 Cor 5:18–19). The gratitude that follows then animates Christians—and their God-ordained covenant communities—to accept their role as "ambassadors for Christ" in bringing holistic reconciliation to others (2 Cor 5:20–21).

But Christian mission must never be treated as the means for gaining salvation. Mission is a response to what God has already done for Christians in sending Jesus as the divine-human bridge to wholeness. Our Worship of God and our mission for God must, therefore, be understood as a unified task of the church and of Christians in a fractured world.

This interrelationship between worship and service may lead to a number of questions. Does a correct understanding of worship lead to faithfulness in mission? Or, does worshiping God on Sundays automatically lead to faithful service during the rest of the week? You know the answers to these and similar questions. Our actions and motives are not consistent, nor are they always pure. Human thought and action can easily be tainted by self-centeredness, sin, and a lack of authenticity. But all Christians are on a pilgrimage to Christlikeness—which our secular society hardly views as a route to success.

Tensions in Evangelism and Social Action

As worship and mission should be viewed as complementary aspects of the church's task or service, so the frequently assumed tension between evangelism and social concern should be understood as allied activities in the church's mission.[38] While I have briefly mentioned the subject of evangelism in chapter 3, I now return to this topic and the related concern of social action because there is an unfortunate tendency on the part of Christians, churches, and denominations to focus primarily on either evangelism or social concern and to neglect the other. Indeed, some Christians openly assert their preference for being either evangelistic or socially aware but then condemn others who emphasize the opposite view as straying from the gospel. In fact, some churches and denominations in

---

Conscience: Why Are Christians Living Like the Rest of the World? (Grand Rapids: Baker, 2005). See also Scott Bader-Saye, *Following Jesus in a Culture of Fear* (Grand Rapids: Brazos, 2020, [2007]).

[38]See for example the helpful essay by Delos Miles, "Social Work and Evangelism as Partners" in *Evangelism in the Twenty-First Century: The Critical Issues,* ed. Thom S. Rainer (Wheaton, IL: Harold Shaw Publishers, 1989), 51–60.

an effort to confirm their commitment to one of these assumed polarities often close effective programs of their rejected area or sell off effective institutions that do not represent their current perspective that may have been initiated by predecessors whose thinking was more holistic. In doing so, Christians mistakenly bifurcate the mission of Christ's work. Such a dichotomy is completely foreign to Jesus who healed the paralytic and forgave sins (cf. Mark 2:1–12). He likewise taught people the message of life and fed empty stomachs (cf. Mark 6:34, 44).[39] To choose only one aspect of the church's mission is to truncate the gospel.

An authentic faith community should reach out and share the message that God has come in Christ to bring holistic transformation to sinful people and free them from the many bondages of life. Communicating the wonderful message of transforming forgiveness and of new life is the work of evangelism and the imperative that is given to the covenant community and to every Christian.[40]

But a church that is truly evangelical (gospel-oriented) will also accept the call of God to care earnestly for people and to assist them in sharing courageously a holistic understanding of the good news of God's saving work, not only in their immediate area but also throughout the world.[41] Christians who are engaged in the mission of Jesus are concerned both for people's "souls" (an inadequate but frequently used description of people's spiritual condition) and for their physical well-being. The correct perspective on salvation means that Christians are involved in bringing "wholeness" to others in our world. Wholeness involves the whole of others. Thus, in his first epistle, John—writing like a contemporary theological ethicist—thunders to his readers: If a Christian has "enough money to live well and sees a brother or a sister in need but shows no compassion, how can God's love be in that person?" (1 John 3 17, NLT). On the other hand, clothing people or feeding their stomachs is also not an adequate representation of the complete gospel. There should be no tension for Christians in caring for the spiritual well-being of others and at the same time also caring for their physical well-being. I have often asked myself if this tendency to choose one side or the

---

[39]See Gerald L. Borchert, *The Dynamics of Evangelism* (Waco, TX: Word Books, 1976). For the synthesis of these stories in Mark, see David E. Garland, *Mark* in NIVAC (Grand Rapids: Zondervan, 1996), 92–100, 252–265.

[40]For a further analysis of evangelism and church growth, see Lewis A. Drummond, *The Word of the Cross: A Contemporary Theology of Evangelism* (Nashville: Broadman, 1992) and Thom S. Rainer, *The Book of Church Growth: History, Theology and Principles* (Nashville: Broadman, 1993).

[41]For further insights into the worldwide task of mission, see for example J. Herbert Kane, *Christian Missions in Biblical Perspective* (Grand Rapids: Baker,1976).

other may be the way of the devil and part of the cultural captivity of Western Christianity.[42]

The world is not a friendly place. It squeezes people—including Christians—into its self-centered molds as it blindsides the followers of the caring Jesus into multiple patterns of divisiveness and of indifference concerning those in need. People need Jesus for spiritual healing and food and health care for physical healing.

Many people today scarcely recognize the refugee status that was once central to the existence of the church and perspectives such as in 1 Peter, which John Elliot aptly describes as providing "A Home for the Homeless"[43]—a setting in which the devil seems to wander at will, confusing Christians concerning Jesus and that God does not really care for them in the midst of difficulties (1 Pet 5:8). The devil continues to do so today but often seeks to convince unwitting believers that they can avoid responsibility for those in need by focusing our attentions only on worship, or on preaching forgiveness, or on caring for the poor and homeless. Our covenant communities (churches) need a holistic gospel and a holistic Jesus. Let us not settle for a truncated message, a truncated sense of service, or a truncated mission. If we do, we will be members of a truncated church facing a confused society.

… And these perceptions of the church's nature, structure, message, and service naturally lead me to the subject of the church's sacred actions.

---

[42]For some thought-provoking views on this topic, see Soong Cha Rah, *The Next Evangelicalism, Freeing the Church from Western Cultural Captivity* (Downers Grove, IL: InterVarsity, 2009). See also his *Prophetic Lament: A Call for Justice in Troubled Times* (Downers Grove, IL: InterVarsity, 2015) and Mark Charles and Soong Char Rah, *Unsettling Truths: The Ongoing Dehumanizing Legacy of the Doctrine of Discovery* (Downers Grove, IL: InterVarsity, 2019)

[43]For a helpful analysis of the sociological setting of 1 Peter, see John H. Elliott, *A Home for the Homeless: A Sociological Exegesis of 1 Peter, Its Situation and Strategy* (Philadelphia: Fortress, 1981. For my comments on the powerful closing section of First Peter see: Gerald L. Borchert, "The Conduct of Christians in the Face of the 'Fiery Ordeal' (4:12–5:11)" in *RevExp* 79.3 (Summer, 1982): 451–462.

Chapter 11

The New Covenant Community— The Church's Sacred Actions

Tensions in the Sacred Actions of the Church

The Church's Sacraments or Ordinances

The church has long battled the issue of sacraments or ordinances. This subject is filled with tensions, disagreements, hostilities, and major theological differences among Christians. By instituting these experiences/acts/sacraments/ordinances, Jesus and his early disciples undoubtedly intended to bring a sense of unity and vitality to Christians. Instead, these sacred acts have engendered a great sense of disunity and hostility among Christians throughout the ages.

The Sacred Acts of the Church Defined

One aspect of the disagreement revolves around the question of the Lord's presence in these sacred acts or actions of the church. Few Christians would deny the presence of the Lord Jesus Christ in the lives of the believers. The issue, then, becomes one of the nature, extent, and significance of that presence of Jesus in these activities themselves. Moreover, questions are frequently raised concerning these actions: Are they in fact directly able to communicate Jesus' presence in the church practices or functions and/or through appropriately designated or installed church functionaries such as priests and ministers? Or contrarily, are these actions or activities done primarily as an obedient response on the part of Christians who seek to follow the commands or orders of their Lord and Savior, thereby becoming intimately identified with him? Furthermore, the range of possibilities between these two alternatives is exceedingly wide and permits opportunity for various modifications of these two interpretations.

As we approach this issue or tension, the options are manifold: Should we interpret these sacred actions as conveying the transforming presence of Jesus in the elements such as the bread and wine and through the water? Or, is the presence conveyed through the words of the ceremony by the officiating officer? Or, is the presence of Jesus to be understood as being there in the nature of the event as an expected fulfillment of a sacred promise from God in Christ?

Or, should the focus be on Christ being powerfully proclaimed as symbolically present in the sacred action for those who obediently respond with humble hearts and wills? Or, should the actions be interpreted as genuine symbols of the transforming experiences of Jesus' presence as the Lord of Christians? The descriptors can be expanded and multiplied considerably, but they can also form overlapping understandings in the minds of Christians.

I should here mention one other interpretation that I have repeatedly encountered during my years as a Christian: a view that uses the terms "a mere symbol." It is a type of protest that grows out of an honest attempt to reject the "thingification" of grace that I discussed earlier. Such a view, however, suffers from an opposite problem. I suggest that the proponents of this view should reflect upon what is being actually implied in such an approach. To argue that the sacred acts of the church are "merely" symbols is to imply that they really may not be important and that they do not have any powerful symbolic or real significance.

Yet one can hardly read the Gospel of John and interpret the signs of Jesus as hardly important. It would also be hard to argue in Romans 6 or 1 Corinthians 11 or in other texts that Paul would have viewed acts such as baptism or the Lord's Supper as merely symbols. So, while many of my closest Christian friends tend to espouse such a view, I would recommend that we should delete the word "mere" from our Christian vocabularies. There is nothing mere about Christianity or its sacred actions (in spite of the significant work of C.S. Lewis when he delivered his radio messages that became titled *Mere Christianity*). Such verbiage is a form of reaction to what is perceived as magic in the same way that some Protestants have referred to the mass as "hocus pocus," which was a reaction against a magical interpretation of using the Latin words "*Hoc est corpus meum*" ("This is my body") in the consecration of the mass!

But I would also add that those who espouse a sacramental perspective sometimes unfairly criticize the nonsacramental view as lacking in meaning, although I was intrigued when I taught in the Chicago area by the number of young people attending Wheaton College who came from nonsacramental family traditions that were drawn to the patterns of Orthodox worship. It clearly points to the lack of understanding among the nonsacramental laity concerning their experiences of the sacred actions of the church. My assumption has been that for those young people their previous encounters with the sacred actions of the church were not much more than "mere symbolic actions of the church."

This fact should give those who lead worship in nonsacramental churches a sharp call to wake up and realize their lack of attention to the way they lead worship. It reminds me of Robert Webber's early experiences in worship that left an emptiness in his spirit and understanding of worship and one reason why he wrote his early book on the Canterbury Trail.[1] We do not need to go back to Canterbury or to Constantinople or to Rome if we will pay close attention to the importance of worship! Worship is not about us or about performance. It is about making God the center of our lives and coming humbly before the Almighty in gratitude and offering ourselves in service to the Lord.

The Number of Sacred Acts of the Church

While many churches celebrate or recognize baptism and the Lord's Supper (Eucharist) as the two domically instituted acts of Christianity, the historic Eastern (Orthodox) and Western (Roman Catholic) Churches have regarded seven sacraments as ordained by Christ.[2] These seven, as defined by various church decrees such as by the Council of Trent, are: Baptism, Confirmation, the Holy Eucharist,[3] Penance, Extreme Unction, Holy Orders, and Matrimony.

One of the most interesting phenomena in Christianity is that although Jesus specifically instructed/commanded his disciples to wash one another's feet in John 13:14, this act has not been regarded by most churches as a recognized sacrament or ordinance. It certainly has been remembered in connection with Holy (or "Maundy," a defective transliteration from the Latin *mandare*, meaning "to command") Thursday and by Jesus giving or "ordering" the "love command" (John 13:34–35). But, although this command/order is practiced by some Christians as a symbol of servanthood, the practice of foot-washing has not been formalized as one of the major sacred actions of the church. Given the human tendency on the part of Christians to assert strongly their views concerning many aspects of their faith, however, perhaps this ordained practice by Jesus of being a servant should be one that receives more attention.[4]

---

[1] For the new edition, see Robert Webber and Lester Ruth, *Evangelicals on the Canterbury Trail: Why Evangelicals are Attracted to the Liturgical* Church, rev. ed. (New York: Morehouse Publishing, 2012, 1985).

[2] See for example Donald Attwater, ed., *A Catholic Dictionary*, 3rd ed. (New York: Macmillan, 1958), 441.

[3] The Nestorian Christians refer to their rite more particularly as the "Holy Leaven," and they begin their Eucharistic service with "an elaborate process of making the holy bread" that they regard as a continuation of the Last Supper. In St. Thomas Christianity (particularly in South India) the Eucharist is referred to as a Qurbana, which means for the Indian mind that it is fundamentally a sacrificial "offering" that is rather parallel to Hindu ancestor sacrificial ceremonies. The bread is leavened, and a little oil and salt are used. Instead of wine, a juice from soaking raisins has been used. For Eastern rites, see Aziz S. Atiya, *History of Eastern Christianity* (Notre Dame, IN: University of Notre Dame Press, 1967), especially at 295–96 and 384–86.

[4] I recognize that in some churches there are several practices that relate to this dominical command but not at the level of importance that I am suggesting.

With these comments in mind, I turn now to discuss briefly the ordinances or sacraments of baptism and the Lord's Supper (Communion or Eucharist). While both of these rites have multiple patterns of interpretation and each could require a full book of exposition to do justice to their significance in Christian practice, I have tried in brief to take seriously the manifold views related to these sacred actions.

Tensions in the Rite of Baptism

There are great differences of opinion among Christians in their understanding of baptism.[5] Not only do those differences involve the significance of this sacred action, but they also extend to the mode and to the persons who are being baptized.

While the Greek word *baptizo* clearly means to dip (oneself) or to wash, because of the great theological controversies that have ensued concerning its meaning in Christianity, translators have chosen to create a transliterated word "baptize" and leave the meaning to the arguments of theological interpreters. Accordingly, some churches employ the mode of sprinkling candidates, others employ the mode of pouring over the head of candidates, some completely immerse candidates, and still others accept multiple modes of baptism.

But perhaps the most significant theological differences concerning baptism involve the issues of those who should be legitimate candidates for baptism and the age or time at which candidates should be baptized. Some churches assert that infants of believing parents (or church members) may be baptized and become a legitimate part of a believing community if the parents and the community (in many cases represented by chosen "godparents") promise to bring up the child in the nurture and admonition of the Lord. For some Christians, infant baptism is a completed act in itself because of the effective work of the priest or minister or the appropriate words being said during the rite. For others, infant baptism constitutes a kind of proleptic action in the expectation that the child will "confirm" or "be confirmed" in a true faith expression when the child is personally able to affirm such a faith in Jesus as Savior and/or Lord.

---

[5]See for example Thomas J. Nettles, Richard L. Pratt, Jr. Robert Kolb, and John D. Castalein, *Understanding Four Views on Baptism in Counterpoints* (Grand Rapids: Zondervan, 2007); and Donald Bridge and David Phypers, *The Water That Divides: Two Views on Baptism* (Christian Focus Reprint, 2008). See also Attwater, ed., *A Catholic Dictionary*, 3441. See p. 181 for the important dialog beginning with Karl Barth's stunning lecture that was delivered to his student in 1943, *The Teaching of the Church Regarding Baptism*, trans. Ernest Payne (London: SCM Press, 1948) that led to the response by Oscar Cullmann, *Baptism in the New Testament* (London: SCM Press 1950) that in turn was followed by a series of responses, perhaps highlighted by the large work of George R. Beasley-Murray, *Baptism in the New Testament* (Grand Rapids: Eerdmans, 1973).

Some churches that practice infant baptism normally assert that there is a difference between a missionary or a pagan family setting where there is not an established community or family of faith into which a child may be born as over against a setting where there is an established community or family of faith into which the child is birthed. There is usually a direct link made between the Old Testament concept of a covenant people (Israel) and the New Testament understanding of the covenant people (the Church).[6] Moreover, there is frequently a coordinated theological link made between circumcision in the Old Covenant and baptism in the New Covenant. Biblical support for the legitimacy of infant baptism among these Christians is usually sought in texts such as Jesus' command to "Allow the children to come to me . . . for to such belong the kingdom of God" and the further words, "whoever does not receive the kingdom of God like a child shall not enter it" (Mark 10:14–15; cf. Matt 18:3, 19:14; Luke 18:16–17; contrast 1 Cor 14:20, 1 Pet 2:2).

The Impact of Karl Barth and the Issue of Faith in Baptism

Karl Barth, perhaps the leading Reformed theologian of the twentieth century, delivered a bombshell in a lecture to his students in 1943 that was quickly circulated in Europe in the form of a pamphlet and was translated by Ernest Payne as *The Teaching of the Church Regarding Baptism.*[7] In that lecture Barth decried the fact that there was in the practice of infant baptism the obvious absence in the recipient of the necessary cognitive element of faith. Since Barth had led the call for a return of Protestantism to the centrality of faith in salvation through his highly acclaimed commentary on Romans, his pamphlet engendered a huge storm of protest. Barth's work was primarily a theological statement about faith and not a New Testament analysis concerning the specific topic.

Scholars from a number of denominations rushed to counter his work. Among them was Oscar Cullmann, a renowned Reformed New Testament scholar who had challenged Christians to reconsider both the issues of time and the state following the Hitler period. He tried to stem what he thought was the possibility of a "schism"[8] in the church by seeking to answer the question of

[6]See for example Paul K. Jewett, *Infant Baptism and the Covenant of Grace* (Grand Rapids: Eerdmans, 1986) and Geoffrey Bromiley, *Children of Promise: The Case for Baptizing Infants* (Grand Rapids: Eerdmans, 1979).

[7]See the earlier footnotes and especially Karl Barth, *The Teaching of the Church Regarding Baptism* (London: SCM, 1948).

[8]See Oscar Cullmann, *Baptism in the New Testament* (Chicago: Alec R Allenson, 1950), 7, 47–55. Cullmann is well known for his use of the V-Day and D-Day motif in reference to Christ's incarnational coming and his parousia, or return in power. See his work, *Christ and Time* (Philadelphia: Westminster, 1950).

whether infant baptism was compatible with the essence of New Testament faith. But Kurt Aland, the well-known Lutheran editor of the Greek New Testament, countered Cullmann because he was not convinced that early Christians of the New Testament era conceived of such a concept as infant baptism. He strongly asserted that the baptism of infants was a later development among Christians in the second and third centuries.[9] By the time of Constantine and his successors, however, the practice of infant baptism was regularized. While the arguments have and will continue, Aland's thesis was then further supported by the major New Testament study on baptism by George Beasley-Murray of Britain.[10]

Over the centuries, not all Christians have followed the pattern of baptizing infants. Among those Christians who have rejected the baptism of infants and who often sought a rebaptism after declaring their faith (and consequently were viewed as heretics by infant baptism advocates) are the later Anabaptists, some Mennonites, and most Baptists. They practice a believer's baptism and belong to Christian groups that are often designated as believers' churches.[11] Because many of them have been persecuted for their views by "state churches" in Europe, many have also taken a strong stance over against state and church alignments and have espoused the concept of freedom of conscience, a view that has been built into the founding precepts of the United States of America.

The fundamental theological building block of believers' churches is that each individual must make a personal confession that Jesus is his/her Savior and Lord before being baptized.[12] As Robert Walton, writing for a committee of British Baptists, stated: "We do not baptize children who have no power to

---

[9]See Kurt Aland, *Did the Early Church Baptize Infants?* (Philadelphia: Westminster, 1963); contrast the views of J. Jeremias, *Infant Baptism in the First Four Centuries* (Philadelphia: Westminster, 1960) and *The Origins of Infant Baptism: A Further Study in Reply to Kurt Aland* (London: SCM, 1963). For a few additional views concerning infant baptism, see: James D.G. Dunn, *Baptism in the Holy Spirit* (Naperville, IL: Allenson and Philadelphia, Westminster, 1970); Martin E. Marty, *Baptism* (Minneapolis: Fortress, 1962); Kilian McDonnell and George Montague, *Christian Initiation and Baptism in the Holy Spirit* (Collegeville, MN: Liturgical Press, 1991); Rudolf Schnackenburg, *Baptism in the Thought of St. Paul* (New York: Herder & Herder, 1964); *Orthodox Perspectives on Baptism, Eucharist and Ministry* (Brookline, MA; Holy Cross, 1985); Alexander Schmemann, *Of Water and the Spirit: A Liturgical Study of Baptism* (Crestwood, NY: St. Vladimir's, 1974).

[10]George R. Beasley-Murray, *Baptism in the New Testament* (Grand Rapids: Eerdmans, 1973); see contra the discussion in Arthur S. Yates, *Why Baptize Infants? A Study of the Biblical, Traditional and Theological Evidence* (Norwich, UK: Canterbury, 1993).

[11]See for example Merle D. Strege, ed., *Baptism and Church: A Believers' Church Vision* (Grand Rapids: Sagamore, 1986).

[12]Ibid.

choose or reject Christ's way of salvation." Then he continued, "God created the Church but he compels no one to enter its fellowship."[13]

In theory there may seem to be little distinction made by some of these believers' advocates between baptism and becoming a member of the church and between those who come from a non-Christian family and those from a Christian family since everyone must make a personal confession of Jesus before being baptized. Yet they admit that the context of children's development can be very different and those contexts can have radically different implications for their lives. To be brought up in a Christian family and within a covenant community is a great blessing, although it does not mean that one has accepted that community as one's home or the designation of a Christian as one's own identifying marker. So, what seems to be crucial for believers' church members is their conviction that until a person reaches the age of accountability, the issue of that person's security rests in the wise understanding of God. Many of those believers' churches were founded when membership in churches was almost the equivalent of state citizenship and when accountability in the Christian community was marginal at best because church membership and citizenship were not actually separated in the minds of most people.

This discussion naturally leads us to back to the haunting issue of security that was raised in chapter 7 This issue of security actually involves our understanding of faith. Humans by nature are troubled by insecurity and seek multiple ways to overcome their insecurities, and it applies to Christians—both to those who baptize infants and those who do not. Clearly while humans can be agents in dealing with insecurity, ultimate security is not really settled by the church's sacred actions or by our fallible human responses (often called faith).

Yet dealing with insecurity is an important aspect of the grace-and-faith relationship or tension discussed earlier. While God is faithful to God's covenant, history is replete with examples of humans being unfaithful to those covenants. So, even covenant does not provide the security that is sought without authentic faith. The crucial question, of course, is: Whose faith are we discussing? Here then is the point that Barth and others were pressing.

The question concerning a believer's faith or decision to follow Christ, of course, resides in the integrity of one's confession and at what age or in what condition a person can legitimately make such a confessional decision to follow Jesus. Some would argue that salvation or belonging to the family of God does not depend on faith. But such an argument is truncated and flies in the face of

---

[13]Robert C. Walton, *The Gathered Community* (London: Carey, 1946), 164.

the New Testament witness, especially in Romans concerning human responsibility. On the other hand, pressures are often placed upon young people to make this important life decision (or confirmation of faith in infant baptism churches) often too early and either in the unworthy interests of meeting certain church goals and practices for baptism or confirmation or because of family insecurities in attempting to make sure children are "secure in the faith." When such skewed patterns are practiced, the basic foundation faith in believers' churches has been compromised and the basic meaning of confirmation in infant-baptizing churches has been vitiated. This issue points to the real tensions that are present among all who are baptized into Christ Jesus.

God understands the frailties of Christians and of our convoluted arguments that seek to justify our practices. But we as God's children should never fail to be thankful for the Lord's understanding and patience with our feeble assumptions and our immature attempts at colonizing the reality of God and God's work in Christ with our experiences and intelligible responses!

Remember, the Christian life is a pilgrimage and authenticity in that pilgrimage is not automatic nor are the church's sacred actions insurance policies against human insecurity nor a guarantee of the Lord's approval in all human sacred actions. Humans are not the creators, suppliers, or authors of salvation. We are only servants of the Lord and recipients of the divine actions.

Tensions in the Rite of
the Lord's Supper/Eucharist/Communion

As with baptism, the Lord's Supper is an equally divisive concern for the church. Even though the Supper was intended to be symbolic of the church's community, service, and oneness (cf. John 13:12–14, 34–35), the Apostle Paul had to condemn the early Corinthian believers for their misunderstanding and misuse of the Supper as a means for causing divisiveness in the community of faith (1 Cor 11:17–22). The situation has hardly improved since that time. On October 1–3, 1529 an important meeting took place in Marburg between Martin Luther and Ulrich Zwingli for the possible purpose of exploring the working together of two branches of early Protestantism. Their agenda included fifteen doctrinal articles. They agreed on fourteen and most of the fifteenth one (which dealt with the elements of the Lord's Supper, but on the last point the conversation collapsed and the conversations were never renewed. Disputes over the Supper have since multiplied. We can simply review the many meanings attached to the

Supper to sense the range of differences in the positions of the various churches and denominations.

To begin, for many Christians the Supper is understood by the meaningful term "the Eucharist" (from the Greek *eucharistia* meaning "thanksgiving") that emphasizes the gracious prayer of Jesus at the Last Supper in giving thanks to God for the shared elements at the Table (Luke 22:17, 19; Matt 26:27) and for the divine plan of redemption. Moreover, the church continues to express its gratitude for the divine gifts, especially in the giving of Jesus' life for our salvation.[14]

Various Views of the Supper

Although implications have continued to evolve since Vatican II, the usual understanding of the Supper for Roman Catholics has been designated as "transubstantiation," which implies that in the mass there is a transformation: "Under the appearances of bread and wine, the body and blood of Christ are truly, really and substantially present, as the grace-producing food of our souls."[15] Accordingly, the Council of Trent declared concerning the species or elements: "it is very true . . . for Christ, whole and entire, exists under the species of bread, and under each particle of that species; and whole under the species of wine, and under its separate parts" (*Lauda Sion Salvatorem* xiii, 3).

Most Protestants have regarded such a view with grave questions, including the amended position that has frequently been termed "consubstantiation," which rejects the direct transformation of the elements into the body and blood of Jesus and asserts Christ's very "Real Presence" as accompanying ("in, with, and under") the elements. Traditionally, Lutherans have asserted that in the eating of the elements Christ's body and blood are actually received orally (*manducatio oralis*) and not in some insubstantial, incorporeal, or spiritual form. They also have held that in order for the real presence of Christ to be experienced on earth at the altar, there is a direct current conjoining of the humanity and the divinity of Christ on earth (*communicatio idiomatum*).[16] Moreover, Lutherans normally

---

[14]As I indicated in Gerald L. Borchert, *Worship in the New Testament: Divine Mystery and Human Response* (St. Louis: Chalice Press, 2008), 40, one of the themes of Luke is prayer, and here Jesus is said to have given thanks for both elements. The order of the elements differs from Matthew, leading some scholars to speculate about which Passover cup is meant. The problem with undestandig the Jewish order, however, is that the Passover ceremony is *haggadah* and not *halakah* (legally determined). Concerning the various views of the Lord's Supper, I also with to acknowledge my indebtedness to several former doctoral students for sharing with me their understandings of the various views of the Supper. Traditions here are also somewhat varied.

[15]See Attwater, *A Catholic Dictionary*, 177. For a further discussion on the Roman Catholic view of the Supper, see Joseph Ratzinger, *Feast of Faith* (San Francisco: Ignatius, 1986).

[16]See Philip H. Pfatteicher, *Commentary on the Lutheran Book of Worship* (Minneapolis: Augsburg-Fortress, 1990) and John Reumann, *The Supper of the Lord: The New Testament, Ecumenical Dialogues, and*

assert that the eating of the elements does not depend on faith that guarantees the objectivity of the rite (*manducatio indignorum*).

The Anglicans likewise generally reject transubstantiation but hold to a clear view of the "Real Presence" that is regarded neither as local nor physical.[17] Although many do not regard the Thirty-Nime Articles to be determinative, some would assert with article 28 that "Transubstantiation (or the change of the substance of bread and wine) in the Supper of the Lord, cannot be proved by holy writ; but is repugnant to the plain words of Scripture, overthroweth the nature of a sacrament, and hath given occasion to many superstitions." Because there is no clearly defined statement/understanding concerning the meaning of the Real Presence, however, there are a number of interpretations as to what the Real Presence means in the Anglican Communion. Furthermore, having been an invited observer of the workings of the Anglican Consultative Committee, I have witnessed views range from an Anglo-Catholic perspective of a "virtualism" in which the Holy Spirit descends on the elements to a more evangelical view in which the elements become the body and blood of Christ only when they are received by faith.

The Supper for those in the Reformed tradition has a very different meaning. They assert that the elements of bread and wine are sacred or sacramental, physical "signs" that point to Christ's presence but that these signs have no objective efficacy in themselves without the accompanying Word of God.[18] Rejecting both the Catholic view of transubstantiation and the Lutheran view that relies on a theory of the union of the two natures of Christ present in the elements, these Reformed/Presbyterian Christians yet assert that the sacred rite is not to be interpreted as just an intellectual apprehension as over against those who regard the Supper as an ordinance. Instead, they generally follow John Calvin who clearly asserted that even though Christ's human body is with God, the Spirit "transfuses life into us" and the elements "represent to us the invisible nourishment . . . from the body and blood of Christ" and "[i]n the mystery of the supper . . . Christ

---

Faith and Order on the Eucharist (Philadelphia: Fortress, 1985). For further insights comparing Lutheran and Roman Catholic views, see Paul C. Empie and T. Austin Murphy, eds. *The Eucharist as Sacrifice*, vol. 3, Lutherans and Catholics in Dialogue (Minneapolis: Augsburg, 1974).

[17]For several examples of Anglican/Episcopal thinking, see Marion Hatchett, *Commentary on the American Prayer Book* (New York: Seabury, 1981) and Eric L. Mascall, *Corpus Christi*, 2nd ed. (London: Longmans, 1965).

[18]For further information on the Reformed view of the Supper, see for example Oscar Cullmann and F.J. Leenhardt, *Essays on the Lord's Supper* (Richmond: John Knox, 1958) and J.J. von Allmen, *The Lord's Supper* (London: Lutterworth, 1969). See also Robert J. Stamps, *The Sacrament of the Word Made Flesh: The Eucharistic Theology of Thomas F. Torrance* in Rutherford Studies in Contemporary Theology (Edinburgh: Rutherford House, 2007).

is truly exhibited to us . . . procur[ing] our justification." Thus, it demonstrates "that we may be united into one body with him, and . . . made partakers of his substance" (cf. Calvin's *Institutes* 4. 17. 1 and 4.17.11). These Reformed believers thus interpret the Lord's Supper as a revitalizing seal in which faith "is refreshed by spiritual food" (*Second Helvetic Confession,* c. 21).

The Methodist-Wesleyan view of the Supper reflects an intriguing mixture[19] in that John Wesley adopted Article 28 from Anglicanism's Thirty-Nine Articles and rejected both the Roman Catholic and Lutheran perspectives. He affirmed the real presence of Christ and the Supper as a means of grace, but he also rejected a memorialist view such as affirmed by Ulrich Zwingli. But Wesley accepted the concept of the "Spiritual Presence" of Christ's body and blood in the sacrament, somewhat akin to that of Calvin. Reflecting his multifaceted roots in the Anglican traditions, Wesley focused on the spiritual presence of Christ while at the same time viewing Communion both as a means for converting the unbeliever and equally as a means of sanctifying the believer. Fitness for taking the sacrament, he held, was not a requirement, but a clear perception concerning "our utter sinfulness and helplessness" was necessary (*Wesley's Works*, 1:280).

Finally, I turn to the broad spectrum of Evangelical, Believers,' and Free Church traditions.[20] Baptists in Great Britain tend to adopt a view that the Supper is a sacrament, whereas many Baptists in the United States view the rite as an ordinance" (which they understand as an obedient response to the command of Jesus Christ). Many evangelicals consider that the words "Do this in remembrance" mean that the Supper is interpreted as a memorial of Christ's death, while others add the proclamation of the resurrection. Many would prefer to employ the term Communion for this sacred action and emphasize the aspect of Christian fellowship (*koinonia*) in the Supper.

There is a difference in some churches between those who practice "Open Communion" and those who practice "Closed Communion." Some of the former may accept anyone who is baptized into Christ from other denominations if they currently profess Christ as their Savior and Lord. Others in the former category may accept only those who have been baptized as believers, considering that infant baptism is really not baptism. Those in the latter category, however, tend

---

[19]For examples of the Wesleyan perspective, see Laurence H. Stookey, *Eucharist: Christ's Feast with the Church* (Nashville: Abingdon, 1993) and Geoffrey Wainwright, *Eucharist and Eschatology* (London: Epworth, 1971).

[20]For a helpful review, see Millard J. Erickson, "The Lord's Supper," in *The People of God: Essays on the Believer's Church,* eds. Paul Basden and David S. Dockery (Nashville: Broadman, 1991), 51–62.

only to accept those who have been baptized and are members in good standing in their own church or community of faith.

Additional Comments

At this point it is appropriate to add a few general comments concerning the Supper. Many evangelicals tend to focus the experience of Communion on introspection and remember the sacrifice that Jesus made for us as humans rather than also considering the aspects of joy and proclamation. As a result, the Supper has become a very solemn time in the worship experience. This pattern, obviously, involves examination (1 Cor 11:28) that is present in other Christian faith communities. But in evangelical traditions many Communion tables are enshrined with the words "In Remembrance," which gives the impression of going to a funeral or visiting a cemetery. But I frequently suggest to these Christians the need to reflect on Paul's profound three-dimensional view of the Supper. The Table definitely looks back in remembrance to Christ's sacrificial death, but the Table is also a present act that reaffirms a commitment to the living Christ. And, the Supper is equally a futuristic proclamation that anticipates Christ's glorious return (cf. 1 Cor 11:26). I would thus encourage all Christians to express the multiple dimensions of the faith in their celebration.

But have you pondered why so many Protestant churches have restricted their practice of the Table to once quarterly. Have we forgotten its meaning? Is it a mere "tack-on" to an already crowded service? Has it lost its celebrative focus? Do we long for the return of Christ, as Paul did? I doubt that Paul viewed the Supper either as a rare event or a commonplace experience. Maybe we need to rethink what we are doing in this sacred action of the church. Are we glorifying God in our encounter around the Table?[21] And, how do those thin wafers in some churches or neatly sliced pieces of bread in other churches represent the broken or ripped-apart body of Christ? And how do we communicate the precious pouring out of Christ's blood with our little plastic cups of prefilled wine or grape juice?

I understand our health concerns on the one hand and the necessity of delivering the elements by a fleet of servers in large congregations on the other. But how can we make this experience of the painful upper room event and the later joyous meeting of the risen Christ in that room more meaningful today? How

---

[21]For some interesting insights into the Supper from Max Thurian, a brother of the Community of Taizé, see *The Eucharistic Memorial*, 2 vols., in Ecumenical Studies (Richmond, VA: John Knox Press, 1960, 1961). See also A.J.B. Higgins, *The Lord's Supper in the New Testament* in SBT (Chicago: Alec. R. Anderson, 1952).

can we bring the two events together in a strategic service for believers? That question should be a haunting tension challenge for the church.

But even more serious is the issue concerning the fact that the Lord's Supper has been effectively separated from the actual meals of the church. Why do we not celebrate the Lord's Supper when we have church meals together? I could, of course, ask many more questions but let me end this section with a forward look.

As we all move into the future, how can the church's celebration of the Lord's Supper become even more effective in communicating the multidimensional nature of the death, resurrection, and return of our Lord? How can we as Christians so divided in our interpretations of the Supper proclaim that Jesus has called Christians to love one another (John 13:34–35) and to exhibit the unity as Jesus prayed (17:21)? How can we move beyond rationalistic approaches to the Supper to a greater emphasis of the communal nature of the Supper? The sense of oneness and community that Jesus in John 13 so vividly portrayed in washing the disciples' feet is a picture that should be scorched into our psyches as Christians. We are a people with a message of a living self-sacrificing Jesus, not a mere past remembrance of death. We are a people who celebrate a community of caring for others, not a group of tired veterans who tell stories from our past. And we are a people who joyously proclaim Christ today and anticipate the eschatological Supper with our Savior in the future.

An Illustration on the Church's Sacred Actions

In concluding this brief discussion on the church's sacred actions, I turn to an instructive illustration. As I indicated elsewhere,[22] at the close of the last century, the world experienced a growing sense of protectionism and provincialism among the nations that in a large measure was a reaction to the fact that the world was also experiencing a contrasting psychological sense of shrinking into a global community. In the church another phenomenon was also taking place.

During the eighteenth and nineteenth centuries the Western churches in their missionary goal of converting the "heathen" had agreed to carve up the two-thirds world in order not to overlap too much in their evangelistic efforts. The idea was perhaps admirable in that missionaries would not have to compete in their mission efforts. During the early twentieth century, however, a number of church leaders realized that their perspectives on church relationships needed to be revised becase Christians in the two-thirds world were becoming more mobile. This mobility led to the beginning of cooperative efforts among some

---

[22] Gerald L. Borchert, "Review of the 20th Century and the Church" in *RevExp* 96 (1999), 347–355.

international missionary executives. Questions then naturally arose about differences in theology. The leaders called an international meeting at Lausanne in 1927 to discuss differences in theology, and the topic chosen was the Lord's Supper. Each denominational family presented its statement on the topic, after which total confusion reigned since all the groups outlined their crucial understandings of the Supper and what was for them non-negotiable.

The original plan of the organizers was to conclude the conference with a joint celebration of the Supper, but instead the meeting was ready to be dissolved because of the discord. Prior to the break-up, however, Anglican Bishop Brent asked the representatives to join him in an extended silent prayer for the Christians in various parts of the worldwide church. Then finally he asked them if they might close with the Lord's Prayer. Perhaps, he suggested, as Christians they could at least pray together. As the result of that prayer meeting, the conference did not break up. And amazingly the conference did conclude with the Lord's Supper, although not all participated in taking the elements.

Prayer saved that theological meeting, and the outcome of the Lausanne meeting ultimately led to the formation of the World Council of Churches in 1948.[23] The strengths and weaknesses of that later body have been vigorously debated, in part because of disagreements over fundamental issues beyond the general confession that "Jesus is Savior" and a lack of agreement over the meanings of "Baptism, Eucharist and Ministry," the title of a significant document that has seen countless dialogs and papers since 1982.[24]

But perhaps what can be learned from this illustration is the fact that genuine Christian love does not demand conformity as the foundation for fellowship and perhaps we can learn again that prayer may be the most powerful "sacred action" that God has given to the church. Perhaps, also, as the Church emerges into the future and faces new transitions yet unknown it will truly discover the secret of unity in diversity.

And these perceptions of the church and its structure, message, service, and sacred actions naturally lead me to the subject of living a transformed life as a citizen of two kingdoms.

---

[23]For the early history of the World Council of Churches, see David Gaines, *The World Council of Churches: A Study of Its Background and History* (Peterborough, NH: Richard R. Smith, 1966), especially 145–56.

[24]See *Baptism, Eucharist and Ministry* (Geneva: World Council of Churches, 1982).

Chapter 12

Living with Dual Citizenship[1]

Tensions in Living as a Part of the Kingdom of God and of an Earthly State

The Nature of Dual Citizenship

I was born a Canadian but a number of years later, after having finished both arts and law degrees at the University of Alberta, I moved to the United States to study theology. Then I married a wonderful American woman student of theology and also became a professor and a United States citizen. When I applied for U.S. citizenship, a unique Canadian law at the time indicated that I would not lose my Canadian citizenship. The U.S. immigration agent clearly understood that fact, so I have had the somewhat fascinating privilege of being a citizen of two countries. As a result, I have often carried two passports as I have traveled to countries around the world. But because I have been a citizen of two countries, some people have asked if that has caused me any problems. Not really, because most of the state requirements are very similar and I have never tried to test any issues that might be in conflict

As I reflect on the issue of Christian citizenship, I want to emphasize with the Preacher in his sermon of Hebrews that Christians should have a vision like Abraham of a city "whose maker and builder is God" (Heb 11:10).[2] Indeed, Christians have a dual citizenship: they are citizens in the phenomenal world (a country on earth) and of a non-earthly, eternal realm of God. Could this fact cause any tensions? The answer could be different than that regarding my earthly dual citizenship. Dallas Willard identified this tension in his reflections on the Sermon on the Mount in Matthew as a divine conspiracy on the part of Jesus by likening Christians to apprentices with Jesus. Believers are in training to become the "salt of the earth" and the "light of the world" in Christ's mission of human transformation.[3] Willard's views were then enhanced by Scot McKnight who

---

[1] A significant amount of material contained in this chapter arises from the Russell Bradley Jones Lectureship that I delivered at Carson-Newman University, "Are Christians Captured by Jesus or Culture," in *Carson-Newman Studies* 11.4 (Fall 2009): 7–18, a revision of which is to be published shortly in *PRSt*.

[2] For a helpful discussion of this text, see William L. Lane, *Hebrews 9–13*, WBC (Dallas: Word, 1991), 351–53.

[3] See Dallas Willard, *The Divine Conspiracy: Discovering our Hidden Life in God* (San Francisco: Harper, 1998).

viewed this kingdom conspiracy in terms of conversion as humans surrendering to King Jesus, discipleship as being mastered by the biblical story and mastering it for themselves, and the eschatological expectation as humans sensing in part the reality of the coming kingdom and being impelled forward to God's new world.[4] Those who have read my earlier chapter 6 will immediately recognize the close connection of McKnight's three segments here to what I have indicated as Paul's three stages of salvation.

The Basic Character of Authentic Christian Citizenship

What then does it mean to be the people of God or citizens of Christ's realm? Christians are expected to evidence God's characteristics. Particularly are they to emulate God, who loved the world and gave his one and only Son (John 3:16) to be the Savior of the world (4:42) so that the people of the world might not be condemned (3:17). And in writing his first epistle, John further declared that authentic people of God are to be known by their lives of love and not merely by their talk about loving others (1 John 3:17–18; cf. John 13:34–35). The difference was crucial because John's recipients were not acting like Christians. For John, rejecting others was akin to the behavior of Cain who was a murderer and was aligned with the devil (1 John 3:12, John 8:44). Now, our society does not like to hear such remarks. They are not "politically correct." In fact, George Barna's research indicates that 71 percent of people surveyed do not believe in the devil.[5]

But the Bible is clear that theological talk alone does not make humans into the people of God. Jesus knew that humans can piously murder, cheat, rape, steal, and destroy (people, things, and reputations) in the name of God. It happens repeatedly. The God and Father of Jesus is hardly the author of a Jihad or the originator of warring crusades. The God of the New Testament likewise is scarcely an advocate today of cheating people out of their savings by cleverly manipulating the stock market, of despoiling the creation in the name of progress, of contemporary ethnic cleansings, of apartheid, or of the subjection of women. Such a god is a pseudo-god, one fashioned after selfish, human desires. Such a god is nothing less than an idolatrous apparition and is characteristic of the devilish ways of Satan who is a liar, indeed a murderer from the beginning (John 8:44) and prowls the world like a ravenous lion seeking to destroy all that is good (1 Pet 5:8–9).

---

[4] See Scot McKnight, The Kingdom Conspiracy: Returning to the Radical Mission of the Local Church (Grand Rapids: Brazos, 2014), 36–42.

[5] See the comments of George Barna concerning, How can we believe in demons if we don't even believe in the devil? in The Barna Report: What Americans Believe (Ventura, CA: Regal Books, 1991), 206.

Being Citizens of God's Kingdom While Living in the World

More precisely, as John Elliot in his work on 1 Peter has clearly enunciated, Peter challenges Christians to recognize that they are like exiles, displaced persons or homeless people (1 Pet 1:1) awaiting their ultimate entry into their heavenly home.[6] Christians are in fact citizens of another world, born anew to a "priceless" destiny (1:4–5). Because of this destiny, Christians can live in a hostile, tainted world as models of another realm. They can accept persecution and suffering, as Jesus instructed in the Beatitudes (Matt 5:10–12), because they know life in this world is for a short time in comparison to eternity (1 Pet 5:10; 4:12–14).[7]

Furthermore, Christians acknowledge a king who is not of this world (John 18:36). Because of Christ Jesus, they are citizens of another world; they can contribute to the betterment of this transient world while also critiquing its evil patterns, both religious and secular. And, Christians do not seek to escape from this world, just as Jesus did not pray that his followers should be taken out of the world.[8] Instead, Jesus' concern was that his followers should be kept from evil and from the clutches of the evil one (17:15). Thus, the Christian perspective is neither a denying escapism from the world nor a compromising syncretism that involves the self-seeking, misguided, culturally-controlled way of this world. Christians are called to challenge the world with the model of Jesus who came to be a light of the world (John 8:12, 9:5). But to follow Jesus means that Christians must be authentic in their lives and in their approach to the world. Accordingly, Christ's kingdom actually involves the great tension inherent in a counter-revolution to the work of the devil in our culture.

Clues to this kingdom were given in the brief incarnation life of Jesus. When Jesus cast out the unclean spirit from the man in the synagogue, humans were totally stunned (Mark 1:27). In another episode, when Jesus was sleeping peacefully in the boat and a great storm arose on the Sea of Galilee, the disciples were terrified. But when they wakened Jesus, he stood up and shouted to the storm "shut up" or "be muzzled" (as the Greek states)! Were the disciples ready for such a display of power? I think not! In shocked amazement, they asked: "Who is this guy?" (Mark 4:35–40). They concluded: "He's spooky! As I retell this story, I remind my students that in the academy we have a special Latin expression for

---

[6] See John H. Elliot, *A Home for the Homeless: A Sociological Exegesis of 1 Peter, Its Situation and Strategy* (Philadelphia: Fortress, 1981).

[7] For my discussion on persecution in 1 Peter, see Gerald L. Borchert, "The Conduct of Christians in the Face of the 'Fiery Ordeal'" (4:12–5:11) in *RevExp* 79 (1982): 451–62.

[8] See my comments in Gerald L. Borchert, *John 12–21*, vol. 25B, NAC (Nashville: Broadman & Holman, 2002), 200–01.

that phenomenon. We call it the *mysterium tremendum*. Yet even though we may identify it, we hardly comprehend such power. It really means "Jesus is spooky!"[9]

We need to admit that Jesus and the Kingdom are actually a mystery to us and that reality leaves us in a quandary because there is a power in Jesus that we cannot explain. When Jesus said "if I by the finger of God cast out demons," he expected his listeners would recognize that it was a sign of the Kingdom (cf. Luke 11:20). Pharaoh learned what the little finger of God could do (cf. Exod 8;19) and when he did not respond correctly, Pharaoh experienced fear, the death of his son, and ultimately the destruction of his cavalry. God is not some toy that we can direct by remote control. Nor is Jesus a spineless St. Nick who supplies all our wishes. Jesus is God. When God sent Jesus, God was not playing games with humans. God was sending a divine message. Paying attention to this message is crucial.

Jesus' kingdom is not like any other kingdom, and its citizens are intended to be transforming persons in the world. They are strangely akin to the *anawim*, the Hebrew for the poor and the dispossessed. Yet they are heirs of God's kingdom (Cf. Matt 5:3) and of Father Abraham (Gal 3:29). Therefore, even though they appear to be meek, hungry, and persecuted, they are in fact the strong of the world (Matt 5:4–10; cf. Rom 15:1–6) because they are the salt of the earth and the hope-filled lamps of the world (Matt 5:13–16).[10] Nevertheless, as members of the Kingdom, Christians live in a genuine state of tension. They live in two worlds. They should not need the praise and adoration of other humans to affirm their commitments to true piety (cf. Matt 6:1–18, 19-21; John 12:42–43), but in their humanity they must repeatedly ask the haunting question: Are we after the praise of humans and the wealth of culture?[11]

And I must quickly add that both Jesus and Paul indicate that this kingdom is not marked merely by words but by power (cf. 1 Cor 4:20). Jesus commissioned his followers not only to preach but also to confront the powerful realm of the evil one so that the restoration of the sick and the oppressed might take place (cf. Mark 6:7–13, Matt 10: 1–15, Luke 9:1–6). That mission of Jesus has

---

[9]For a further analysis of this text, see Gerald L. Borchert, "What Is God Doing in the Storm?" in W.H. Gloer, ed., *Following Jesus* (Macon, GA: Smyth & Helwys, 1994), 7–11.

[10]For an excellent treatment of these verses, see Robert Guelich, *The Sermon on the Mount: A Foundation for Understanding* (Waco, TX: Word, 1982), 119–133. See also Donald A. Hagner, Matthew 1–13, vol. 33A, WBC (Dallas: Word Books, 1993), 91–102 and Charles Talbert, *Reading the Sermon on the Mount: Character Formation and Decision Making in Matthew 5–7* (Grand Rapids: Baker, 2006).

[11]It is easy to be drawn into cultural relativism and sacrifice the way of Christ. For further insights into our task as Christians in confronting the accepted norms of our society, see for example Paul Chamberlain, *Talking About Good and Bad without Getting Angry* (Downers Grove, IL: InterVarsity, 2005).

not changed. We are to be authentic agents of transformation in a broken and conflicted world. Yet you may ask: What really do we find?

Christians and Inauthentic Citizenship

When the world sees Christians fighting among ourselves while at the same time claiming to be the followers of the Prince of Peace (cf. Isa 9:6, Luke 2:11, Eph 2:14), it easily recognizes that Christians are simply play-acting, just like the hypocritical Pharisees in the time of Jesus. I cannot help but add here an experience I had while living and teaching in Jerusalem.

On a Palm Sunday after attending a worship service at a nearby church, I walked over to the Church of the Holy Sepulchre. There, two priests of different Christian traditions were pushing and fighting each other because they both thought that it was their time to control access to the traditional site of Jesus' tomb. Their concern, of course, was to gain the maximum amount of time for donations from pilgrims. One group had obviously gone over time. Just think about the implications: fighting over the tomb of Jesus whose body was not even there!

Then, I learned a sad story about that church. When the Israelis recaptured Jerusalem in their War of Liberation, they took over the keys from the Muslim family who had been the church's doorkeepers for more than a hundred years. Then the Israelis gave the keys to the Roman Catholics in trust for all the Christian traditions that had access to the site. But the jealousies that emerged were so intense that the Roman Catholics actually gave the keys back to the Muslim family to calm the tensions and disputes that had arisen among the Christians. Do not think that the Jews and the Muslims in Jerusalem are unaware concerning the pettiness of the Christians in that church!

But, as Protestants, please do not be too ready to dismiss such illustrations as pertaining to Orthodox and Roman Catholic Christians alone. Instead, consider: How do you think the world regards Protestants in their cultural, self-righteous squabbles in the name of Jesus? Do you think the world does not know about our pettiness and in-fighting? Perhaps it would be well for us to reread some texts from the New Testament and apply them to ourselves and not simply direct arrows of guilt toward others (see John 13:34; Rom 12:9, 13:8; 1 Cor 13:1–13; 2 Cor 5:14; 1 Pet 2:17; 1 John 2:10, 3:17, 4:7; cf. also Gal 5:6; Eph 4:15, 5:2; Phil 1:9; Col 1:4, 3:14; etc.).[12] Do our patterns as believers and churches actually represent the Jesus of the New Testament?

---

[12]While Christians may take sides on issues related to theological differences, we should be aware of the

I have taught Baptists, Episcopalians, Lutherans, Methodists, Presbyterians, Orthodox, and many other Christians including various charismatic students over the last number of years and many of those students have told me that they wonder whether their church is messed up. I appeal to all of us that we present an authentic model of Jesus to our young people. We should ask ourselves: Which model of citizenship will we choose: the human side of our citizenship or the model of citizenship demonstrated by Jesus? That question is very crucial as the church faces the future.

If we verbally, organizationally, or otherwise castigate others with whom we disagree, it is only a small step in following the devil to destroy their reputations, to ruin them economically, and ultimately to eliminate them. Many Nazis were faithful Protestant churchgoers. But here I do not need to focus on the well-known stories concerning German Lutherans because when I taught in Germany, I discovered some very disturbing facts concerning my own tradition. It became clear that colleagues in my tradition also sang the praises of Adolph Hitler because he promised to clean up the morals of the country. They also pandered him with attention in order to achieve some of their political and religious goals.

I have told my students a number of stories, but one has always stood out. It was finding a picture in the archives of the seminary in which the principal/president was wearing a "Nazi brown shirt." I trust you know what such a picture means! I, as a dean in an American seminary, could not help but ask myself: How had that German Christian leader handled the tension over citizenship? Had he modeled the pattern of Jesus, or had he sided with cultural nationalism? What would I have done if I were in his place?

This experience has haunted me since those times I taught in Germany and has forced me to remember that we are only one step removed in our American democracy from following in the path of the Christians who accepted Hitler in hopes of obtaining an ethical renewal of Germany. So, I read with appreciation the perceptive editorial in *Christianity Today* by Timothy Dalrymple[13] where he sought to explain why evangelicals related to the 2020 presidential election in two ways. He categorized well-meaning Christians as either viewing themselves as part of the Church Regnant (those who recognized the weaknesses of the presi-

---

impact that such disputes have on the integrity of the Christian witness to the world. See for example the sad story of Protestant in-fighting—illustrated in Harold Lindsell, *The Battle for the Bible* (Grand Rapids: Zondervan, 1976)—which continues today.

[13]See the editorial by Timothy Dalrymple, "Why Evangelicals Disagree on the President: The Reason We're Divided, and How We Can Come Together," *Christianity Today*, Nov. 2, 2020.

dent with the hope of protecting the Christian way of life) and the others as part of the Church Remnant (those who refused to accept the president's weaknesses as a justification for his unchristian behavior, especially with the weak among us). Although Dalrymple correctly admits oversimplification here, initially his categories starkly remind me of the German confessing church and those Christians who went along with Hitler in hopes of purifying Germany. They both believed, at least at first, that they had good motives.

So, I would hardly single out for criticism my German brothers and sisters, because we in the United States of America could easily have done the same. Therefore, I must ask us as Christians: How does the world regard some of us as Christian leaders when we pander to politicians in order to be recognized and achieve our political goals? While we have different opinions on what it means to be the "salt of the earth" and the "light of the world," we must never excuse greed or immorality or agree to override the needs of the poor and helpless among us. Perhaps, as the result of the Covid-19 pandemic, God will awaken Christians to remember long after it passes the plight of the needy in our midst.

We are called to be authentic. Will we heed that call? Prejudice and intolerance can be found around the world. The devil and his servants will do all in their power to keep Christians from being true citizens of God's kingdom and the realm of Jesus Christ.

The Significance of Authentic Christian Citizenship

I must point out here that the Baptists of Germany since the Second World War have learned a significant lesson from their Hitler experience. They no longer permit national flags in their church sanctuaries. But what about our patterns of flags in Protestant churches in North America? Look around your church sanctuary and then ask: Does our church represent a citizenship with Jesus or with culture It is a tough, unsettling question.[14]

I would challenge us to ask another question: What about our worship? Is it actually focused on Jesus or on performance—an important aspect of cultural acceptance? Both in music and preaching, where is our focus? Do we croon or yell into microphones to gain the attention to us? Or, are we actually centered on Jesus?

---

[14]Where do you stand on the issue of allegiance? See for example the work of David Crump, *I Pledge Allegiance: A Believer's Guide to Kingdom Citizenship in the Twenty-first Century* (Grand Rapids: Eerdmans, 2018). See also "Church and State," chapter 5 of D.A Carson, *Christ and Culture Revisited* (Grand Rapids: Eerdmans, 2008).

So, while focusing on authentic citizenship, I am reminded that the Apostle Paul understood very clearly the nature, characteristics, and benefits of citizenship. He was a Roman citizen by birth and when they beat him and incarcerated him in Philippi without knowing his citizenship, he knew it was a serious breach of his political rights (Acts 16:22, 38–39). His citizenship was also a determining factor in the way the Tribune halted Paul's "trial by beating" in Jerusalem's Antonio Fortress (22:24–29) and in his subsequent assignment of a huge protective force to assure that he would be delivered safely to the governor's headquarters in Caesarea (23:23). His citizenship also gave him the authority to appeal his case directly to the emperor, and no provincial governor or local king could stand in the way of his direct access to the throne of Caesar (25:10–12; 26:32).

These rights of citizenship gave Paul a strategic perspective in his discussions concerning Christian citizenship. Even the concept of the Roman Empire as the household of Caesar (cf. Phil 4:22) is crucial to his understanding of God's kingdom as God's household in the Pauline letters (e.g., Eph 2:19, Gal 6:10). Thus, as Caesar was Lord of his household (empire), Paul understood Christ as the Lord of his divine kingdom (household) on earth. But notice the important point here: The early Christians refused to call Caesar their Lord, and they were willing to suffer death for their loyalty to Jesus.

But that reality only mirrors the fact that Paul regarded Christian integrity as crucial and that is the reason he discusses so many issues in the Corinthian correspondence that deals with authenticity. Both Paul and John clearly asserted that the early Christians should be fearless even in the face of persecution. They were convinced that Jesus, as the Son of God, was their Lord and was equal with God (Phil 2:6; cf. John 5:18). The reason for such a lofty understanding of lordship and preeminence is that Jesus was active in the creation itself and therefore the indisputable Lord even of the earthly Caesar (cf. Col 1: 15–20; John1:1–5; 20:28, 31). Paul would willingly acknowledge Jesus as sovereign but not willingly anyone else (Rom 1:1). Moreover, Paul firmly believed that at the end every tongue would confess that "Jesus Christ is Lord" to God's glory (Phil 2:11).

But I have been asked what such a confession means. Does "confess" (*exhomologēsētai*) here include unbelievers and enemies of Jesus? Does it mean that unbelievers will finally confess "Jesus is Lord"? Does it mean that such people will begrudgingly admit they were on the wrong side? Does the statement include judgment? That concept may be gained from the book of Revelation when the rider on the white horse—whose name is the "Word of God"—slays his enemies (Rev 19:11–21). Yet I doubt that these views provide the meaning.

Gerald Hawthorne[15] would also doubt such speculations, and he translates the Greek as "thankfully acknowledge." I am of the opinion that the statement was meant to be understood as a universal acclamation of Jesus. Acclamations were common in the Roman world, but this acclamation goes far beyond the empire-wide acclamations that the Roman Caesars expected from their subjects, because it involves every tongue (*pasa glōssa*). To press the statement further, however, requires great care because other answers are speculative. Yet as an assertion of faith, Paul's universal acclamation of Jesus in the context of Jesus' *kenōsis* (his emptying) is truly a magnificent contrast.

Living with a Two-Kingdom Perspective

The issue of God's realm involves a serious tension that Luther, Bonhoeffer, and others have since identified as the doctrine of the two kingdoms.[16] Christians are citizens of these two realms, a matter Jesus addressed briefly in the question raised concerning paying taxes to Caesar (cf. Mark 12:13–17, Matt 22:15–22, Luke 20:20–26). While Christians owe national allegiance to the nations in which they are citizens, their ultimate loyalties belong not to Caesar (or some nation) but to God. They ought to pay their legitimate taxes to civil governments and obey the laws of the land in which they live. But when issues of morality and loyalty to Christ collide with loyalty to the state, then as Oscar Cullmann and Walter Wink have indicated, Christians are duty-bound to engage the conflicting powers and give the priority to God (Mark 12:17).[17]

The issue of conflicting priorities of obedience is often encountered for Christians in such matters as the bearing of arms and service in the military, including the use of weapons to kill others. In this regard, it is interesting to note in the Apostolic Constitutions (c. 380) that although the labors of many were condemned as less than Christian, the role of being soldier was affirmed with Constantine.[18] While scholars continue to debate the legitimacy of just war

---

[15]Gerald F. Hawthorne, *Philippians*, vol. 43, WBC (Waco, TX: Word Books, 1983), 75, 93–96.

[16]See for example Dietrich Bonhoeffer's views of the *regnum gratiae* and the *regnum naturae* in his *Ethics*, ed. E. Bethge (New York; Macmillan, 1965), 196–207.

[17]See the discussion in Oscar Cullmann, *The State in the New Testament* (New York: Charles Scribner's Sons, 1956/London; SCM, 1957) and Walter Wink, *Engaging the Powers* (Minneapolis: Fortress, 1992).

[18]The *Apostolic Constitutions and Canons* (the *Ordinances of the Holy Apostles through Clement* [of Rome]) was undoubtedly not early but was probably written in Syria sometime around 380 AD/CE. This work indicates that a soldier is not to be rejected as a believer if he fulfills the moral obligations outlined by John the Baptist (Luke 3:14), but such a dispensation is not given to athletes and actors. Thus, "If one belonging to the theatre ... whether it be man or woman, or charioteer, or dueller, or racer, or player of prizes, or Olympic gamester, or one that plays on the pipe, on the lute, or on the harp at those games, or a dancing master, or a huckster, either let them leave off their employment or let them be rejected" (*Apostolic*

theories with Paul Ramsay and others,[19] it seems more appropriate not to attempt to justify war, but to recognize as with divorce that war is tragic. Moreover, we should not forget that in the Beatitudes Jesus reminds us that peacemakers are blessed and designated as children of God (Matt 5:9).

In democratic countries, change of national perspectives can be effected by elections. But not all nations are democratic or offer citizens an irenic means for changing national policy. Witness the tragedy of Tianamen Square in China where human life confronted national policy and lost. But whatever form of state government exists, the general principle for Christians is attempting to be good citizens in their earthly realm while confessing they are citizens of two realms. Christians live in the God-given tension of offering honor to whom honor is due and seeking to be obedient to the laws of the land unless and until they conflict with obedience to God (cf. Rom 13:7, 1 Pet 2:13–17). In this respect it is significant to notice the important distinction that Peter makes concerning those who are to be honored (all people), to be loved (the community of believers), and to be feared (only God). And note that the emperor is placed by Peter in the first category of those who are to be honored—not in either the second or the third (1 Pet 2:17)!

Relating to Demonic Government Patterns

While government organizations are recognized as legitimate institutions by Jesus, Paul, and Peter (cf. Mark 12:14–17, Rom 13:1–3, 1 Pet 2:13–16), it would be highly unwise to designate all or indeed any government as sacred or holy. Emil Brunner argued that "it is dangerous and fantastic to imagine that sinful [people] are capable of making the reign of justice and eternal peace a reality." And, "the prudence of Scripture does not contradict historical experience which shows that human evil … bursts forth in huge and concentrated eruptions."[20]

Indeed, some governments can be exceedingly demonic and can engender horrible dehumanizing pogroms or ethnic cleansings. Think not merely of Germany but also of places such as Afghanistan, Azerbaijan, Iraq, Rwanda, Somalia, Sudan, Syria, Yemen, and the former Soviet and Yugoslav republics—to

---

Constitutions, Book 8, Section 32).

[19]See for example Paul Ramsay, *The Just War: Force and Political Responsibility* (Lanham, MD: University Press of America, 1983 or the earlier version by Scribners, 1968). Contrast Walter Wink, *Engaging the Powers*, 209–29.

[20]See Emil Brunner, *Justice and the Social Order* (New York: Harper, 1945), 256. I think that it would be wise for all who have doubts about the possibility of the Western nations falling into devilish patterns should read Elie Wiesel's stirring account with the Preface to the twenty-fifth edition by Robert McAfee Brown, *Night* (New York: Bantam Books, 1986, 1960).

name a few. Christians must take great care not to support the legitimacy of any such activity, even at a distance or even if countries committing atrocities are supportive of the Christian's home state. Could such patterns happen in the United States? Did the Germans think it could happen in their state?

Following the destruction of Jerusalem, the Jews sought to reconstruct the Jewish religion on the basis of what became Mishnaic traditions rather than on the Temple sacrificial system. Christians were then systematically singled out and excluded from worship in the Jewish synagogues and condemned by what some have designated as the councils (the *Beth Din*) of Jamnia. Tracing this period and the history and significance of such councils is difficult today, but it is clear that after AD/CE 70 Jewish Christians were condemned by the Jews. Christians became marked people in the notorious curse of the heretics,[21] which was inserted into the twelfth of the eighteen benedictions that formed a significant aspect of Jewish worship practice. Since Christians were thus excluded from synagogues as heretics, they were no longer protected as members of a *religio licita* (a licensed religion) in the Roman Empire. And, according to Pliny, the Jews and others in hostility reported the Christians both to imperial and local authorities as practicing an unlicensed religion.[22] This conflict is one reason why John in Revelation twice categorized the Jewish religion as a "synagogue of Satan" (cf. Rev 2:9, 3:9).

This hostility to Christians is certainly reflected in the Fourth Gospel in stories such as the excommunication of the blind man (John 9:22, 34).[23] The subsequent hostility that has occurred against the Jews including the holocaust, however, is hardly justifiable, even if it had its roots in earlier historical incidents on the part of Jews. But some contemporary scholars, distressed over the Nazi pogrom, have unfortunately been far too willing to accept the Jewish criticisms that the Johannine writings are patently anti-Semitic or anti-Jewish. John was not anti-Semitic. He was a Jew who knew well the Old Testament and was highly critical of Jewish brokering of hostility against Jesus and Christians.

The negative attitude of western Europeans to Jews in the years since early Christianity is well illustrated by the figure of Shylock in Shakespeare's *The Merchant of Venice*. The audiences undoubtedly cheered as Portia entrapped the Jewish loan shark and enabled his daughter to marry outside the Jewish faith.

---

[21]For a copy of the curse of the *minim*, see C.K. Barrett, *The New Testament Background: Selected Documents* (New York: Harper, 1961), 166–67.

[22]For Pliny's correspondence with Tajan, see Henry Bettenson, ed., *Documents of the Christian Church* (London; Oxford University Press, 1943), 3–6.

[23]See my discussion concerning the blind man's exclusion from the synagogue in Gerald L. Borchert, *John 1–11*, vol. 25A, NAC (Nashville: Broadman & Holman, 1996), 319–21.

With those embedded feelings among Caucasians in Europe, it was not difficult for Hitler to argue that the Jewish ghettos ought to be eliminated.

But by way of contrast to some contemporary one-sided arguments, I should here point out the issue of the distinctions in automobile licenses used for many years in Israel between the yellow ones on Jewish cars and the green ones on Palestinian cars, perhaps legitimately representing the Green line established by Lord Balfour's separation. The problem as recognized by anyone who has lived in Israel, however, is that the green-plated cars have often been harassed at checkpoints and made to wait for very long periods of time, whereas the yellow ones were not even required to stop. It reminds me of the Nazis who forced the Jews to wear yellow stars of David. The Jews who suffered so much in the Nazi period have themselves not given justice to the Palestinians. Instead of "building bridges of peace," the Jews have built walls. The result is discouragement among the Palestinians and the enhancing of terrorism. Such is the way with humans who do not understand the way of God's love and the nature of being citizens of two kingdoms. And I should add that the situation is not different in the Muslim world where separation among Muslims has been the name of the game for centuries and has now been heightened by the oil-rich groups.

Yet we should be reminded of the ethnic mistreatment evidenced in North America by the imprisonment of natural-born and naturalized Japanese-American and Canadian citizens and the seizure of their properties. Most Christians stood silent, just as their soul-partners in Europe did with the Nazis, while the authorities and news media proclaimed lies and half-truths about all Japanese people in the name of national interest. I grew up in a German-speaking Baptist church in Canada during the Second World War, and I know what it is like to be fearful and have our churches stoned.

Since the Second World War, at least Canada has passed a constitutional amendment to the effect that a singling out of a race or an ethnic subgroup should no longer be tolerated. Yet manmade laws cannot guarantee the integrity of non-discriminatory human treatment of others—particularly minorities. Discrimination is an easy option for people who do not choose to accept differences among people. The devil, as John states, is always ready to spread lies and messages of hate (cf. John 8: 43–47 and the warnings against lying in Rev 21:8, 27 and 22:15). Christians, therefore, must learn to recognize the demonic nature of much in culture that is interpreted as national self-interest.

The Ultimate Question of Christian Citizenship

The ultimate question for Christians is: What citizenship will we choose? To whom or to what will we give our ultimate allegiance? What will tension in citizenship mean for us? Will we choose Jesus or culture? Will we model our lives according to the love of Christ or on personal and corporate self-interests that can be very powerful weapons in the hands of the devil and his servants?

In setting this series of questions in an easy framework, I turn in closing this chapter to a personal reflection on a conversation I had at Princeton with my doctoral supervisor, Otto Piper, who was a personal friend of Albert Einstein. Both were forced out of Germany and later periodically discussed their histories on a local park bench. During my study at Princeton, I served as Dr. Piper's assistant and met with scores of well-known professors from Europe who came to his home. After one meeting while sitting in his office, he told me that because he had written a major German work on Christian integrity and ethics, he was marked by the Gestapo. During the rise of the Third Reich, he was visited several times by authorities and then one day he was told he had twenty-four hours to get out of the country or be imprisoned.

As a result, he had to leave one son behind in Germany. Thus, in that war he had one son in the German military and one son in the American forces. He said to me: "Jerry, I know what God experiences when he has children on both sides of wars. You know, during the war, we had the tradition at Princeton of reading in chapel the names of those service men and women killed in action who either attended this school or were related to anyone working at this school. Well Jerry, my son in Germany was killed in that war and they read out his name in chapel. When they did so, a number of people protested that the enemy was being honored… Jerry, that young man was my son! I know a little of what God experiences in war and bloodshed."

I will never forget that story or the expression on Dr. Piper's face. And I have recounted this personal reminiscence many times because I need to ask myself the pointed question: Am I primarily a citizen of the realm of Jesus or of my cultural and national heritage? It is an ultimate question and both you and I will have to face it for the rest of our lives. But we will also have to face it when we stand before God at the end of time.

… And that statement brings me to the next chapter on Christian hope.

Chapter 13

Living with Tensions
and the Christian Hope

The Ultimate Tension of Acceptance and Judgment

The Difficulty of Communicating the Future

The concluding words of the last chapter raise for Christians a number of strategic questions concerning the future. There have been many books written on the subject of apocalyptic literature,[1] on the *parousia,* the coming of Jesus, the end of the world, and the coming judgment. And many sermons have been preached about escaping from the clutches of hell.[2] Many interpretations of the Book of Revelation have also been written,[3] including a number indicating various views of interpreting Revelation.[4] The subject is expansive, and I could add more to

[1]See for example the classic by H.H. Rowley, *The Relevance of Apocalyptic* (New York: Harper and Brothers, n.d.) as well as Leon Morris, *Apocalyptic* (Grand Rapids: Eerdmans, 1972); Paul D. Hanson, *The Dawn of Apocalyptic: The Historical and Sociological Roots of Jewish Apocalyptic Eschatology* (Philadelphia: Fortress, 1975, 1979) and J. Richard Middleton, *A New Heaven and a New Earth: Reclaiming Biblical Eschatology* (Grand Rapids: Baker Academic, 2014).

[2]For some popular works, see chapter 11 of Andrew Root, *The Pastor in a Secular Age* (Grand Rapids: Baker Academic, 2019) where he uses the theme of Jonathan Edwards' "Sinners in the Hands of an Angry God" as a basis for dealing with eschatology and escaping judgment. See also Hal Lindsey, *The Late Great Planet Earth* (Grand Rapids: Zondervan, 1970), and his even more pointed *The 1980s: Countdown to Armageddon* (King of Prussia, PA: Westgate Press, 1980); John F. Walvoord, *Armageddon, Oil and the Middle East Crisis* (Grand Rapids: Zondervan, 1974, 1990) and Tim LaHaye and Jerry B Jenkins, The Left Behind Series in 12 vols. (Carol Stream, IL: Tyndale, 1995). For an exchange on hell, see Preston Sprinkle, ed., *Four Views on Hell,* 2nd ed. (Grand Rapids: Zondervan, 2016). See also my discussion on p. 217 and C. Marvin Pate, *The End of the Age Has Come: The Theology of Paul* (Grand Rapids: Zondervan, 1995).

[3]See for example C.B. Caird, *The Revelation of St. John the Divine* (New York: Harper & Row, 1966); John F. Walvord, *The Revelation of Jesus Christ: A Commentary* (Chicago: Moody Press, 1966); Isbon T. Beckwith, *The Apocalypse of John* (Grand Rapids: Baker, 1967); Adela Yarbro Collins, *Crisis and Catharsis: The Power of the Apocalypse* (Philadelphia: Westminster, 1984); John P. Newport, *The Lion and the Lamb: A Commentary on the Book of Revelation for Today* (Nashville: Broadman, 1986); Philip Edgecumb Hughes, *The Book of Revelation: A Commentary* (Downers Grove, IL: InterVarsity, 1990); and Arthur W. Wainwright, *Mysterious Apocalypse: Interpreting the Book of Revelation* (Nashville: Abingdon, 1993). See also the magisterial work of David Aune, *Revelation 1–5, Revelation 6–16,* and *Revelation 17–22* in 3 vols. (Dallas: Word Books, 1997, 1998, 1998). For interpretations of the Book of Revelation as a drama, see John Wick Bowman, *The Drama of the Book of Revelation* (Philadelphia: Westminster, 1955); James L. Blevins, *Revelation as Drama* (Nashville: Broadman, 1984); and *Revelation in Knox Preaching Guides* (Atlanta: John Knox, 1984).

[4]See for example George Beasley-Murray, Herschel H. Hobbs and Ray Frank Robbins, *Revelation: Three Viewpoints* (Nashville: Broadman, 1977); George Eldon Ladd, Herman A Hoyt, Loraine Boettner

the bibliography because I have taught the Book of Revelation for many years and also written a commentary[5] on it. But rather than continue to cite endless bibliographical references and arguments about when the *eschaton* (the end of time) will happen, and discuss at length the nature of heaven or the temperature of hell, I propose to take you on a journey to exercise your thinking.

"How could Jesus communicate the future to his disciples?' To answer this question, we must recall that people in the Mediterranean societies during the time of Jesus were not future oriented but were present oriented, while most of us in America, Canada, and Europe are geared to thinking futuristically. But that issue leads me to a further question: How can I lift our thinking beyond the phenomenal world in this era of the "immanent frame"?[6]

Before Jesus was crucified and died, he sought to provide his followers with some insights into what they should expect in the future. But it was virtually impossible for Jesus to provide the kind of information they or we could understand or a time chart, a road map or a futuristic GPS reader that could supply dates concerning the end of time and compass coordinates and space travel directions on how to reach heaven.

Peter, James, and John in their present-oriented thinking did ask for such information concerning when events such as the destruction of the Temple would happen and even for signs of its approach (cf. Mark 13:4). Jesus did confirm that the cosmic structure would surely collapse, but he announced that not even the angels of heaven were privileged with that information. Perhaps more shocking was the fact that even he, the Son of God, did not know the time because that information was privileged to God (13:32). Moreover, Jesus warned the disciples not to be led astray by so-called predictors who would offer them phony information and wow them with tantalizing acts of power that might suggest these pseudo-prognosticators were also privileged (13:22, 32–33). Jesus strongly cautioned the disciples to remain alert and await his coming (13:33–36).[7]

---

and Anthony A. Hoekema, *The Meaning of the Millennium: Four Views*, ed. Robert G. Clouse (Downers Grove, IL: InterVarsity, 1977); and Stanley N. Gundry and C. Marvin Pate, eds., *Four Views on the Book of Revelation* (Grand Rapids: Zondervan, 1998, 2010).

[5]See Gerald Borchert, "Revelation" in the NLT Study Bible (Carol Stream, IL: Tyndale House, 2008), 2160–2205. See also my discussion on "Revelation: Anticipating Eternal Worship" in *Worship in the New Testament: Divine Mystery and Human Response* (St. Louis: Chalice Press, 2008), 214–232.

[6]The task we face today is relating to a world that has set its mind on the secular world. Perhaps the writings of James K.A. Smith, *How (Not) to be Secular: Reading Charles Taylor* (Grand Rapids: Eerdmans, 2014) and his thesis concerning the "immanent frame," as well as Andrew Root, *The Pastor in a Secular Age*, can be of assistance.

[7]For a discussion of this strategic chapter on eschatology, see for example Robert H. Stein, *Jesus, the Temple and the Coming Son of Man: A Commentary on Mark 13* (Downers Grove, IL: InterVarsity, 2014).

Yet even though Jesus tried to enlighten the disciples concerning his *parousia* (coming), the whole idea just seemed to cloud their minds because they were not really prepared for the possibility of his "departure," which Luke called his "exodus" (9:31). When Jesus suggested that they knew the way where he was going, Thomas, the realist, voiced for all the disciples that they did not have the slightest clue where Jesus was going. Then Jesus responded that he was "the way" to the Father, to which Philip replied in exasperation: "Just show us the Father!" (John 14:4–8).[8] Bewilderment had captured their minds, and they probably forgot that if Jesus granted the wish, they would be dead! They would be in the numinous presence of the "holy" (Hebrew *qodesh*) God.[9]

The sacrificial death of Jesus (the Son of God) was hardly in their image of a messiah (cf. Mark 8:31–33, 9:30–32). So, when Jesus submitted to being arrested, Peter tried to intervene by using his puny sword. Yet he hardly understood the power of this Jesus who could cause the arresting band to fall in helplessness before him (cf. John 18:5–11) or could summon an army of angelic warriors to protect him (cf. Matt 26:53). But the disciples—who boldly asserted that they would be faithful to the end (cf. 26:35)—fled the scene in fear for their lives (cf. 26:56).

Then just as readiness for Jesus' death was not part of their thinking, neither was his resurrection part of their anticipation. The scheming Jewish authorities, however, were anticipating some sort of a plot from the disciples—such as stealing the body—so the shrewd enemies set a guard at the tomb. As it turned out, the soldiers were helpless before the power of God's angelic messenger (cf. Matt 27:62–66, 28:4). But the disciples were clearly terrified because they expected to be arrested by the Jewish secret service and hauled off to prison, so they locked their chambers (cf. John 20:19). The promised resurrection of Jesus (cf. John 14:1–3, Acts 1:11) and victory over death were hardly in their minds. Dissolution was.

Concerning an Understanding of the *Parousia*

With these thoughts in our minds, let us reflect briefly on how significant the resurrection and the return of Jesus (his *parousia*) are for us. I question seriously

---

[8]See my further discussion on this Johannine text in Gerald L. Borchert, *John 12–21*, vol. 23B, NAC (Nashville: Broadman & Holman, 2002), 107–115.

[9]For a discussion of God's holiness See for example Norman H. Snaith, *The Distinctive Ideas of the Old Testament* (London: Epworth, 1944), 42–50. All one needs to recall concerning holiness is the fact that the men of Beth Shemesh died because they looked into the Ark of God's Covenant (1 Sam 6:19) and that Uzzah died when he touched the Ark in trying to keep it from falling (2 Sam 6–7). For the Hebrew people, it was an awesome and terrifying thought to encounter the presence of God (cf., for example, Gen 28:17, Exod 34:10, Deut 7:21, Ps 131:1, Dan 9:4).

whether the transcendent is much a part of our normal thinking today because it does not fit our "immanent frame" of reference. It may be that for many people God hardly permeates our thinking in the way it did for Paul in Philippians (cf. Phil 1:6, 20–23; 2:10, 16; 3:8–10, 20–21; 4:5). Perhaps this reality is one reason why we are a worried and troubled generation of Christians and why we do not evidence the great joy and confidence Paul expressed in this same letter (1:4, 15–18, 19, 29; 2:2, 11, 17–18; 3:1, 14; 4:1, 4, 9, 10–11, 13, 19–20)—even though he was in prison (1:12–14)![10]

As I indicated in chapter 12, it is really hard to live as a citizen of two realms, especially since we live in such a complex world and seek to meet all our commitments and care for the needs both of ourselves and those who mean a great deal to us. The pressures are intense and constantly weigh upon us. How can the *eschaton* (the end) compare in importance to the present concerns that constantly face us? And so we are confronted with another gripping tension in our lives: the importance of our future in our present. But in one sense we may not be very different than many of the early Christians, such as the Corinthians or Galatians, who focused on daily issues and forgot about God.

But for us in the post-enlightenment era, the future is a separate category that can easily be divided from our understanding of the present. Is not our idea of the future viewed as something akin to an insurance policy that we have somehow earned and that we put into the safety deposit boxes of our minds as a guarantee of well-being for a later time when we think we will need it? Indeed, does the *parousia* actually impact the way we use our time or spend our money in the present era? These questions go to the heart of who we are as Christians, although they may hardly be on the front burners of our minds. Yet they are concerns with which we have to deal. They cannot be treated by others.

Reflecting on the Future: From the Temporal to the Eternal [11]

So, for some perspectives on these questions I turn now to one of my intriguing hobbies. I enjoy reflecting on the state of reality beyond the normal considerations of our human experience. Will you join me in this adventure? I think it may be an intriguing opportunity for you.

---

[10]For studies on Philippians, see for example David Chapman, *Philippians: Rejoicing and Thanksgiving* (Focus on the Bible, 2012). See also Gerald F. Hawthorne, *Philippians*, vol. 43, WBC (Waco, TX: Wood Books,1983) and Gordon D. Fee, *Paul's Letter to the Philippians*, NICNT (Grand Rapids: Eerdmans, 1995)

[11]Some of the materials in this chapter reflect my earlier thinking in "Excursus 33: Questions of Eternity: Where Is the Place? What Is It Like? How Do We Get There?" in G. Borchert, *John 12–21*, 360–67.

Introducing the Concepts of Time and Eternity. While I have already introduced the subject of time in an earlier chapter, I turn now to ask you to consider first the concept of eternity. For many of us the idea of eternity is regarded as a continuum of time. But such an idea does not actually represent an adequate Christian perspective.

The Greeks had, in fact, no clear idea of eternity or even the idea of "forever." Their view of time was cyclical and repetitive, and it involved their concept of recurring eons or ages.

Christians, however, are indebted for their basic concept of time to the Hebrew understanding that time is linear. Time has a beginning and will have an end. Moreover, the Christian understanding of time is that God is working out a divine purpose for humans in the context of time. Accordingly, when the Christians came to write about their idea of eternity and "forever" in the New Testament, they were faced with a complex problem. No word existed in Greek for that idea of "forever." They had to rely on a complex expression for "forever" such as *eis ton aiōna* (unto the ages), or to a terminal view of the cycles, Thus, they took the Greek cyclical idea and extended it linearly.

The problem is that the Christian idea of eternity does not exactly mean an infinite extension of the current cycles or ages. Emil Brunner envisioned it this way: "Here on earth there is a before and an after and intervals of time which embrace centuries or millenniums" But, he continued, "on the other side, in the world of the resurrection, in eternity, there is no such divisions of time"—of which he adds—"is perishable."[12] The Christian concept of eternity means that there is another reality outside of time that is not continuous with time.

Relating to the Issues of Space. To make my point clearer, permit me to introduce the issue of space that is perhaps easier to understand. As a youth in the sixth grade, I devoured books on space. My mind was greatly stretched when I encountered the startling idea of the astronomer Sir James Jeans that "space was expanding."[13] That idea stopped me cold but as I tried to reflect on its meaning, it wiped out my understanding of a stable and secure universe with set limits. Since that time we have learned about the existence of black holes in space and Einstein has set us on the path of dealing with the interconnection between matter and energy, the nature of the atom, and atomic subparticles in addition

---

[12]See Emil Brunner, *Eternal Hope* (Philadelphia: Westminster, 1954), 152.

[13]That book, which I read in grade school, was published in 1932 by the renowned Cambridge astronomer and has since been revised and republished under the same title as Sir James Hopwood Jeans, *The Mysterious Universe* (Muriwai Press, 2017).

to such phenomena known as quasars. These phenomenological discoveries have forced me to a much deeper level of thought about God and reality.

But my goal is not to remain in the realm of scientific discussion. Rather, it is to make my thinking on God, space, and the future a little clearer. I realize that I am again shifting the base system from observation of a phenomenal reality to theology, but I trust that I will not become simplistic. So, let us consider space for a moment, not the space of interplanetary travel but the space of my office and particularly my office chair. When I sit on my office chair, my wife cannot sit on the chair. There is not enough room. The space is limited. To sit on the chair, she would have to sit on my lap. But here is my point: God can sit on the chair with me! Indeed, God can be in me.

There is something about God that transcends the phenomenological world or the limitations of what we call space. God is not bound by space concerns. Do you wonder why it says in John that the risen Jesus was able to come into the room where the frightened disciples were meeting without opening the doors (John 20:19, 26)? In other words, he could go through solid objects. Indeed, when the risen Jesus suddenly appeared to the disciples, he was not merely a spirit: he could be touched and could eat a piece of fish (John 20:27, Luke 24:36–42). Those experiences do not make sense to our mortal minds. But God is not mortal. God became a mortal for a brief period in the incarnation, but that period has ended.

Thinking about God in Categories of Time and Space. Now, let me return to the issue of time and space in relation to creation. The first chapters of both Genesis and John assert that in the beginning God existed and began the creative process. Unlike the early Mesopotamian and Greek literature, however, in the Bible there is no story of the creation of God or the gods. God's existence is assumed in the Bible. But what is important to note is that neither Genesis nor John assert that in the beginning there was God and time. Time is not eternal, but like space it is the result of God's creativity. Accordingly, God, the Creator, is neither bound nor limited by the created phenomena of time and space.

Now even though Jesus became limited for a short time, the Fourth Gospel indicates that Jesus boldly announced to the hostile Jews who relied for their support on Abraham that "before Abraham was, I am" (John 8:58). But such a statement is not merely a theological assertion; it is also a supra-chronological statement that does not compute for humans who are subject to time. Yet neither does the idea of the divine Word becoming flesh make sense nor the fact that he was active in the creation of "everything" (cf. John 1:2, 14; Col 1:16). So, I invite you to pause for a moment and reflect on the incredible idea that Jesus was active in the creation of his mother—a proposal that we can readily assert theologically but that idea does not really make sense logically.

Perhaps, trying to wrap our minds around this exercise will help us understand how ridiculous to the natural human mind the assertions of Christianity concerning Jesus seem to be. Yet if these ideas are what the biblical writers are asserting, they have some profound implications.

Transcending Phenomenological Thinking

Assuming the eternal reality of Jesus is not bound by the limitations of time and space, consider the possibility that eternity also coexists with the so-called space and time of the phenomenological world. Such an idea has further implications for the Christian. If it is possible for God and heaven to coexist in the dimensions of our space and time warp, it would mean that God does not age! It would also mean that God could be present in our space, in our churches, and in our homes all at the same time. Many Christians have come to assert this concept.

It can also mean that spiritual battles can be taking place not only in our society but also in our covenant communities and in the so-called safe environment of our homes. The devil could actually be seeking to do battle with God in our sacred or protected contexts—even if the devil is not almighty.[14] My point is that many today find it difficult to "imagine" that the spiritual realm actually could impinge on the phenomenal realm.

The Starkness of Death

But let me return to Brunner's work, which I read many years ago while I was in seminary and thankfully I was reminded of his work by one of my colleagues. In that work Brunner posited "The date of death differs for each [person], for the day of death belongs to the world." But, he added, "Our day of resurrection is the same for all . . . for these time-intervals are here, not there in the presence of God, where a thousand years are as a day."[15]

---

[14]According to the seer of Revelation, the devil is hardly to be considered almighty or equal to God. He can hardly conquer God, which is the reason that in the superhuman battle God is not the combatant. Instead, Michael the archangel is sent to dispatch the devil/Satan /the dragon/the ancient serpent (Rev 12:7–9). On earth, however, the situation is portrayed a little differently. When the devil attacks the children of God, God uses whatever means necessary to protect those children (Rev 12:11–17). This story is a fascinating portrayal of the earthly battle between the children of God and the devil.

[15]Brunner, *Eternal Hope*, 152.

There is a concern here among many people with respect to death and dead bodies. When I worked in a cemetery or graveyard as a teenager, the burial crew (we called them gravediggers) dug up people who had been in the ground for years in order to bury someone else from the family in the same plot. What comes vividly to my mind is the nature of one woman's body. She had been a blond in life, and her hair seemed still to be there. But when the air and the shovel hit her hair, to the shock of gravediggers, it dissolved immediately. It was there in form one moment, and the next moment it was completely gone. The substance had disappeared.

So, I asked myself: In the "afterlife"—if she had one—would she have needed her earthly hair? Although people spend fortunes on the preservation of their bodies, the question remains as to what kind of body would be appropriate to preserve for the afterlife and at what age would we want our bodies to be represented. Do you understand our problem? As we grow older, some parts of our bodies do not work very well and we actually can lose an eye or a hand or our hearing or our mobility and ultimately the heart stops beating. Do we still want those nonfunctioning parts of our bodies?

The Resurrection vs. the Immortality of the Soul

Paul sought to answer such a question for his struggling Corinthian children in the faith as they wrestled with the problem of death. His answers included that what is sown in mortality will be raised in immortality (cf. 1 Cor 15:35–50). And the anticipated change in the resurrection would come in the smallest indivisible moment (*atomos*)—as in the blink of an eye—and the mortal body would be given a new transformed immortality (15:52–54). Now, the neighbors of the Corinthian Christians were probably not interested in transformed dead bodies (cf. the Athenian debaters in Acts 16:32). Like most Greeks, they doubtless believed that the body was similar to a tomb in which the human soul was trapped and that at death the body was sloughed off, allowing the soul to ascend and become absorbed into the "eternal soul."[16]

But unlike the Greek philosophers, Christians affirm the belief in the resurrection of the body. That affirmation is strategic because Christians boldly maintain that no part of the earthly human is divine whether on earth or in heaven. Life in the present realm is a gift from God, and eternal life in the resurrection is also a gift. Not all Christians are aware of this crucial distinction, however, and some

---

[16]See Plato, Phaedrus, 246–54, for his discussion on the soul as it assumed its wings and escaped the process of reincarnation.

folk traditions among Christians actually blur the distinction between immortality and resurrection.[17]

Christians should understand that resurrection bodies will be very different from mortal bodies so they should hardly be upset or concerned about the preservation of their earthly bodies. Transporting the temporal into the eternal is scarcely possible, and the resurrection depends not on our efforts of preservation but on God's transforming power. So, North Americans who have large tracts of land for burial purposes should not criticize Christians in places such as Japan or Singapore where the scarcity of land makes it necessary to have earthly bodies cremated.

Such issues remind us of the proud Sadducees who posed a problem for Jesus concerning a woman who had been married to multiple men before her death. Scornfully they asked Jesus: To whom would the woman belong in the resurrection (notice the male-oriented question)? Jesus simply responded that in the hereafter there was a different pattern to life (cf. Mark 12:18–27, Matt 22:23–33, Luke 20:27–38). So, I repeat, we can *not* transport earthly and mortal bodies or concepts into heaven. They are just not appropriate in the resurrection life with God. The Egyptians perfected the preservation of the body ,but I doubt those bodies would be of any use in the realm of God.

The Coexistence of Time and Eternity

Let me push here the idea further concerning the coexistence of time and eternity. It can have radical implications for our understanding of death and what follows. Many Christians are deeply concerned about the state of a person *between* the time of death and the resurrection (notice the time reference!). The thought of a person and the body rotting in the tomb simply terrifies people's sense of well-being. Accordingly, some have proposed the strange concept of "soul sleep" in an effort to placate human uneasiness and to explain the so-called "time differential" between the two events. The fundamental problem with such an idea is that humans have attempted to squeeze their ideas of the afterlife into the limitations

---

[17]For a very significant discussion on this issue, see Oscar Cullmann, *Immortality of the Soul or Resurrection of the Dead? The Witness of the New Testament* (London: Epworth, 1958). Because there are many misunderstandings concerning resurrection and immortality, I recommend this little book should be on the shelves of pastors and Christians who are interested in a clear distinction between the two ideas. For more recent discussions on resurrection, see several works by N.T. Wright, including *The Resurrection of the Son of God*, vol. 3, Christian Origins and the Question of God (Minneapolis: Fortress, 2003), especially 476–479; *Surprised by Hope: Rethinking Heaven, Resurrection and the Mission of the Church* (New York: Harper-Collins, 2008); and the brief work of Craig A. Evans and N.T. Wright, *Jesus, The Final Days: What Really Happened* (Louisville: Westminster-John Knox, 2009).

of mortal time. Yet such a proposition again involves the transporting of the created reality of "time" into the eternal reality.

Instead of trying to manipulate mortal realities so that they might fit into eternity, the better approach is to view death as an exit from the created order—including time! Now unlike the Greek philosophers, who viewed death as a part of an eternal continuum and immortality of the soul as an inherent possession of most humans (unless they were beasts with no soul), death by contrast for the Christian is very real. So, just as God breathed into the red clay (the probable meaning of Adam) and this dirt became a living being (*nephesh hayah*; try not to use the word "soul" here—Gen 2:7), so in the resurrection God will re-breathe into humans new life. Thus, death is very real for Christians, but resurrection is more real and lasting! Yet resurrection is not dependent on humans or on human power. Resurrection is completely dependent on God and divine power. Humans in their thinking and formulations about the future generally try to control God, but let me assure you that such a proposition does not actually work now in our phenomenal reality and it certainly will not work in the hereafter.

The Reality of Two Resurrections

The crucial point is that in giving resurrection life to humans God does not make earthly distinctions (*diastolē*) such as are familiar among humans (cf. Rom 3:22). God cannot be controlled, manipulated, or intimidated; God cannot be bought, and God is not impressed by pseudo-goodness. Resurrection life is dependent upon God, and a human's authentic relationship with Jesus is crucial. To Jesus, God has given the right of judgment in the matter of resurrection life. Jesus made that fact eminently clear when he said that the Father had "given all judgment to the Son" (John 5:22). But Jesus also indicated that after death there are two resurrections: the resurrection of life and the resurrection of judgment (5:28–29).[18]

The first resurrection is clearly desirable because it is the realization of eternal life, and the second is totally undesirable because it means condemnation. Humans, however, often have difficulty imagining that a good God would render condemnation and death upon them. But God does not play games with humans. God understands that humans are self-centered, disobedient, and basically think that divine reality revolves around them. So, they usually think that they can use God and God's creation for their own selfish purposes. Since humans have continuously failed to honor God and God's purposes (cf. Rom

---

[18]For my further discussion of this subject, see Gerald L. Borchert, *John 1–11*, vol. 25A, NAC (Nashville: Broadman and Holman, 1996), 237–242.

1:18–32), God sent his own Son to reconcile them to God and to forgive their sin and disobedience. That Son, Jesus, is both our savior and our model for a new life of being properly related to God. Therefore, the way one deals with Jesus is the basis for determining which type of resurrection is delivered to a human at the end of their or our "time" on earth (cf. 1 John 4:13–21, Phil 2:5–11).

Therefore, we humans actually determine our own resurrection by the way we live. Jesus pictured himself in a judgment scene as a shepherd separating people like sheep to his right (acceptable) and goats to his left ("sinister"), and that the latter group would experience condemnation (Matt 25:31–46). Likewise, we read in the Book of Revelation that those who have become God's children through Jesus, the Lamb, are blessed and will experience the "first resurrection" but that the others will experience "the second death" and condemnation (cf. Rev 20:6, 14).

The Conclusion to Time

I turn now to another set of word pictures related to time that may seem strange and have been the subject of misleading interpretations: the "Lake of Fire" and numeric period called the "Millennium."[19]

Hopefully you have followed my thinking and have understood my suggestion concerning the possible coexistence of time and eternity. You should then realize that many of our ideas related to the question of "when" are stuck in the phenomenal world of time and should be reoriented. Of course, it is difficult for us to extricate ourselves and our thinking from the context of time. But if time and eternity are coexistent and if when we die we exit time, then time really should no longer be a factor in our thinking. Naturally such an idea does not compute in our space-time framework, but such an idea is precisely why I posited earlier that God does not age. God may be called "the Ancient of Days" (Dan 7:13), but this does not mean that God is old and decrepit.

And this conclusion should bring us to the issue of the way we communicate our ideas concerning death and the future. Let me again ask: How could Jesus communicate the coexistence of time and eternity to people who were bound by the reality of time? And how would the biblical writers even begin to fathom what Jesus might be trying to say? It would be incredibly difficult, especially

---

[19]For my further discussion on the "Millennium" and the "Lake of Fire," see G. Borchert, "Revelation," 2194–2196. In the midst of confusing views on these word-pictures, Craig S. Keener's discussion can be helpful in sorting out the strange populist views from the more reasonable ones. See his *Revelation*, NIVAC (Grand Rapids: Zondervan, 2000), 462–482. See also William LaSor, *The Truth About Armageddon: What the Bible Says about End Times* (Grand Rapids: Baker, 1982) and Arthur H. Lewis, *The Dark Side of the Millennium: The Problem of Evil in Revelation 20:1–10* (Grand Rapids: Baker, 1980).

since most of the people were members of the peasant class in the Mediterranean world of the first century and therefore had little view of the future, let alone of our advanced concepts of space and dimensional thinking. And even if they were among the elite, most had not developed their concepts much beyond plane geometry. But that statement is not meant to demean them nor to elevate us to the position of being "superior knowers," as our knowledge still remains partial and clouded (cf. 1 Cor 13:12). Moreover, our lives are also mired in sin and manipulative ways of thinking.

But for a moment let me posit for you another possible scenario to help us understand our dilemma in trying to understand God and time in relation to death. Can you conceive of the possibility that when you die that you not only exit time but that you also are given the entrance into a new dimension of reality that is beyond time? When you die, somehow God calls you to the resurrection perhaps "immediately" but that "time" term is basically meaningless in eternity. Those then who die "later" (a time term) will also enter the non-time immediacy with you. Thus, when Paul was writing to the early Thessalonians and wanted to assure the Christians—who had watched their fellow Christians die—he told them that those who died first would not precede the later ones to the trumpet call of God. Do you see how non-time designations become difficult to integrate into our thinking concerning the "end of time"? Time is only meaningful in the realm where time is experienced (1 Thess 4:15–18).

Such an idea may also assist us in understanding the concepts in Revelation of the Lake of Fire that burns forever and more particularly with the many arguments over the Millennium. These latter arguments have created great splits in the church, but the thousand years is a time designation for a long period of "time" that is basically irrelevant when dealing with eternity, even though such a thought may be significant for us who live with time.

As I indicated in my commentary on Revelation, it seems that the devil has used this thousand-year time designation that involves a mere seven verses (Rev 20:1–7) in the entire Bible to confuse Christians and to promote our fighting with each other. The result is that the devil has effectively turned our attention away from the fact that God will surely deal with all the evil enemies, including the devil's self. Yet many Christians seem to be more interested in trying to understand a small-time statement in eternity than praising God for the promise of the devil's demise![20] Christians, let us stop fighting and constructing theolog-

---

[20]See G. Borchert, "Revelation," 2195–96 and G. Borchert, *Worship in the New Testament,* 229–230.

ical systems based on the use of one-time term in seven verses that is swallowed up in eternity and our expectation of Heaven!

I must also pause to add a brief comment concerning the word pictures of the lake of fire and hell. I am slow to detail much beyond the reality of punishment in terms of these two concepts/places. People have asked me to provide extended information pertaining to hell and while some interpreters have been happy to speculate on the many aspects of the destruction of the enemies of God or on the annihilation of the impenitent, [21] I have learned from my legal training that I should be careful to recognize the nature of biblical silence on such matters— beyond the fact that punishment is pictured here as an unquenchable fire.

What that means in terms of eternity for those who are consigned to the resurrection of judgment and condemnation may be interesting and fodder for speculation and research. But I have been intrigued by the thinking of C.S. Lewis who pictured hell and evil in one book as sheer noise and in another as the presence of the white witch and a freezing winter with encompassing snow and ice.[22] While fire and molten lava are great symbols of destruction derived from our phenomenological world, I would not want to speculate on the temperature of hell or the length of its "time warp." I must admit the sheer brilliance of John's word picture of throwing "death and hades" into the "lake of fire" (Rev 20:14)! What a magnificent image! But let us all pray that our names are written in the Book of Life so that we do not end there (20:15).

The Concept of Heaven[23]

Here again I would invoke the name of my philosopher brother, Don, who periodically reminds me that one of his former Princeton supervisors, the late Emile Cailliet, often warned his students not "to colonize reality with the intelligible."[24] In this chapter and elsewhere I have sought to remind myself and you

---

[21]For some interesting views, see Sharon L. Baker, *Razing Hell: Rethinking Everything You've Been Taught About God's Wrath and Judgment* (Louisville: Westminster, 2010); Christopher M. Date, Gregory M. Stump, et al., *Rethinking Hell: Readings in Evangelical Conditionalism* (Eugene, OR: Cascade, 2014); Preston Sprinkle, Denny Burk, et al., *Four Views of Hell*; Steve Gregg, *All You Want to Know About Hell: Three Christian Views About God's Final Solution to the Problem of Sin* (Grand Rapids: Thomas Nelson, 2013)

[22]See the works of C.S. Lewis, *The Screwtape Letters and The Lion, the Witch and the Wardrobe*, in the following sets: The C.S. Lewis Signature Classics (New York: HarperOne, 2017); and *The Chronicles of Narnia* (HarperOne, 2002–2005).

[23]For my further interpretations of heaven in chapters 21 and 22 of the Book of Revelation, see G. Borchert, "Revelation," 2196–2199.

[24]I am exceedingly grateful for this advice because it often cautions me from assuming that our perception of reality may not be what it actually is. For some excellent insights into the thinking of Emile Cailliet, see, *The Christian Approach to Culture* (New York: Cokesbury, 1953).

that we cannot transport the concepts of the phenomenal world into the eternal realm. That warning applies most importantly to our understanding of heaven.

Our major problem is that we have not been to heaven and we do not possess the language of heaven required to describe that realm. So, what the New Testament writers and particularly John in the Apocalypse did was to present heaven in earthly terms. John's vision of heaven was limited by his understanding of his world. How else could he describe his experiences and his visions? Does heaven have streets? If it does, then what better perspective on streets could there be than that they would be made of precious gold which the ancients (and we) have regarded as incredibly valuable. But the gold of these streets was not the same as our gold: it was clear as transparent glass (cf. Rev 21:21). Moreover, heaven is pictured not as an eternal city (not like Rome) but as a magnificent "new" Jerusalem given by God as God's place of peace (21:2), and each of the twelve gates of this Holy City was constructed of a "single pearl" (21:21). Intriguing! I often ask my students to imagine the size of the oysters that produced them. Or, could they be from "mother of pearl"? But such a question is pointless. The point is that heaven is pictured in earthly terms.

Yet what is most important concerning this picture is not the physical attributes of heaven but what the seer thought the descriptions meant. Anyone who has lived on the edge of the desert knows the importance of water. In this vision of heaven water was available from a gushing fountain in abundance and it was given without cost to the accepted inhabitants (21:6). And the river that provided life came directly from the throne of God (22:1). The "Tree of Life" that was barred from humans because of sin in the beginning of the Bible (Gen 3:22–24) in this description of heaven is restored to the residents. Moreover, it produces fruit in every month of the year so that there is not a lean month in heaven. But these descriptions are time terms. Yet even more impressive is the fact that the tree is present on both sides of the river so that there is no wrong or impoverished part of the great city (22:2). It is further fascinating that the structure of the city is in the form of a huge cube! I know of no city in that shape, but the seer was trying to say that the city was perfectly constructed (21:16).

Most intriguing are the names on the gates and foundations. The foundations are identified as the twelve apostles (seems appropriate), but the gates are said to be the twelve tribes (cf. 21:12–14). It seems to be completely reversed until one understands that while they may seem to apply to the ancient children of "Israel" (7:1–8), that interpretation hinges on the meaning of the 144,000 discussed in both 7:4–8 and 14:1. In the first text the priority of the tribes goes not to Ruben, the firstborn but to Judah, the tribe of the kings and of the Messiah (Jesus). Also, Levi and two tribes from the Joseph clan are included. The result is that the tribe of Dan is omitted. Speculation is that he was regarded as the symbol of a deviation that some early Christians thought could be the tribe from which the Antichrist would come.[25] But more significant is the fact that in the second text John clearly identifies who the 144,000 are (cf. 14:1) when he states that they have the names of the Lamb and the Father inscribed on their foreheads. They are none other than those who have been "redeemed" by Christ.[26] When we read the Book of Revelation, therefore, we must read it as a Christian book and not as a Jewish book since the Jewish synagogue was regarded by John as an instrument of "Satan" (cf. Rev 2:9 and 3:9). But this statement is not a call to anti-Semitism, as I argued in the chapter on citizenship; it is a reality statement.[27]

Finally, what becomes absolutely crucial is that one must try to understand the symbolic nature of the descriptions of heaven and not press them into literal constructs. Similarly, in John's gospel we must try to understand that when Jesus speaks of preparing a place for us we should not press the idea of having "a mansion" in heaven—as the King James translation of John 14:2 suggests or is pictured by the twentieth-century gospel song about a mansion in heaven. But perhaps the most significant idea concerning the picture of heaven in Revelation is that no "temple" will be necessary: God and Jesus will be the inner sanctuary or *naos* (Rev 21:22), just as Jesus said that his body was the authentic *naos* when he cleansed the Jewish Temple (John 2:19). And the seer sums up his description with the forceful reminder that since the divine presence is in heaven, nothing evil will be found there and no lying or falsehood will be permitted (Rev 21:8, 27; 22:15).

While the New Testament writers may not have actually visited heaven when they wrote their works and did not supply us with stunning video clips of the site, they have provided us with powerful insights into the presence of God and

---

[25]See G. Borchert, "Revelation," 2177. The story of the tribe of Dan is not a pretty one. After failing to resist the pagan ways in the southern territory near the Philistines, the people moved north with captured idols and obliterated the unsuspecting residents of Laish/Dan in the north (Judg 18–19). It also became one of the two worship centers with a golden calf set up by Jeroboam, the son of Nebat (1 Kgs 12:28–30). Jacob's farewell address to his sons in Genesis 49 may provide some insight into Dan being viewed with suspicion since he is likened to a serpent and a viper (49:17).

[26]See G. Borchert, "Revelation," 2186.

[27]For my comments on the hostility to Jewish worship centers in the messages to Smyrna and Philadelphia as synagogues of Satan, see G. Borchert, "Revelation," 2168 and 2170. Concerning the references to the "curse" directed against the followers of Jesus by the Jews that was added to the twelfth of the eighteen benedictions, see C.K. Barrett, *The New Testament Background: Selected Documents* (New York: Harper and Brothers, 1956), 166–167.

the Lamb that is the ultimate goal of Christians. And I am convinced that they joyfully anticipated their "post-time" experience when they would join the hosts of heaven in the sevenfold praises to the Lamb (Rev 5:12) and to God of "blessing and glory and wisdom and thanksgiving and honor and power and strength" that belongs to God forever and ever! Amen (Rev 7:12).

A Prayerful Summation

As believers move into the future in the name of Jesus Christ, my earnest prayer is that the God who created time and our earthly context will help each of us to use our gifts wisely, not disputing with others over temporal words but proclaiming the grace of God to others while we have been granted this brief period of living on earth. And may we join the hosts of heaven who praise the living God.

 … And so, I turn now to the empowering challenge of living with tension into the future.

Living with Tension into the Future

Observations on Our Formulas and the Future

As we reach the concluding chapter of this study on "Tension: Empowering Christian Thought and Life," it should have become apparent that we as humans have a major difficulty in accepting tension. But as we move further into the future, I am firmly convinced that we will be challenged with ever-increasing situations that will produce tension or dissonance in our lives and force us to review our preconceptions and perspectives as Christians. Yet in confronting these tensions, I am also convinced that God—through the Spirit who represents Christ's presence—can lead us to move forward with both boldness and humility in seeking to engage our puzzling tensions because they can become some of the most creative periods in our lives as we seek to bring new syntheses and appropriate blends to the disparate and incongruent aspects of our realities.

Not all differences require either/or answers. Now I am not referring to good and evil. But sometimes harmony can be achieved with both/and answers, and this does not mean one lacks decisiveness. Instead, it can mean an ability to see partial truth in more than one alternative. I recommend that we consider such a possibility. It may lead to new insights and greater harmony among those who have taken the name Christian seriously!

The fact is that any form of dissonance, cognitive or other, is frustrating to humans, including Christians. We want to resolve issues into our preconditioned formulas, perspectives, or patterns of life. We do not like to admit or to live with the fact that there are no easy answers or solutions to some matters that can be set into what we consider are acceptable or solvable patterns of reality. Yet life and thought are often far more complex than is often recognized. And when we add God and the person of Christ to our equations, the answer to a tension becomes far more complex. Our hopes for easy and simple answers frequently mushroom beyond our early comprehension, and such is certainly true of any pre-arranged solutions or pre-formed answers within our physical or phenomenal world settings.

But even the complexities of modern astrophysics and of our genetic systems warn us that simplistic answers to many of our alternatives are hardly adequate. Of course, in time we may indeed discover answers or at least acceptable solutions to some of our current complex physical questions such as the black holes of our universe. But our probable solutions to some of these questions do not mean that other seemingly insoluble problems will not then emerge as a result.

It is for this reason, as we move into the expanding future, that we need to be aware of the great limits of human understanding and experience—in spite of our contemporary vast increase in knowledge. In this respect, I cannot help but reflect again on the fact that when I was in law school, the half-life in terms of knowledge for some engineers and scientists was then estimated to be approximately ten years, but since that time we must remember that it has shrunk considerably. And you are aware that for a number of those professions half the information they need to know for the future in the period of those short years was not yet available.

Nevertheless, the present is certainly a wonderful time in which to live. But it is also a time of great anxiety and a time of making incredibly complex decisions that impact not only us but also many others around the world. Indeed, it is becoming much clearer that in addition to the joys of modern conveniences we also possess the devastating potentialities for self-destruction and the annihilation of even our own society.

Of course, many people—including some Christians—would gladly welcome the opportunity to crawl back into the past where right and wrong, good and evil appeared to be far clearer than they seem to be today. In that pattern of retreat from the future some Christian parishioners, ministers and theologians long for a return to the "safe" theologies of the Middle Ages and/or of the Reformation when alternatives were complex but at least seemed to be more easily defined. Yet while a retreat to such theologies may soothe the troubled minds of some Christians, such a retreat will only provide a shaky stability unless it is accompanied by a theology that is also able to envisage the emerging future as well.

Retreat to a defined set of propositions is often suggested as the hope for the church in times of unrest and change. But propositional faith, while satisfying on the surface, is not sufficient for life. We must never forget that even though living is much more complex today than it was in the past, decisions for our great-grandparents were also not easy for them because they were humans and the tensions of life were very present then as well.

Directing Our Reflections into the Future

So, in this final chapter as we envision the future, it is crucial that we review briefly our earlier reflections as stepping stones for our approach to what may lie ahead. In this journey into the unknown, Christians should all agree that we must have at least a clear commitment to seek divine help in ascertaining for the future the ultimate and radical difference between matters of good and evil that hide in the issues of life. These differences will surely confront us in the world of tomorrow with new faces and forms.

To play the ostrich game and avoid seeking to understand and deal with the difference between these two polar opposites would ultimately render the Christian witness on earth innocuous at the least and patently irrelevant in facing the critical questions of life. New questions will undoubtedly confront us as Christians who, at this stage in life, may have gained some fairly clear perception of evil or the negative reality in the world. Hopefully, it should also have initially prepared us to face the future with a sense of confidence that through the power of the Holy Spirit we will be able to discern the presence of future evil.

But more strategic is the fact that we should become God's instruments of sharing the amazing gift of forgiveness that has become available in Christ Jesus, not only for us but also by extension in this instantaneous communications era can become available to many other confused and anxious humans who long for security in an insecure world that constantly seems to be changing.

Insecure humans, however, will always tend to make distinctions and seek to repress others as they seek blindly to convince themselves that they are better than others and are correct in their misguided perceptions—and that they should be proud of their superiority. Yet scarcely do they often recognize their own humanness or the fact that they have been duped into falsely thinking that their view of superiority is a self-achieved reality. In actuality such a view of superiority is nothing but a fake smokescreen that hides them from honesty and that will disappear in the winds of tragedy and death as a flimsy vapor that has no substance. Moreover, such a view of superiority is in the long run of little value in building an acceptable new future, and it will face the ultimate judgment of God.

The only satisfactory answer for human insecurity is the assurance that comes from a living relationship with God in Christ Jesus who died and was raised from the dead to provide a guarantee of salvation or wholeness in life. Such wholeness, I would remind us, is available only as a promised gift in this life and in the life to come and that it is received from God by active believing in Jesus the Christ— usually described as being obtained through faith. It cannot be earned simply by human goodness or achieved by human effort or gained by human relationship or inheritance (cf. John 1:12–13). It always remains a gift and thus allows no one to boast. Moreover, it is a life-changing process with God of growing into that new and exciting wholeness or salvation that is the fruit or result of authentic life with Jesus in this phenomenal world.

In response to this gift of new life, the receiver can hardly fail to express an overwhelming gratitude for this incredible gift of life. And in return, the recipient is not only duty-bound but also joyously willing to invest that new life in grateful service towards others in the name of the giving God who has loved humans beyond their most fanciful expectations. These transformed believers are God's way of preparing reconciling ambassadors (2 Cor 5:20–21) to the multitudes in the world who uneasily face the unknown in the future. These ambassadors of Christ Jesus are also confident not in themselves but in the God who created the world and who is hardly ignorant of the challenges that humans now face and will face in the future.

As we move into the period of the not yet, authentic ambassadors will live in response to the gentle leading of the Holy Spirit who directs Christians to use both their endowed talents and God-given abilities in love for the benefit of their Lord and others and not merely for their own personal advancement. Such a pattern of living, however, will hardly be promoted on the Fleet Streets, Wall Streets, or Madison Avenues of the future because such living does not focus on building economic investment portfolios for the self. The investment pattern that Jesus would continually still recommend is one that should not lay up "treasure on earth" that is subject to market crashes, stock manipulations, pandemics, earthquakes, or tsunamis that can wipe out human possessions in a few moments of earthly time (see Matt 6:19–21; cf. 6:33–34; Luke 12:21, 32–34).

Instead, living in response to the Spirit means that Christians are people who regard prayer as a quality that marks their lives as dependent upon a power beyond themselves. Moreover, their time is regarded as a God-given gift that is hardly meant to be wasted or squandered but is to be used for the self-giving purposes of God in the world. Such a goal for Christians is not an unrealistic pious way of life but is one that is rooted in a genuine understanding that all of life belongs to God in Christ Jesus who is in fact the only one who can bring wholeness and meaning to life.

These authentic followers of Jesus should then impact not only their Lord's covenant community but also many in society beyond the community with the reconciling message of God that points humans everywhere to a future full of expectancy. Many false models of Christian integrity will undoubtedly emerge in the future and will attract those who are looking for an easy Christianity that will soothe their insecurities and allow them to mix Jesus and the goals and desires of a "me-centered" society. The authentic ambassadors of Christ instead will be challenged to confront those pseudo-models of Christianity with the living Christ and the true *kerygma* or message of the Lord.

In the future, words will not be sufficient to convince the unconvinced. Only authentic living will convince future generations of the reality of the living Jesus. I already sense that among the new generation there are a number who are longing for the authenticity that goes beyond the words. Accordingly, our prayer should be that Christians today would learn the lesson of living the truth so that they will be prepared for the future that is emerging in our midst.

In this task of preparing for what is ahead of us, the ambassadors of Christ must learn the important lesson that they are in fact citizens of two realms. Clearly living in these two realms will continue to produce further major tensions for Christians because the goal of each realm is very different. Periodically these realms will surely be engaged in open confrontation with each other in what will lead to a clear face-off in the wills of their advocates. The early Christians encountered such face-offs and were called to choose between Jesus and Caesar at the cost of their lives.

Some of our future confrontations will be quite subversive and therefore will demand Christ-centered insight in believers. Accordingly, Christians will have to stay in close touch with their Lord through prayer and worship so that they do not fall prey to the subtleties of cultural temptations that will assail them in the future. Such a warning before hand, however, is hard to envision in its implications. But as I have traveled in many parts of our contemporary world, I have learned the stark reality that becoming a Christian can cost persons, their families, their jobs, and even their lives. The enemy of Christ is not asleep!

But this last statement brings me to the fact that there will come a point when the present and the future will be merged and the created reality of time as we know it will cease to exist. At that point the Lord Jesus will emerge from his heavenly realm and will deal effectively and conclusively with his enemies and with all those who have rejected him.

To live as though such a reality is unlikely or impossible is simply to play the ostrich game that in no way will prevent the anticipated end from coming. Yet the future in time is not the ultimate future. It is only a brief span on the way to judgment or the reality of the new heaven and the new earth. This latter reality that we call heaven will be an eternal gift from God to those who have trusted their lives to Christ Jesus and have been faithful even in their deaths.

May all Christians live in the wonderful expectation of their ultimate life with Christ Jesus before whom everyone shall bow and acclaim Jesus Christ as Lord (cf. Phil 2:9–11). At that point, the current created orders of reality will have come to an end and God will provide the final gift of that new order in which the Lord will actually dwell with believers (cf. Rev 21:1–4). Then all who live will proclaim their ultimate acclamation: "To God be the glory!" And all creation will bow and confess a resounding "Amen!"

Selected Subject Index

CPSIA information can be obtained
at www.ICGtesting.com
Printed in the USA
FSHW021229180421

9 781635 281415